CAREGIVING
WITH GOD

22 Months with Jerry

The story of one couple's journey through 22 months of a serious stroke
and the beautiful way God provided everything needed and then some!

Lois A. Cox, PhD

Dedicated to the Memory of
Jerry David Cox
June 14, 1940-December 30, 2017.
He will always be remembered
for his smiles, hugs, song, and love for all.
Blessings abounded during the
twenty-two months spent caring for this sweet guy!

Contents

Acknowledgments

Many thanks to my family and friends who encouraged me through the twenty-two months of caregiving for my husband. My daughters, Aimee Lynn Herbel and Kara Talley, loved their dad throughout the days of the stroke and carry his legacy on in their lives. To my dear friend Kelly Ann Rozmin, who helped me through every week of Jerry's care; I will be forever grateful! My son-in-law, Tim Herbel, sang with Jerry, as did Aimee Lynn. The grandkids, Alex and Cassidy Talley, Kinsey Herbel, David Manning, and Sharayah and Savannah Sikkema, gave lots of hugs and love to their grandpa. My readers on CaringBridge were amazing in their daily prayers and encouraging comments to my journal.

The editors I was blessed with—Linda Brooks, Jack Thomas, Diane Mauck, Mara May, and Amy Treadwell— were such an integral part of having this book make sense to you, the readers. Thanks to all of you for helping to make this possible.

The biggest thanks must go to my editor and wordsmith husband, Jerry. He helped me so much through our marriage regarding learning how to write more effectively. His editing on my first book and my doctorate writings was marvelous. He is truly the reason this book exists. I will love you forever, Jerry!

Introduction

When God Rewrites Your Story

My life was planned. After many moves around the country for Jerry's job, I was finally in a career in which I thrived: technology integration specialist for the school district in Minnesota, where I was employed as a teacher. Then Jerry's erosive osteoarthritis was so severe that a move to a warmer climate was needed. I completed my doctorate degree as we were moving back to Oklahoma City. The move was also to be closer to our oldest daughter. I got busy searching for an encore career to use my fresh degree, and I got involved in our new church and community, but then Jerry couldn't wake up.

Mark 5:19 tells the story when Jesus talked to a man just freed from a terrible demon. The man wanted to follow along with Jesus. However, Jesus's response to the man was, "Go home to your own people and tell them how much the Lord has done for you, and how he has had mercy on you."

The reason for writing this book on my experiences taking care of my husband, Jerry, is just such a testimony. God wants us to tell others how wonderful He is when He rewrites your story! We have plenty of other scriptures encouraging us to do that as well.

I will give thanks to you, Lord, with all my heart; I will tell of all your wonderful deeds. (Psalm 9:1)

Come and hear, all you who fear God; let me tell you what he has done for me. (Psalm 66:16)

One generation commends your works to another; they tell of your mighty acts. They speak of the glorious splendor of your majesty—and I will meditate on your wonderful works.

They tell of the power of your awesome works—and I will proclaim your great deeds. (Psalm 145:4–6)

Other scriptures also telling us to proclaim God's good works include Psalm 26:6–7, Psalm 73:28, Psalm 73:28, Psalm 75:1, Psalm 105:2, and Psalm 107:2.

Do I need any more reason than that to write this book? Psalm 145:4–6 emphasizes that not only do we need to tell our stories to those adults around us, but it is also crucial to pass them on to younger generations. How else will they know God's care for us? We tell our children and grandchildren about our accomplishments in life, our careers, and our hobbies and interests, but how often do we tell them of God's care for us when He rewrites our stories?

This book aims to do just that: tell of God's mighty deeds in my life as I cared for my husband of over fifty years at his death. God did not stop the struggles and affliction. He did not take away the delusions and loss of memory. He did not keep us from the ten inpatient hospital stays. He did not give Jerry total recovery. But He did draw me closer to Him every day of our twenty-two months together, and He gave us a beautiful and special relationship. This book cannot be long enough to tell all the magnificent things He did for me. My prayer is it will be uplifting to you no matter what struggles you have faced, are currently facing, or will face.

Being confident of this, that he who began a good work in you will carry it on to completion until the day of Christ Jesus. (Philippians 1:6)

When I read this, it hit home personally. Throughout my life, I have felt God directing me in many ways. During the caregiving days, He gave me even more direction. I know we will not be complete until Christ's return, however God is continuing to work a good work in me leading to that day. The caregiving led me to the next chapter of the good work God had planned for me.

Praise be to the God and Father of our Lord Jesus Christ, the Father of compassion and the God of all comfort, who comforts us in all our troubles, so that we can comfort those in any trouble with the comfort we ourselves receive from God. (2 Corinthians 1:3–4)

In this verse is one of the best reasons I believe God put me in this position of caregiving. He knows there are others in the same position or going through some other difficult time. This scripture lets me know I now have a responsibility and opportunity to comfort others. But it is not my comfort. I am to share the comfort of God. Every day I was able to take care of Jerry was a credit to God's strength. Every day I got up depressed but ended up praising God at the close of the day was a credit to God's presence. Every day I had enough wisdom to make the right decisions was a credit to my Bible study and prayer. Every day I responded to Jerry with love and patience was a credit to God's answer to my daily prayers. The twenty-two months were all credited to God never leaving my side. Our daughter Kara said as part of her talk at Jerry's celebration of life service, "As hard as the stroke was on everyone, especially Mom and Dad, it allowed us the chance to see the sweetest finale of a great man's life."

The following verse gave me a different future hope.

I will repay you for the years the locusts have eaten. (Joel 2:25)

God was telling the people He would repay their years of tribulation. I knew God would repay my twenty-two months of caregiving with a fulfilling ministry of sharing my testimony with others who needed to hear of God's amazing care of His children. I pray this book will do that for you.

God may choose to rewrite your story as well!

1 - The Day Our Lives Changed Forever

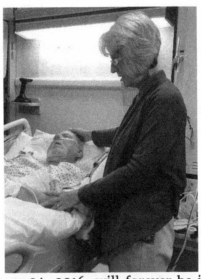

Wednesday, February 24, 2016, will forever be in my memory. February 23 was a normal day with my husband of forty-eight years. On Tuesdays, Jerry attended a men's Bible study at church and filled the rest of his day with activities at his computer, reading, or singing. I had attended my weekly leader's meeting for Bible Study Fellowship (BSF) as preparation for the Wednesday class with the whole group. We studied Revelation that year. How appropriate to study the end of this world as we know it when my world as I knew it was about to end.

For the entirety of our marriage, Jerry was a night owl, and I needed much more sleep. As usual, I was in bed hours before Jerry, and I don't know when he came to bed the night of February 23 or the morning of February 24. Once asleep, I slept soundly, rarely knowing when he joined me in our king-sized bed. Our morning schedules were different as well, because going to bed early also meant getting up early for me. That Wednesday, I was up and getting ready to go to BSF class. I walked through the bedroom a few times, telling Jerry he needed to wake up.

After living in Onalaska, Wisconsin, for seventeen years, we moved back to Oklahoma City to be closer to family. Jerry's severe erosive osteoarthritis was affected adversely by the cold in Wisconsin. I also foresaw I would need help in the future with Jerry.

On Monday, Wednesday, and Friday, Jerry volunteered in our eldest daughter's classroom. Lynn was teaching high school choir in Moore, Oklahoma, carrying on the vocal talent passed down by her dad. Jerry loved being in her classroom for several reasons.

First, he loved to sing and was an absolutely phenomenal bass. Remembering Jerry's bass voice took me back to when we first met. His singing had delighted me for those fifty years. The bass voice captivated me on a Sunday in early 1966. He was leading singing at the church I attended and was wearing a blue sports coat, which caused his gorgeous blue eyes to pop. I knew I had to get to know this man better—and get to know him I did! (To hear Jerry sing pre-stroke, go to YouTube and search for "Lois Cox I'd Rather Have Jesus.")

Second, Jerry loved people but especially teenagers. He spent seven years of our marriage as a youth minister for three different churches in Midwest City; Tulsa, Oklahoma; and Fort Collins, Colorado. He was like the pied piper because teenagers were drawn to him, and he was drawn to them. He was genuinely interested in teens—a love they felt and reciprocated. Volunteering in Lynn's classroom was a natural fit for Jerry.

Because the male teens in a high school choir are still developing their adult voices, Jerry's deep and resounding voice was a great addition to the male section, encouraging students to sing better. He was loved by all the students and generously gave out hugs to any who needed or wanted them. Lynn loved having her dad in the classroom those three days a week. Because Lynn called

2

him Dad in class, so did most of her students. One name of endearment also used by some students was Papa Smurf.

Third, Jerry loved watching our daughter do what she does so well: be a choir teacher. He came home bursting with pride and telling me how she got the kids to work and achieve excellence. It was a match too short for them both because it lasted only eighteen months from the time we moved back to Oklahoma City in 2014 to the day of the stroke.

But here we were in our new home, and Jerry was not waking up. It was not unusual to have to wake Jerry up multiple times in the morning because of his late-night routine. After going through the bedroom several times telling him to wake up, I noticed he had one leg out of the bed like he had tried to get up, but he never moved at my encouragement. Finally, as I was ready to head out the door, I went over to him, leaned over, and told him to wake up so he would not be late for school. When that didn't get any response, I took an arm and pulled it up. That was when I realized this was more than just a deep sleep. After trying without success, I called our son-in-law, Tim, and then 911. The emergency responders were working on Jerry when Tim and Lynn arrived. Lynn was just getting ready to leave for school herself. I was fortunate to catch her.

The EMTs also tried to wake him but to no avail. Of course, I couldn't tell them when he went to sleep the night before or what he was doing when he went to bed. He was dressed for bed, which was his norm, so I inferred nothing was wrong when he went to bed. We will never know what time during the night things happened. It took several paramedics to carry him out on a draw sheet to the waiting stretcher as they navigated through the house and out the front door. They headed to the Oklahoma University Medical Center in Oklahoma City, and so did we. I don't remember taking anything with me except his phone. I remembered his medication list was in pictures on the phone.

Time in the emergency room stops when you are in a crisis like this. It was a little while before he was settled in a room and we could go back to be with him. There had been no signs of any increase in consciousness, and he was snoring deeply. They began to run every test possible; connected IVs; performed an EKG, a CAT scan, and an MRI; took X-rays; and ran blood work and a urine sample. I answered all the questions for admissions as well as anything I could tell them about his medical history. He had been hospitalized at the OU Medical Center previously in December 2014, presenting with stroke-like symptoms at that time, however no stroke was diagnosed then. I was asked whether we had a do not resuscitate (DNR) and do not intubate (DNI) in place along with a medical power of attorney (POA). These documents were in our files, but I explained to the doctor that neither of us wanted food withheld because we believed it would be hard on the family to watch that happen. The doctor told me, "That is the kindest thing to do at times." I completely disagreed with him but would find out twenty-two months later he was right. I never saw that particular doctor again, and the doctors on the floor did not restate that belief.

Decisions about DNR, DNI, and whether you want your body to be sustained with food and water when the body is naturally shutting down should be made before medical emergency situations occur. Jerry and I had discussed these at length many years before the stroke and had come to the decisions we did. One of Jerry's brothers had, in the last few weeks of his life, refused to eat, causing him to starve to death. He was suffering from dementia and made the decision to not go on living. We observed how difficult that was on his caregivers, which resulted in our decision to not include that in our healthcare power of attorney document, along with DNR and DNI.

The doctor's observation of withholding food being a "kind thing" was poorly timed for me in the stressful situation of the day. Looking back on his comment, I believe he was suggesting I should withhold food and water and let Jerry pass peacefully because of the severity of the stroke. Given Jerry's condition that first day, he was not able to independently take food and water. Had the doctor convinced me to change my mind at that point on withholding food and water, I would have missed out on the many blessings of the twenty-two months I had with Jerry before his death.

These decisions are important and should be discussed with your spouse if you are married, but you should also discuss them with close relatives who might be called on to make these decisions for you if you are incapacitated. I remembered my sister was the one to make the decision to end life support for her father-in-law years ago. Her husband was an only child and had died in a car accident. To make matters worse, her mother-in-law preceded the father-in-law in death, leaving the decision to my sister to turn off life support for her father-in-law. Even believing this was the best decision, she struggled emotionally with the finality of it.

Such important decisions need to be discussed with your children and any others who might be called on. The forms are available through your doctor, hospital, or attorney, and the form content varies from state to state. It is an easy process to complete but is extremely important when a stroke, heart attack, car accident, or other life-threatening situation happens. If you have a will or a trust, the healthcare power of attorney can also be included in those documents. The important takeaway is to be sure it is done!

One last recommendation is to review your decisions about every three to five years. During that time frame, medical science could have made some advancements, resulting in improved quality of life in areas previously not possible. One example of this is a clot-reducing drug, tissue-plasminogen activator, which can be administered very soon after a stroke if the time of the stroke is known. For certain types of strokes and with some patients, this drug can reduce the effect of the stroke. Cancer research is also providing newer treatments often more successful than previous ones.

These decisions were discussed and documented with the doctor. Then at about 3:00 p.m., the diagnosis came in: Jerry had suffered a bilateral thalamic stroke. Later tests would indicate plaque had broken loose, moved up an artery in the back of his neck, broken in two, and split to both sides of the thalamus. The affected area was small, they explained, but this was a very serious and rare stroke. We were given little hope that day Jerry would leave the hospital or even wake up. The words went into my hearing, but the complexity of what I was being told did not totally register in my mind. It had already been a very long day, and a deep fog seemed to settle over my thinking. Lots of phone calls were made to family, including our younger daughter, Kara, in Savannah, Georgia, and to Jerry's two living brothers in California. The word spread quickly, bringing in much love and prayers to our God to help us.

Of course, I knew nothing about the thalamus or bilateral, or strokes for that matter. Yes, I knew stroke patients usually had a compromised body, with different handicaps developing from paralysis of legs and arms to speech difficulties, and most definitely brain damage. However, I knew few people personally who suffered a stroke. This gave me no expectations of what was to come. I simply knew the doctors were not the least bit encouraging about Jerry's future, which was my future as well.

How was I even to pray to God about this situation? Did God share the same lack of hope for Jerry as the doctors? Did God want to call this sweet man home to Him? Did God know how much I depended on Jerry for wisdom, companionship, maintaining the house, spiritual guidance, and my identity as his wife? What did God have planned for Jerry's and my life moving forward? How was I to carry on with my life at this point? How should I even pray? It is hard to pray for God's will to be done when I truly wanted it to be my will. I wanted my husband to miraculously wake up from his long nap and be ready to go home and resume our lives. No answers to any of my questions were there that day. The meaning of faith began to come into focus.

The first indication Jerry was still in there was when Lynn played Dean Martin music on her phone for her dad, and we saw Jerry's foot move to the beat. Being in a comatose state does not mean a person's brain is not active, even when the body is asleep. I talked to him, assuring him of my love. When anyone called, I told him who it was and stated they were praying for him—for us. I knew I had the prayers of the more than four hundred ladies who attended the BSF class that morning. Our church in Oklahoma City and our previous church in Wisconsin, as well as my daughter's church in Moore, Oklahoma, were also praying for us. Family and friends were praying. Leaning on God was all we had because medical science wasn't giving us any hope. Because the hospital was full, it caused a delay for Jerry to get into a room on the stroke unit. He was still in his room in the ER when I left that night to go home for some desperately needed rest for what was to come.

Once home, I called on God to help me get the rest I needed, which He did. It was one of the first blessings I received from God to show me His ability to meet all my needs because He was and is ever present in our lives. I went to sleep in a daze and woke the next morning in a daze. Everything I was doing in my daily life before the stroke that seemed so terribly important was suddenly left behind. Everything I needed to do was forgotten. I was given one task: to be with Jerry and work on his recovery. Nothing else was important!

On the second day of Jerry's hospitalization, one of my BSF classmates said I should start a site called CaringBridge: Personal Health Journals for Any Condition (CaringBridge 2018). Through the years, I had followed others who had created a CaringBridge site, so I was familiar with this wonderful tool. I started it that second day of the hospitalization and journaled daily until the time of Jerry's passing. It turned out to be therapeutic for me to share my day, my struggles, God's presence, meaningful scriptures, and prayer requests. In return, so many people followed me on CaringBridge, leaving encouraging posts and praying. By the time I stopped writing after Jerry's death, there were 44,290 hits on my site. The site was also a great way to communicate to everyone at once rather than having to retell the same story over and over to the many who wanted to know Jerry's progress. In rereading the first few days of my entries, it had been my goal to read this to Jerry one day when he recovered, to let him know what we went through during those twenty-two months. It would be many months before I realized he would never read it—the journaling was for me. As I was reading through my journal, reliving the twenty-two months and remembering things for this book, I found that on day 150 of the stroke, I commented I should write a book with all the things I was learning. I guess that was a good idea!

Jerry was hospitalized for fifteen days. The OU Medical Center is a teaching and research hospital. At some point during each day, two resident teams (neuroscience and medical) would check on Jerry, as well as the neuroscience team, resulting in three team visits each day. This gave me many different perspectives about what a bilateral thalamic stroke was and what it did to a patient. I would not appreciate its severity for quite some time. I learned the thalamus is the control center of the body. I read that

8

the thalamus is often compared to a switchboard, holding all the connections for the body. The processes of the entire body go through the thalamus, and when it is damaged, the connections with or from the thalamus cannot be made easily or at all.

A good reference I found told me, "A thalamic stroke is a type of lacunar stroke in a deep part of your brain. Thalamic strokes occur in your thalamus, a small but important part of your brain. It's involved in many crucial aspects of your everyday life, including speech, memory, balance, motivation, and sensations of physical touch and pain" (Seladi-Schulman 2018, para. 2).

> The thalamus performs the following functions for our bodies:
> - It manages our sensitivity to temperature, light, and physical touch;
> - It controls the flow of visual, auditory and motor information;
> - It is involved in motivation, attention, and wakefulness;
> - It is in charge of our sense of balance and awareness of our arms and legs;
> - It controls how we experience pain;
> - It is also involved in aspects of learning, memory, speech, and understanding language; and
> - Even emotional experiences, expression, and our personalities involve the thalamus. (Casswell 2015, para. 3)

One of the biggest connections I learned right away was the thalamic control over the body's ability to wake up or retain consciousness. Dr. Sidorov, the neurologist who would oversee Jerry's care for the next twenty-two months, told me full recovery of this type of stroke would mean Jerry would be awake one to two hours a day. That was a lot to take in, imagining how our lives would be living with the effects of this stroke. I would learn as we went along that the thalamus controls body temperature, blood pressure, and the immune system as well as other functions. Infections would become a danger to avoid because the result could be fatal—even something as simple as a common cold would result in a hospital visit.

These thoughts kept coming back to me over and over: one to two hours a day of awake time? What kind of life was that for Jerry? What would that mean for me as the caregiver? I did not know what physical therapy could do for Jerry at this point, however I knew enough to know a person who sleeps twenty-two to twenty-four hours a day would not be strong enough to move when awake. Would I be facing a hospital bed at home with a husband who slept day in and day out? Should I pray for pneumonia to take him quickly? Would Jerry want to live in that condition? I believed I knew his answer to that: no. There would be no quality of life with that schedule. However, would I be giving up on my belief that God could do anything if I prayed for something like pneumonia to take Jerry? My faith was about to be tested in ways I never expected!

The neurologist who had seen my husband in December 2014 came in to see Jerry. She was happy to meet me again but sorry for the circumstances. Then she said, "We had to have missed something then." She stood at the end of the bed with her team, and her response was spoken as a statement of facts surrounding his previous visit. Of course, my emotions were at a high with this news and what had transpired since coming to the hospital. Confusion, uncertainty, shock, fatigue, memories, and disbelief flooded my thinking. We might not be here had they not missed it previously.

It was always nice for doctors to admit they had made a mistake, but what was I to do with this information? Should I get upset? Should I consider suing? Should I go storming down to the hospital administrator to voice a complaint? No, that wouldn't help now. If we had known two years earlier Jerry had suffered a minor stroke, we would have simply been expecting the "big one" at some point. I don't know whether we would have done anything differently with that knowledge—maybe, maybe not. There would certainly be nothing to be gained by letting it bother me now. God was in control then, and He was still in control. I had to depend on Him no matter what had happened or what would happen. Trust was becoming real to me as never before in my faith. Jerry was lying there with a rare stroke—the first one these doctors had ever seen.

Jerry always was a one-of-a-kind guy! He was my one-of-a-kind guy, and we were starting a one-of-a-kind journey together through this stroke, as well as my own journey of faith. I watched him lying in bed and sleeping soundly, and the future with him was a mystery to me. But God was there to guide and strengthen me through the months to come—all twenty-two of them.

A lot had happened since our arrival at the ER. Then on the second day, just after Jerry finally got moved to a room on the stroke unit, a member of the praise and worship team from church and her husband came to visit. Before they left, they suggested singing a song with us. Jerry had several visitors around the bed when everyone started singing "Amazing Grace." As the group was singing, suddenly we heard Jerry singing along. His speech was garbled and hard to understand; however we knew what he was singing. Tears flowed down our cheeks as we kept singing. It was hope for us. Jerry was still in there, and his music was going to get out.

During those fifteen hospital days, there were many ups and downs. The doctors often could not rouse Jerry enough to even open his eyes. Some days, he would open his eyes and answer a few questions. IVs were already becoming difficult to start with all the needle sticks in his veins. One morning, it seemed he was seizing, but that was later dismissed. He had a second MRI to see whether there was an additional stroke, but thankfully there was not.

As I quickly learned, Jerry still wanted his kisses and would pucker up for more. His mind was awake, even if he wasn't. He quickly developed a urinary tract infection, pneumonia, and an infection in his ankle. Later, I learned when patients have an internal catheter, they can frequently have UTIs. The antibiotics they put him on made him sleep more, causing some days with no awake time. The neurologists would come in and almost pound on his chest to try to awaken him—an act that worked some times but not others.

One thing that always pulled Jerry out of his unconsciousness was song. Our daughter Lynn would come and sing with her dad. She sang old hymns, and often he would join in, totally asleep but singing. He'd even sing the bass harmony so deeply embedded in his memory. He could usually sing several verses of old hymns from memory, but rarely could he remember the newer praise songs of the last twenty years or so. His singing had a positive effect on his lungs, keeping his oxygen at a normal level, so most of the time he did not require additional oxygen. This was good because Jerry was not fond of the cannula held at the end of the nose with the tubing that wrapped around the ears. He was constantly pulling it off the times the respiratory therapist attempted to put it on him. God had given Jerry the gift of song. Now it was not only helping him physically with adequate lung capacity but also inspiring all those who heard him sing.

As I looked back and read my journal entries from those first fifteen days, there were several scriptures God gave me in my devotional readings that held great meaning for me. Matthew 19:26 was the first one I posted.

> Jesus looked at them and said, "With man this is impossible, but with God all things are possible."

The medical doctors had knowledge and experience to give them a feeling of being in control of Jerry's progress, but I knew better. I held on to the hope of rehabilitation giving us a recovery far beyond medical science's predictions. I was now to not only read this scripture I had read so many times before but also to truly believe it with all my heart. Also, by this time many people were posting daily encouragement and strength for me on CaringBridge as I faced each new day. Psalm 23:4 soon followed.

> Even though I walk through the darkest valley, I will fear no evil, for you are with me; your rod and your staff, they comfort me.

I had entered the darkest valley of my life and desperately wanted the comfort of God's rod and staff. I found great comfort in the hospital chapel, where I would go and cry out to the Lord on a regular basis. The OU Medical Center has a series of sky walks connecting several of their buildings. These pathways provided great exercise for someone sitting in a hospital room all day, and they also gave me time to process, think, reflect, listen to God, and time to unwind. God was providing me comfort for a totally unknown future. I was truly living from day to day, not wanting to think too seriously about what was to come tomorrow, next week, next month, or next year. Today was all I could handle, and it was God getting me through each day.

On the seventh day of the fifteen hospital days of this new life, the men's Bible study group came to see Jerry. I was so encouraged as he named each one of the men in the circle—

something he couldn't do later. There were so many visitors early on to encourage us in our struggles; one of the nurses even said that Jerry must be a special guy to have so many visitors. He truly was a very special guy who loved everyone he met. Others felt his care for them when they met Jerry. But he wasn't just any special guy—he was my special guy. The multiple kisses continued any time he wanted them—as many as he wanted.

Psalm 29:11 was in my day eight entry.

The Lord will give strength to His people: The Lord will bless His people with peace.

I did experience a strength and peace not my own. It was exhausting to get up every morning, head to the hospital, wait on doctors throughout the day, go through tests, watch nurses stick Jerry over and over, talk to social workers, enjoy visits from family and friends, and do a lot of sitting. Strength came from the Lord, as did peace. At night, I was always able to go home and sleep peacefully and restfully to be ready for another day by Jerry's side. I also needed strength to keep up with the mounting mail at home, work on bills as Jerry had always done that task, do a little laundry to keep me going, and wonder what to do with everything else at home.

Next was Proverbs 3:5.

Trust in the Lord with all your heart, and do not lean on your own understanding.

What an excellent word from the Lord this was for me. My understanding of what was going on right now with the stroke was certainly very limited. However, the encouragement to trust in the Lord gave me comfort knowing my Lord knew not only Jerry and me but also the body He created, and our future. It also meant I didn't have to struggle to understand everything. Why wouldn't I trust in Him with all my heart?

A few days later, God gave me Isaiah 41:10.

> So do not fear, for I am with you; do not be dismayed, for I
> am your God. I will strengthen you and help you; I will
> uphold you with my righteous right hand.

I was amazed at the scriptures God would put in front of me at the
exact times I needed them. Did I have fears? Of course I did. I was
entering uncharted territory. My personality was and is one of
organization and planning. For the first time in my life, I was in a
situation where I could not plan or organize anything. I had no idea
what to plan for, or how long it would be, or when we would go
home, or whether we would go home, or whether I could handle
him wherever we were, or ... The list of the things I knew literally
nothing about went on and on. I needed to hear there was no need
to fear. God was there, and He would strengthen me and help me—
and He did!

Our time at the hospital had so many ups and downs. Jerry
was fed first through a tube going down his nose. The hospital
speech therapists came in several times to give Jerry a swallow test.
They brought in several thicknesses of liquids and foods to see his
ability to swallow without aspirating on food or liquid—another
risk factor for pneumonia. As asleep as Jerry was most of the day,
he never passed a swallow test. It does require being conscious! For
that reason, the decision was made to insert a percutaneous
endoscopic gastrostomy (PEG) tube to allow for feedings to
continue while he slept.

The procedure was an easy one, inserting a tube directly into
the stomach. This could also be used to give him crushed medicines.
The anesthesia required for the procedure, of course, created more
drowsiness. It seemed everything they did to the poor guy made
him sleep more and more. To keep him from pulling at the tube
while the hole healed, they put an elastic binder around his middle.
It took quite some time for him to adjust to a tube hanging out of

his stomach or to understand how valuable the tube was for me to administer his care.

Early on, the doctors discussed sending Jerry first to an intensive rehabilitation center, where he would receive three to five hours a day of therapy. It also provided the more intense nursing care required at this point in his recovery. As he continued to sleep more and more, however, the decision was made to not send him there, because it was believed he would waste too much of the therapy time. A skilled nursing facility or nursing home was the next placement for Jerry.

The second weekend he was hospitalized, our dear friends Paul and Mara from Wisconsin visited. Fortunately for me, she was a stroke nurse and had also worked for some time in a nursing home setting. God was providing me with a trained professional, Mara, to visit facilities close to my home and provide the best advice in my decision. Mara knew what questions to ask and how to read the reports they provided to the public. (See a future chapter on the practical side for what to look for in selecting a facility.)

I had previously visited nursing homes many times. We took groups caroling for the patients at Christmastime. Through the years, several of our friends or members at church were in a nursing home, and we would visit and often take communion to them. I can tell you that visiting others in that type of facility and selecting one to place my husband in were not even close to the same experience. Some homes seemed to have an instant urine smell. Others were gloomy, and patients sat in the hallways asleep and alone. I understood this was a necessary step for Jerry, who had not been out of bed and only occasionally sat up for brief moments, but it felt like I was putting him in a prison. In actuality, I was putting both of us in a prison!

When the representative from the chosen skilled nursing facility came to talk to me, she said they would do as much with

Jerry as he could tolerate and respond to, but it is difficult when a patient sleeps as much as Jerry did. If I listened to all the negatives I heard, if I focused on the fact that Jerry slept more through the infections and surgical procedure, and if I thought about the future too seriously, it would have been extremely easy to give up and go home. But God kept giving me the right scriptures, the right people visiting at the right times, and even a few encouraging nurses and other staff who would remind me of God's power.

In the initial days of the stroke, it hit me that income tax season was upon us. Life does seem to stop when a medical emergency of this magnitude happens, however the tasks of life must keep going. Yes, I could have filed for an extension on the taxes, but with the future so unsure, I decided to attack them. There were several days I fussed at Jerry's timing. I would tell him if he were going to have a stroke, he could have at least scheduled it for April 16! All the tax papers were sorted out and neatly in a folder. TurboTax was downloaded on his computer, but this would be a first for me in our forty-eight years of marriage. I would have to file the taxes this year. Yikes! I kept reminding myself I did have a bachelor's degree in business education, giving me every skill needed to complete taxes. I needed to take a little time to start exploring that task. One of the men in his Bible study group who had visited earlier had used TurboTax and agreed to be my reference. I slowly began the task of familiarizing myself with the software and the collection of tax papers, and I built my confidence to accomplish this. The work continued into the skilled nursing days until they were complete.

Our first of ten total hospital stays during his twenty-two months was coming to an end. Sodium levels had been an issue (also controlled by the thalamus), but they were getting back to normal levels. The neurologists had written discharge papers before the nephrologist approved them. Jerry would need several more days of IV antibiotics after discharge. The fifteen days of IV sticks had made it difficult to find a vein for a new IV placement. He must have felt like a pin cushion with all the sticks—there were always blessings to being asleep.

Once more, a myriad of questions grasped at my thinking: What would I find in the skilled nursing facility I chose? How would Jerry respond to physical therapy? Would we need to be there the whole one hundred days (twenty days totally covered by Medicare, and days twenty-one through one hundred requiring a $167 per day copay before no coverage was provided at $350 per day). What was my role to be in his care? I remembered my vows made on August 6, 1967, to live with this man in sickness and in health. We had forty-eight years of relatively good health, and now I was facing the sickness part of those vows. The commitment was made, and for me there was no other choice but to care for the man who now slept away his days.

God continued to give me guidance through a scripture on day fifteen, our last full day at the hospital.

> Peace I leave with you; my peace I give you. I do not give to you as the world gives. Do not let your hearts be troubled and do not be afraid. (John 14:27.)

Peace—was it really a possibility in my situation? How could I even think about peace during all these unknowns? Is this what faith is all about—having peace when that is the last thing you feel at the moment? I was sitting beside a sleeping man who might never stay awake for long periods of time, who hadn't been out of bed in fifteen days, and whose stroke had changed the course of our future in one night, and I was to have peace? I needed to trust totally in God to move ahead.

Things I Learned While Caregiving with God!

1. I have learned life is unpredictable. Be sure you end each day with those you love knowing it!
2. I have learned to extend forgiveness to any who have wronged you before it is too late to do so.
3. I have learned if you don't make that call today to reach out to someone, you may not get another chance.

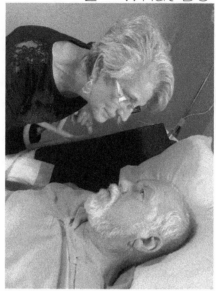

On day sixteen in the afternoon, we arrived at the skilled nursing home. Jerry was taken by ambulance. I drove by a friend's thrift shop to pick up some lounge pants. Jerry never wore these, but they were needed at the facility. Zippers would just not work during this stay or for the rest of his life. Lounge pants— the title didn't quite match what Jerry would be doing. Yes, lots of sleeping, but you normally think of lounging as a chosen activity, not planned therapy and sleeping when your brain insisted on it. I checked on Jerry in his new room before I was instructed to go to admissions to check in Jerry and sign all the needed paperwork.

My son-in-law met me there because he wanted to be in on the financial end due to his background in financial planning. I had all my paperwork ready, including values of what we owned, bank account information, and investment accounts. I felt like I was heading into a financial meeting and preparing to ask for a big loan for a new business. I was to convince these people I would sign my life away if needed for my husband's care. I wondered whether all the financial planning for retirement we had carefully done would all be for naught at the end of Jerry's stay here, however long it would be.

This meeting was very unpleasant to sit through because it seemed the admissions staff was much more concerned about how the bill would be paid than how they would care for my husband. They had insurance information from me but needed to know how I would pay the federally assigned $167 per day copay for days twenty-one through one hundred. The skilled nursing facility also wanted a plan for payment if he stayed longer than one hundred days. When I left the admissions office, they had in hand the value of everything I owned plus the value of my investments. In essence, I committed to pay for his care even if it required everything I owned. What an awful feeling to put the value of Jerry's life in dollars, but that was what I did. (See a later chapter on the practical side for how to know how much of your financial portfolio and property can be taken, and what is protected.)

Our secondary insurance did not cover the skilled nursing home copay of $167 per day, which resulted in a bill of thirteen thousand dollars. God had provided for this in His great planning. The district where I taught for seventeen years in Minnesota created a health savings account for me because I did not take the school district's insurance plan, opting to take Jerry's. The school district added one thousand dollars per year for each year employed. When I retired in preparation for our move to Oklahoma for our new life, I received an incentive of twenty-five thousand dollars from the Minnesota school district added to my health savings account. We considered long-term care insurance at one time but decided against it due to the cost at that time. Long-term care insurance has changed in the last few years due to the high cost involved. A warning to readers: read the coverage closely.

When I finally left the admission process and got back in the room with Jerry, I found him agitated from the move, pulling on his tube, and probably wondering where I was. The nurse said to have Jerry push the call light when he needed something. I thought, *Hmm. Can she not see he is asleep most of the time?* In addition, I soon discovered his eyesight was very poor, with intermittent double vision at that time. The call light was not something he would ever learn to see or push. Jerry was never a complainer, which in this case was to his and my disadvantage. I was the one who needed to anticipate his needs to communicate with the nurses. The quality care he would receive here based on these initial observations was already a question in my mind.

There was a lot more stimulation involved in settling into the facility, which added to Jerry's initial agitation. When nighttime came, I decided there was no way I could leave him. The rules here were so different from the hospital. In the hospital, beds had side rails to keep patients from getting up or falling out of bed. Here at the skilled nursing facility, it was considered as violating the patient's rights. He had the right to fall out of bed! As stupid as that sounds, it is true. The staff had his bed as low to the floor as it would go and a mattress on the floor beside the bed in case he did fall out. My thought was, yes, it would cushion the fall—but then what? If he couldn't get up on his own, couldn't see the call light, and the nurses checked on patients every only two to three hours at night, he could lie on the floor for a very long time unnoticed. I opted to sleep on that mattress to be able to reach his hand and hold it through the night. Little did I know that the end of our journey would mirror this night.

There are difficult decisions made daily when your spouse is in this condition. I knew from our fifteen days at the hospital that his mind had not completely shut down. He could probably hear everything we said even when he appeared to be in a deep sleep. I

22

kept talking to him, explained things, and assured him of my love. I wanted him to feel safe in the new environment. Feeling my hand in his, I believed, would assure him of my presence.

God was at the same time assuring me of His presence. God gave me Psalm 130:5, "I wait for the Lord, my whole being waits and in his word I put my hope." Waiting has never been one of my talents or skills. As a planner and doer, when given a job, I attacked it and got it done. Now God was teaching me while I was caregiver for my husband. So many promises in the Bible were about to become more real than ever before in my life. My whole being was in this—not just a part of me. Never had I been so focused on one thing: Jerry! My only hope at this time was in the Lord as I experienced a long, difficult night.

The first difference in the care from the hospital and the skilled nursing facility was the time between checking on Jerry. In the stroke unit, Jerry was watched hourly, and call lights were answered quickly. Now he was on a longer list of patients to be seen by the nurse and nurse's aide. I would push the call light and get ready for a nurse to appear at the door. There was no way to call the desk as in the hospital. That first weekend there (we arrived on a Thursday afternoon), I waited as long as two hours to get a response to the call light. Retraining happened quickly for me. If I needed something, it was best to go to the desk myself and find help if possible.

We did see the doctor who took care of the patients at the facility on Friday. He was an interesting man, wearing a ponytail and Birkenstock-type sandals, making me uncertain of how to take him at first. He said I was probably told that whatever rehabilitation results we had in three months would most likely be what we would have for the rest of his life. Then he said, "Well, I believe in God, and we can get more than three months." Yeah! At last some encouragement. I was told that over and over how crucial the first few months of rehab were for their maximum physical achievement in therapy. Some doctors said six months of rehab were needed for results, and a few even stretched it to a year. However, I knew we were on a tight schedule for rehab, and Jerry wasn't awake enough yet to benefit fully from therapy.

The first weekend gave me encouragement by having lots of visitors who came to see him, which provided good stimulation for him to stay awake. Lynn was there as well, and the singing began. When I ran home to work on taxes and other financial matters, I came back to find the news of how involved he had been with his visitors and with singing. Of course, I was saddened to have missed all the excitement. They sang together for some time, and Jerry was awake for part of it and sang with eyes closed for part of it. Once I arrived back, the exhaustion of the day put him back to sleep. Still, we needed a lot of encouragement to keep focusing on recovery.

A stroke provides a very long road to recovery for the patient and caregiver. I was beginning to see caregiving was not going to be a short-lived job. It wasn't like teaching in school, where I had a semester to teach students with an exam at the end that showed what was accomplished, and then I moved on to the next class. Progress would be very slow, and discouragement and disappointment would be daily battles. I learned to rejoice with the smallest progress made and thanked God for each blessing that came my way.

Jerry's singing was one of those blessings. Nurses would stop in to see who was singing and were surprised to find it was Jerry. There were days he would sing more than others and some days not at all, but every time I heard that deep bass voice, I was touched, encouraged, and blessed. The wake-up narcotic he was on provided longer periods of wakefulness, which was also a blessing. I cherished times to talk to him and have him hopefully talk back to me. Conversation had never been his strong suit, but any words now were a delight to all of us who heard them.

A verse I read early in our skilled nursing stay was Romans 8:28, "And we know that in all things God works for the good of those who love him, who have been called according to his purpose." I was having a hard time seeing how Jerry's stroke would work for our good, but I had to believe this promise of God, along with the others. As of now, I could see his singing bringing joy to others there and to me. But the rest of the promise in the days and months to come was not clear to me yet. It would take my total faith to believe how a stroke could be worked for my good or for Jerry's.

As I have mentioned, one of my skills was being an organized planner. It helped me through my careers as a teacher, a printer for a large church, and a medical secretary. When we went on vacations, my planning kicked into high gear, having all the details worked out before we left the front door. Our move to Wisconsin in 1997 took me back to the classroom teaching high school business classes. Eventually, a position was created for me at the Minnesota district, where I taught just across the Mississippi River from where we lived in Onalaska, Wisconsin. I served as a technology integration specialist for the entire district. I wanted to go back to school and finally found a master's program in instructional technology and completed that in 2009.

It turned out to be such fun (yes, I did say fun), I decided to go on pursuing academic degrees. Most local PhD programs required attending school every other weekend from Friday night through Sunday. This didn't fit either my desire to be in church on Sundays or wanting to spend all the time with Jerry that I could. Jerry was sixty-nine when I started an online program. Even at that age, I realized my time with him was a gift and didn't want to waste any of that time being away for that many weekends. The

PhD program was in instructional technology and online learning and was completed in September 2014 when I was sixty-eight years old—only four months from turning sixty-nine. Upon moving to Oklahoma, I was armed with a bachelor's degree, two master's degrees, and now a doctorate degree. Teaching in a university was in my planning, however I unsuccessfully looked for eighteen months for a job using my new education.

Then came the stroke, and my future had only one plan: caregiving for Jerry. How could God let this happen? It wasn't that I needed the salary from working, but I wanted the fulfillment it gave me. Teaching was the career I enjoyed the most and giving it up was certainly not in my long-term planning. Perhaps Jerry would recover to the point I could return to the classroom. I was already scheduled to teach an online class for St. Mary's University in Winona, Minnesota, that June as I had taught for the previous six years. Hopefully, by June I could handle caregiving for Jerry and my online class.

The unknowns were more than the knowns. My husband was sleeping his life away before my eyes with snippets of awake time and small bits of encouragement from time to time. Why couldn't the doctor tell me when I could expect results? Why couldn't the therapists work him harder or for longer periods of time? Were my prayers of recovery being heard? Why do strokes hit Christians? Why had God taken Jerry out of Lynn's classroom, where he was having such tremendous results with her students? Why did I have to give up my dream of continuing to teach in a university?

A devotional book I was reading at that time provided a partial answer to some of my questions. The verse one day was John 15:2.

> [My Father] cuts off every branch in me that bears no fruit, while every branch that does bear fruit he prunes so that it will be even more fruitful.

One comment from the book about the verse was,

> Father God, I often ask myself, "Why is this happening to me?" when in fact, I should be asking You, "What are You trying to teach me?" When You need to remove something from my life—particularly something I don't want to release—remind me that this pruning is necessary for my spiritual health, growth, and well-being. (Drennan 2015, 73)

At the time we were settling into the skilled nursing facility, I couldn't see I was learning anything. I was simply being detoured from my life's plans and especially my retirement plans. Another verse came up in my reading.

> Your eyes saw my unformed body; all the days ordained for me were written in your book before one of them came to be. (Psalm 139:16)

God, being omnipotent, knows all things about all people. Even before I was born, He knew what was going to happen in all the days of my life. He knew that I would be an organized planner and would marry Jerry. He knew about his stroke, my caregiving, and his death. There must be something I was supposed to learn from all this. Where was I to go from here? The nursing home days were just getting started, as were the questions.

Lynn was reading *Kisses from Katie* (Davis 2011) at the time and shared some of Katie's story with me. Katie was an amazing young woman who moved to Uganda soon after high school graduation against the wishes of family and friends, and she fell in love with the orphaned children there. Her book tells of her struggles and triumphs. In one of her chapters, she reminds the readers of God's promise not to give you more than you can handle even though this scripture is talking about temptation (1 Corinthians 10:13). She said she believed God gave her more than she could handle to cause her total surrender to Him.

There was no place else for me to turn but to God. This situation was far beyond my capabilities to handle, but not for God. We were not promised easy lives.

In this life, you will have troubles. (John 16:33b)

At the same time, we are promised full, abundant lives.

I have come that they may have life, and have it to the full. (John 10:10b)

Right then, it was easy to accept I would have troubles, but I was struggling to see this as a full life. Faith had to overrule so much right now.

Monday came, and it was time to start with the much-anticipated physical therapy. We were already twenty days into the first month of a limited time to achieve physical recovery. I watched the two male therapists and another aide manhandle him out of bed. His eyes remained closed as they did throughout the session. They moved arms and legs to get movement going. The right side of the body was the compromised side, causing the leg and arm not to move on their own. This right-side deficiency also caused the double vision, as we would learn later. Watching the movements made by therapists enabled me to continue doing therapies in the room. The goal seemed to be to get the muscles going to help them remember their tasks.

Jerry was aware of everything going on around him. It was almost like he was watching himself on television—he knew what was happening and what was being said, but he couldn't do anything to make those movements change. Just as the physical therapists were finishing up with Jerry's eyes still closed, the speech therapist came up to him. She was young, pretty, and blonde. As she started talking to him, she asked him to open his eyes, and pop—they opened to see her. This response, I found out when his brothers came to visit him a year later, was a Cox men trait. They were fascinated by beautiful women and responded well to them. The speech therapist conducted another swallow test, which Jerry failed. He would remain on tube feedings for quite some time to come.

A big player who came in my life and into Jerry's recovery was Kelly Ann, Lynn's best friend. These two had met at church, where Lynn encouraged her to join the praise team. Lynn was the music minister at the time, and that started a lifelong friendship. When Jerry and I moved back to Oklahoma City, Kelly Ann also became a part of our lives and served in the role of the family beautician. Kelly Ann loved to serve people and was equipped in caregiving, having taken care of her older sister, who succumbed to cancer the fall before Jerry's stroke. She had started regular visits with Jerry in the hospital and now continued them in the nursing home. Her weekly visits included haircuts when needed, beard and mustache trimming, fingernail and toenail care, and massages for Jerry. Thus began a practice of pampering Jerry to make his life as good as possible. And did he ever respond to the pampering! He loved every minute of it. When I asked one day, at least a year later, if he was worth all this pampering, he emphatically said, "Yes, I am." He soaked up every bit of love and attention given and continued to frequently give kisses to me.

My CaringBridge site provided more support for me than I imagined possible. Writing every day became such a blessing to be able to process the day and talk about my fears, frustrations, hopes, and the scriptures God continued to provide to me for strength. People in my life were becoming more important to me. It had always been my practice to visit people in the hospital or other settings, but now I understood the true value of someone reaching out to you. In many posts on CaringBridge, people would say how they wished they could do more than just pray, because many lived out of town. "Just pray" was a huge help for me and Jerry. I felt the prayers of so many, which gave me strength to get up the next day and come back to the skilled nursing facility for another round of advocacy.

Each day was new and different. The encouragement we had early on with the wake-up narcotic wasn't always as much of a wake-up as we wanted. A particularly awake and active day would be followed by one to two days of Jerry being more asleep, less attentive, and much less active. Brain injuries, I was learning, were extremely fatiguing to the body and slow to heal. My routine at the nursing home was in place now, as it had been at the hospital: get up in the morning, have breakfast, arrive at the nursing home between 7:30 and 8:00 a.m., and stay throughout the day until Jerry was asleep at the end of the day.

The time I spent at home was an integral part of my new schedule. My sleep at home was crucial for me to keep going through the days, and God was helping me fall asleep at home. Depending on what time I woke up in the morning (I never set an alarm from the day of the stroke through the twenty-two months, allowing myself to get the sleep I needed), I either had my quiet time at home or brought my devotional books with me to the nursing home. Jerry wasn't normally awake until after ten, but I still wanted to be there for anything he might need.

Early on, my son-in-law, Tim, encouraged me to get an appointment with an elder law attorney. Tim wanted to be sure we all understood what could be used for Jerry's care if it went long-term in the facility. Hearing the legal side was helpful. It was also an encouragement to set up a trust. This was important, the lawyer explained, because people often die "out of order." Caregiving is stressful emotionally and physically and often results in the unexpected death of the caregiver, often leaving the one needing the care without the necessary funds to care for himself or herself.

Another learning experience came from one of Kelly Ann's clients, who was a patient advocate. She visited the skilled nursing facility when I was struggling with the fact that Jerry was not being cared for in a timely manner. I learned a great deal from her example when she insisted on seeing the director of nursing immediately to address these issues. I grew up in a time when authority was not questioned but just accepted. Now I was in a position when questioning was needed and at times required to ensure quality care. My boldness took some time to develop, but with encouragement, especially from Kelly Ann, it did come. Unfortunately, my experience with the delay in care and lack of care in a skilled nursing facility environment is not an isolated incident. It is repeated all too often.

One morning early in our nursing home life, God gave me Psalm 34:18, "The Lord is close to the brokenhearted and saves those who are crushed in spirit."

Some days were so encouraging; others were anything but. For Jerry, I needed always to be positive and encouraging, knowing his mind was working inside the seemingly asleep and unconscious body. He always needed to hear of my love and his progress—that he could do this, that God could do this. But then I wondered, What if God didn't completely heal him? What would that do to my faith? So many were praying for complete healing and restoration back to the old Jerry. When we pray, "If it is your will," are we really saying we will understand if He doesn't answer our prayers as we want them answered? I was already being tested beyond anything I had ever undergone, and I suspected my journey ahead was long.

Another verse to help me was Psalm 27:13–14 (ESV).

I believe that I shall look upon the goodness of the Lord in the land of the living! Wait for the Lord; be strong, and let your heart take courage; wait for the Lord!

I learned—we all learned—to take great joy in the days Jerry was awake more, talking more, and moving more. In our world of instant gratification, waiting is so difficult. I can remember having my knee replaced in 2008 and wanting the physical therapy instantly make it work like new. It was well over a year before I felt completely recovered from the surgery. That was only one part of the body. Jerry was dealing with the control center of the whole body that needed to be healed. I was pretty sure I hadn't prayed for more patience in a very long time, learning years ago that God would send circumstances to teach me patience. However, God was in charge of what He wanted me to learn through Jerry's stroke. It was with God's help that I was to learn what patience really is.

One morning only three weeks after the stroke, the doctor came in on his morning rounds, the content of which provided an illustration of the power of the thalamus. He asked Jerry if he would open his eyes. We could both see him trying to open the eyes, but they wouldn't cooperate. Finally, Jerry took his hand and pulled the eye lid up to see him. Amazing how something as small as opening an eyelid was now a major accomplishment for Jerry. Recovery was moving at slower than a snail's pace, and our job was to wait on the Lord!

With these early days at the nursing home, I realized that I could decide which direction or focus to take my caregiving. The question "What do I do now?" could be answered by deciding I had put too much time and energy into furthering my education to give it all up now. Jerry would have nursing care in the skilled nursing facility—it was in fact called "skilled nursing." Why would he need me there all the time? There were certainly many other patients alone most of the time. Does that mean their loved ones cared less for them? If this happened when I was still working and needed the income, would I have been expected to quit work to be here? People live in these facilities for years. so what was I so concerned about?

Another option of "What do I do now?" was more drastic. A friend of mine who is a physician's assistant shared with me a story from real life. I have no idea the names of these people or anything about them because of patient confidentiality, but I know it happened from her account. A couple entered their retirement years when the husband had an illness requiring caregiving; I don't even know the illness. The wife informed my friend she didn't sign up for this in her retirement and divorced her husband. That was certainly an option.

A third option of "What do I do now?" would be to get him settled in the long-term care side of the facility after he completed his hundredth day in skilled nursing because the progress didn't seem to be consistent enough. And why was I wasting time there? No one expected him to leave the facility anyway. Why should I? Perhaps I should get on with my life.

The option I chose for "What do I do now?" was, for me, the only option. Jerry had been my husband for forty-eight years at that time. We made a commitment to each other, and I intended to keep that commitment. If the tables were reversed, Jerry would not have questioned taking care of me. I certainly wasn't going to question taking care of him. With his limitations, that meant spending lots of time in this facility. I couldn't count on the nursing staff to check on him often enough to anticipate his needs, and he certainly was not able to tell them. No, my answer to that question was to put my life on hold and take care of my lifetime partner. We experienced a lot of life together, and I believed God would get me through whatever was coming next. Caregiving without an end date is difficult, but God's care doesn't have an expiration date. He was going to be with me however long it took.

After a month at the nursing home, a nurse gave us the encouragement to help me stand firm in my decision. He worked at another nursing facility as well and told us he bragged about our family to the other staff. He worked with three or four other bilateral thalamic stroke patients, but they were not doing as well at that time as Jerry. He credited that opinion to our family always being there to encourage and meet his needs as well as we could.

I also read a poem by Helen Steiner Rice titled "What More Can You Ask?" to comfort me in my decision to take on the job of full-time caregiver. Here is a section of the poem.

"God comes not too soon or too late."
So wait with a heart that is patient
For the goodness of God to prevail,
For never do prayers go unanswered,
And His mercy and love never fail.
(Rice 2012, 14)

The poem also talks about God's never-ending love no matter what is going on in your life. He is there to hold you up when your spirits are down in the caregiving. His strength is holding you up each day. He knows our daily struggles and always understands us. He freely gives us these gifts because of His great mercy and love. But we must trust Him.

Jerry was teaching me lessons in his dependent state. He had to have help doing everything from eating, to getting up, to staying clean—all parts of his care. To help me with this, God gave me Psalm 18:2, "The LORD is my rock and my fortress and my deliverer, My God, my rock, in whom I take refuge: My shield and the horn of my salvation, my stronghold." I needed to be as dependent on God as Jerry was on me. Without God, I could do nothing and certainly could never hope to have salvation. God never let me down and with His help, I wasn't going to let Jerry down!

Another scripture that helped me during this time was Ephesians 2:10, "For we are God's handiwork, created in Christ Jesus to do good works, which God prepared in advance for us to do." I read this scripture one morning and thought how timely to follow a scripture I read the day before, which talked about not growing weary in doing good. Our purpose in being here is to do good works in order to show God's love to others. Our good works can in no way save us. It would take more than a lifetime to begin to do enough, and then our sin would still overshadow the good works. God's grace is such a gift to us.

The "prepared in advance for us" part of the scripture came to mind strongly the next morning. Of course God knows the past, present, and future. He knew the day we said our marriage vows that Jerry would have a stroke on February 24, 2016, and that I would be his caregiver. God spent my lifetime preparing me for the job I now must do.

I remembered my first experience with full-time caregiving. It became unsafe for my grandmother to live alone in Dallas. Her three daughters, my mom and two aunts, decided to move her in, with each of them in a rotation. They started out with a month with each daughter. As grandmother's care became more demanding on whoever had her, they went to two weeks with each daughter, then one week, then three days, and finally every day she moved to another home. The daughters were determined to not put her in a nursing home if at all possible. The day they had grandmother, they had to sit with her all day. She was lost, confused, frightened, and wanted her caregiver right there holding her hand all day. When they all reached the point where they could no longer give that care, they put her in a nursing home. She died two weeks later.

Next, my mother cared for my aunt when her breast cancer metastasized into bone cancer. The last year of her life was excruciatingly painful, and Mom was there most days in her care. She died on Easter Sunday 1983. Oddly enough, my mother was diagnosed with pancreatic cancer on July 12 of the same year and died on September 12. My dad was the caregiver, however he seemed ill prepared for the task. He cried for two months not knowing what to do or how to cope. I spent as much time as I could during those two months flying down each weekend and taking my two-week vacation to be with her. This was also a time of caregiving to my father in his distress.

Those firsthand experiences helped prepare me for caring for Jerry. When you vow "in sickness and in health" as a young bride, it is a pie-in-the-sky vow that you make without clearly understanding its meaning. As I sat in the ER on February 24, 2016, my choice was made forty-eight years previously, and the training was provided through my family. God prepared me for this time and prepared the time for me. Now that I was in the middle of it, He continued to provide what I need.

There were still so many days I questioned whether I could keep going or even whether I wanted to keep going. There were days when I asked God why He hadn't taken Jerry home yet. Then I chastised myself for being selfish and wanting my life back all to my own. God prepared me for this. Mine was not to question or to want out but to rely totally on Him to provide what I needed!

Things I Learned While Caregiving with God!
1. I have learned the true meaning of "in sickness and in health."
2. I have learned that what you do today will ensure you have no regrets tomorrow.
3. I have learned how your priority list changes overnight when your spouse has a stroke.

3 - Training for My New Job During the Skilled Nursing Facility Stay

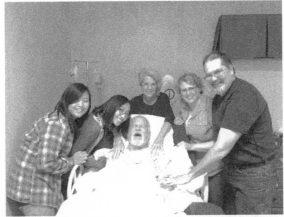

Our adopted family from Minnesota: Savannah, Sharayah, Kim, and Dan Sikkema.

The new job that I accepted was full-time caregiver for my husband. As we moved through the skilled nursing days, there was another choice to make. These people were trained to take care of stroke patients—I wasn't. At the end of the one hundred days, I would be taking Jerry home to be alone quite a bit of the time. I could either sit back, relax, and let the staff do their job here, or I could start my training by being involved in his care in the facility. Of course, the logical thing to do would be to know what I was doing when we left.

My involvement not only helped prepare me but also assured Jerry would get the best of care and attention because I was always watching. A comment from one of the staff as we neared the end of our hundred-day stay gave me cause to think. The person said I would do just fine at home because I was so involved there. When I questioned, "Isn't everyone involved in their family's care?" the answer was a definite no. Most families let the staff do their jobs and didn't want any part of it.

Another reason I decided to be present as much as possible was due to his limitations. Early on, we didn't know the extent of his eyesight loss (we never did know for sure the rest of his life), but it was apparent he was not able to focus on the call light, and his mind did not communicate to him that this was the way to get help. As already mentioned, Jerry was never a complainer, which was pleasant in our forty-eight years of marriage. However, in our new situation, it would have been wonderful for Jerry to start complaining when something was wrong. Because he did not, I needed to be there to anticipate and interpret his needs. Who knew Jerry better than I did?

Jerry's right side was compromised and did not move much at all in the days following the stroke. I watched every one of Jerry's physical therapy sessions through the window; families were not allowed inside the room, or else I would have been sitting even closer to hear everything they said and did. One of the practices I did was continue the physical therapy in the room when he was awake. The therapists worked on the right side a lot, trying different exercises. I would copy them, knowing that getting the right-side mobility back would be crucial for Jerry when we got home. Whoever was there—Lynn, Kelly Ann, or me—would work the right side, including just massaging it to get the muscles limber and thinking about moving. Even the slightest resistance felt gave us great joy in his progress.

I found a small electric massager at home and brought it in to help stimulate the muscles. Each day, I would work in between sessions with the therapists to see if we could get a little more muscle activity. By day forty-two after the stroke, Jerry could swing his legs off the bed. Progress was coming. However, progress was so extremely slow. It was easy to become discouraged at not seeing giant leaps but only tiny bits of progress from day to day. Many days it seemed there was no progress or perhaps even digression.

The amount of Jerry's sleep time was such a huge issue because when you are asleep, you are not actively engaged in physical activity. I knew sleep was a healing process, however with this type of stroke, sleep was normal even in full recovery.

Scriptures on waiting became more meaningful to me during this time.

> I waited patiently for the Lord; and He inclined to me and heard my cry. (Psalm 40:1)

My cries were often, but the waiting patiently was still a learning exercise for me. I heard the therapists tell me daily how long it would be to make headway, but it was so hard to wait day after day after day. The one hundred days were going to be up no matter where Jerry was physically.

Another scripture I leaned on was Lamentations 3:22–23 (ESV), "The steadfast love of the Lord never ceases; his mercies never come to an end; they are new every morning; great is your faithfulness." I had the promise of God's love every day, and those mercies were desperately needed. Yes, every day was new and always started with high expectations of increased mobility, or more awake time, or more talking or better swallowing with the speech therapist. I was reminded again and again of my lack of control over this entire situation.

By the time Jerry was moved from bed baths to showers and whirlpool baths, I routinely helped the staff with them. I also watched intently when they did bed baths because they would be a part of my future care as well. They were typically short staffed, which gave me much-needed hands-on experience for going home later. As Jerry became more aware of his surroundings, he also became more aware of mostly women giving him showers. He felt more comfortable with my presence and my doing most of the washing. Occasionally there was a male nurse aide who was always Jerry's first choice. Nurse aides turn over rapidly in these types of nursing facilities. I should have counted the number of different ones we had in only one hundred days—it was staggering. However, I always jumped at the chance to help with a shower or whirlpool bath.

The speech therapists were also working all this time on Jerry's swallowing issues. He had the PEG tube allowing him to continue to receive the nutrition and calories he needed. We did have some discussions about his weight because they wanted to be sure to keep him at his entry weight. His primary care doctor had urged him to lose about twenty pounds for his blood pressure, causing me to have a different perspective on the number of calories he was receiving. The therapist would regularly work on different thicknesses of liquid to see his ability to swallow. A problem arises when the windpipe doesn't shut down as automatically as it does normally, allowing liquid or food to go into the lungs. When that happens, even minuscule amounts of fluid entering into the lungs means aspiration pneumonia can develop. Aspiration pneumonia is the number one killer for stroke patients (Armstrong and Mosher 2011). He had to be able to swallow 100 percent of the time for their tests before food would be introduced.

I didn't realize until later, when he was in my total care, that he was not getting the amount of water he needed daily, causing several urinary tract infections (UTIs). If you have never experienced UTIs in senior citizens, the side effects of this infection are more severe than in the younger population. Patients can get confused, hallucinate, and can become aggressive. The worst infection Jerry experienced in the nursing home had all these symptoms. One night the male nurse aide, one of Jerry's favorites, brought him back to the room quickly for me to calm him down. Jerry was sure the aide was someone else who was dangerous and could not be trusted.

Because of Medicare restrictions, patients must have at least three symptoms of a UTI before given a urine analysis. For the most severe UTI, Jerry had five symptoms before they tested. Of course, by then it took a powerful antibiotic to knock it out. Once Jerry was home in my care, he had only one UTI, and that was a hospital-acquired one from a nurse performing a straight catherization. I made sure once home he received forty ounces of water a day through his tube (the amount recommended by one of the hospital physicians) to keep him hydrated.

On day fifty-four of the stroke (about mid-April), Jerry's mind was trying to figure out some things. His questions to me that morning included, "Why are you here? Why am I sick and you are not? Are you miserable? I am miserable." This made me very sad to hear his thoughts such as they were, however at least I could understand more of what was going through his mind.

At the same time his thinking was processing these thoughts, he began to ask to "go" to the bathroom, resulting in successful trips. These trips required getting nursing staff there to help, and they also began another training process for me. The nurse aides knew exactly how to get him from the wheelchair using the grab bars, as well as onto the toilet and off again. It was quite an improvement to not require an internal catheter because those often cause infection. One nurse explained patients with an internal catheter either have just gotten over an infection, have one now, or are developing one. In my experience with Jerry, this was the case, but it is not with all patients. Thus, learning to take him to the actual bathroom was huge in the skills I needed at home.

As we progressed through our one hundred days, I took Jerry by myself more and more frequently. I would routinely turn on the call light but then start the process. By the time they answered the call light, we could be finished, getting on the toilet, or needing to get off. The bathrooms were also furnished with a help light. My thinking was what better way to become comfortable with the process than to try it at the skilled nursing facility, where I could call for help? The physical therapists said I could call them for help (they scolded me for doing it myself), however that would have meant a thirty- to sixty-minute wait for them to finish with their current patient.

On day fifty-five, Jerry took his first steps. He was hanging on to bars on both sides and had a physical therapist in front of him and behind him, and he took those steps! The tears I shed that day as I videoed him walking made it challenging to see my phone's camera. I knew this was such a diligent effort on his part to keep pushing himself. It meant so much to me in looking toward going home. Mobility and ambulation meant everything would be so much easier for the caregiver. Could I have done it with a wheelchair? Yes, with God's help, but God made the caregiving much easier for us both.

In speaking with the speech therapist about all the things I was reteaching Jerry, I asked if the brain had simply lost connections or needed total reteaching. She said it was reteaching. The brain loses so much in a stroke and relearning never stops. There was a day later on when I was getting Jerry into the car. He was standing but not putting his foot in to sit down on the seat. When I asked him to get in, he said, "I don't remember how." By that point in our twenty-two months, he had done it multiple times. I asked his neurologist about that incident, and he said Jerry actually did not remember how to get in the car.

My sister had several serious illnesses requiring long hospitalizations followed by skilled nursing stays. She had always been an avid knitter. After one of her stays, she could not remember how to knit. It did come back to her, but it required some reteaching to get there. We take so much for granted in our lives. When I drink water from a glass, I never think about how to swallow it. My windpipe closes at the right time, and the liquid flows through automatically. Not so with a brain injury. Jerry was starting back at the beginning, and I was his teacher.

Another task I took on in the facility was cleaning out Jerry's mouth. When you don't swallow anything by mouth, there is a lot of phlegm and yuck that needs cleaning out. Jerry also wore upper dentures. It quickly became my job to clean out his mouth every morning and evening, taking care of his dentures at the same time. My doing this became more necessary after one morning when I arrived a little later—not until 8:00 a.m. It was unusual, but Jerry had gotten up early that day, and I found him sitting at the nurse's station when I walked in. He was on a soft diet by that time, but the nurse told me he had a difficult time chewing the food that morning, so they were moving him back to pureed foods. I took one look at him and said, "Do you think it would have helped to put his teeth in before he ate?" Yes, I needed to be there to be sure he was taken care of properly.

When I would go home at night, I found myself in a tangle of responsibilities that seemed to wrap around me as I came through the door. What should I attack first? How could I maintain a household when I was never there? When did I get the laundry done or grocery shop for food to eat before I left in the morning? How did I get the bills paid or take care of other internet tasks? Using the open Wi-Fi at skilled nursing or the hospital always came with the warning of it being an insecure connection. For that reason, I never took care of any business while there concerning finances or online shopping requiring my credit card information. Home was more secure, but it was also more time consuming during my times home. The pull to stay home and work on things was always there, tugging at me as I got ready to go back to take care of Jerry.

An additional new struggle was going to sleep alone at night. I married Jerry the summer after I graduated from college. This was my first time to sleep alone in a house except for Jerry's business trips through the years. I knew how important it was to fall asleep quickly and sleep soundly for the next day's activities. Again, God's promises helped me to sleep well at night.

> When anxiety was great within me, your consolation brought me joy. (Psalm 94:19)
>
> I lie down and sleep; I wake again, because the Lord sustains me. (Psalm 3:5)
>
> When you lie down, you will not be afraid; when you lie down, your sleep will be sweet. (Proverbs 3:24)

I learned to turn it over to God when I got into bed and let Him give me the restful sleep I needed.

Jerry developed an infection requiring an antibiotic. The infection caused some swelling around the entry site for his catheter. The doctor at the skilled nursing facility prescribed prednisone and made an appointment for us to see his urologist. When the doctor saw Jerry and found out the medication they had put him on, he voiced his concern for the care patients receive at nursing homes. Prednisone should not be used for swelling. This gave me another reason for being totally involved in Jerry's care and being skeptical about his medical care in the skilled nursing facility.

On day sixty-five, Jerry told his speech therapists he was seeing a duplicity of things. I knew the eyesight was not what it should be, but now I understood seeing double could truly complicate things. He stared at the ceiling a lot, which now made sense. There were no duplicates on the ceiling—just a solid surface. Later, I would also learn Jerry stared at the ceiling when he was delusional or hallucinating. I tried several things to help with the double vision, such as putting an eye patch over the affected right eye. I think it eventually corrected itself, or he got very used to seeing double occasionally. The eye doctor was of little help other than diagnosing he had double vision. A high percentage of stroke patients have eye limitations.

Reading the story of Ruth during the skilled nursing days was timely. Jerry and I included Ruth's pledge to her mother-in-law, Naomi, in our wedding vows. Ruth 1:16 was particularly applicable.

> But Ruth replied, "Don't urge me to leave you or to turn back from you. Where you go I will go, and where you stay I will stay. Your people will be my people and your God my God."

I had pledged that almost forty-nine years earlier, but the deep meaning was becoming real to me. Jerry was in skilled nursing, so I would be in skilled nursing. When Jerry was in the hospital, I was in the hospital. The commitment made to this man many years ago had new requirements now. I could not turn my back from these in our current situation. We stuck together through other struggles and difficulties—this one was simply tougher!

Another reason for my training in skilled nursing was the busy schedule of the staff, which caused long delays in answering our needs. The first time I got Jerry to bed by myself was day sixty-seven. Jerry was so ready to get back into bed, but the call light went unanswered for such a long time. The first transfer was using a transfer board—one of the tools used there. One side slides under his buttocks, and the other end is on the bed. Jerry helped scoot over from the wheelchair to the bed, and he was in bed. Every new trick and skill I learned and developed gave me more confidence as we approached the end of the hundred-day stay.

I also learned the art of feeding Jerry in skilled nursing. There is so much to the swallowing process we don't think about because it is automatic for a healthy person. However, for someone with swallowing issues, any thin liquid can easily go down the windpipe rather than the esophagus. Once Jerry moved to a pureed diet, it was important to feed him small bites and to quit feeding completely once he was too sleepy. It was the same issue of causing food particles to go down the windpipe if he was not alert enough to move the food in the right direction. Once home, I learned this skill very well and was praised by the home health speech therapist whose job it was to watch the caregiver feed the patient.

By day seventy, Jerry was thinking clearly enough to have some depression. He made a comment that made me realize it was more than just being down that day. He had refused to eat for the speech therapist that day and told her, "I feel two of me." Strange thing to say, but I had an idea what he meant. When I questioned him, he could tell me that he was a different person than he used to be. He was remembering the old Jerry but was aware of the new Jerry. The thought of the new Jerry wasn't comfortable to him, and he wondered whether people would still love him that way. The many get-well cards he received helped him realize he was still a much-loved man!

I could only imagine how difficult it must have been for him to realize his limitations compared to his life prior to the stroke. He was involved with lots of people before the stroke, and now he just sat here doing little and sleeping a lot. Food didn't taste good, he couldn't see well, he couldn't get up and walk, and he had to have help to do everything. Depression is very common with stroke patients. An additional part of my nursing now was to constantly remind him of my love for the new Jerry, as well as the love so many others had for him. I took this job seriously and carried it throughout the rest of his life.

In another bout of depression, Jerry shared with me that the recovery process was too hard and was going too slowly. He was ready to give up and didn't want me to see him that way. It was understandable for him to feel that way, and it took some talking and reasoning to assure him how much he was loved and how slow progress was with stroke patients. Then we discussed how recovery was coming from God, and he must turn it over to Him and trust. It was difficult to talk him into a better place when I understood his feelings.

By the time Jerry was in skilled nursing for sixty days, I was working to get him out for activities. The church we attended was conveniently located on the other side of the large block for the nursing home. I could put Jerry in his wheelchair and walk him around to the Sunday evening class when he was awake. At first, when the car was needed, I recruited someone to help me get him in and out of the car. As he progressed and grew stronger, I managed to get him in and out by myself—another huge step for preparing to go home. I watched everything the therapists did and learned the proper techniques to use.

Several of the staff at the facility encouraged to me in their evaluation of Jerry's progress. It was much faster than expected, and the staff credited that to my presence and regularly working with him. It was a sad situation to realize this was not the common practice with many families. They had patients who never had visitors. I realized some of their families lived far away; but when I asked one of those patients, she told me her children never even called her or visited. I would not want to be forgotten and could not imagine that for my sweet husband. One day, he even confirmed my part in his recovery when I complimented him on his wonderful progress. He responded by saying, "I have this woman who loves me!"

Along with all the nursing care I was learning to do, I also dealt with Jerry's thinking abilities. It was clear his memory was not functioning much of the time. He normally remembered who I was, but he saw me every day. At times he didn't recognize the grandchildren, who came less often. Even when he did remember me, it was not always as his wife but as that lady who was always there. One time, he told my daughter I was the "kissing lady" because I always greeted him that way and throughout the day. I was also the one who made him behave, causing him to ask the nurses not to tell me about something he did. There was no memory of home—he asked me why I couldn't sleep there with him. He had no concept of why I left at night.

By day seventy-seven, Jerry was hallucinating. Although it is common for stroke patients to hallucinate, I would learn later in his recovery that his were a side effect of his wake-up narcotic. The dosage was too high. Yes, it was giving us six to eight hours of awake time a day, however the side effects were not worth the extra awake times. Later on, it also caused aggressiveness until the dosage was lowered.

Hallucinations were scary for Jerry, and for me trying to help him get through them. The nurses found him during the night talking to the ceiling. I did not discover he was talking to the ceiling until day seventy-seven. When he had them, he would stare at the ceiling with a look of total fear on his face. How terrible it was to add this to his other recovery issues. Nights of hallucinations caused me to stay later because I could not leave him in fear. I would pray with him, pray over him, talk to him, sing with him, and pretty much do anything I could think of to get his thinking on something different.

All the attention and care I gave Jerry had positive effects on his recovery but also created one very spoiled Jerry. One evening when I was writing in my journal while he was still awake, he said, "I don't like it when you work on your equipment. I don't like it when you aren't busy with me." He got spoiled with all the attention, including manicures and pedicures weekly from his daughter and our good friend Kelly Ann. As spoiled as he was, one day the therapist asked how he was doing, and he said, "They are really bullying me. You should feel sorry for me." He was talking about all the work of therapy. However, none of us felt sorry for him with all the special treatment he was receiving.

Our days at skilled nursing were times of progress, however slow it seemed at times. There were days when Jerry was barely awake and others when he worked hard and moved forward. God gave me more scriptures about waiting on God—a very difficult task for me.

> But as for me, I will look to the Lord; I will wait for the God who will deliver me. My God will hear me. (Micah 7:7)

> It is good to hope and wait patiently for the Lord's salvation. (Lamentations 3:26 ISV)

Waiting for his recovery was a challenge often too difficult for me. I wanted it quicker and more complete.

As strange as it sounds, the more Jerry recovered, the more challenging his care became. When we were only two weeks away from going home, Jerry started wanting to be more independent. This was totally understandable but at the same time dangerous. He wanted to stand up from his wheelchair by himself to get the grab bars by the toilet. He wanted to be left alone in the shower and bathroom. He wanted my help less and less. This took some strong reasoning on my part to help him understand his need for help from me or one of the skilled nursing staff.

A couple of the last things I learned in skilled nursing were how to get him in the car and how to get him off the floor after a fall. The therapists helped Jerry transfer from wheelchair to car several times, but the day came when I was to be tested. I was to take him to a dentist appointment, and they watched me do the transfer and said I did it completely correctly. This was a much-needed skill when we went home because the doctors' appointments never ended.

The occupational therapists taught me how to prevent injury during a fall without hurting either him or me by helping Jerry slide down to the floor if he was falling. When I asked how to get him off the floor after a fall, they said, "Call the fire department." I realized the fire department was very helpful to come and help me, but that was not the answer I wanted to hear. The therapists showed me the process of getting Jerry onto all fours, crawling to the closest chair or bed, moving to a kneeling position, and then helping him put the strongest leg down to push up to standing. I successfully used this method several times at home. I also called the fire department once.

By the time we left skilled nursing, Jerry had suffered through four UTIs, and his PEG feeding tube into the stomach had fallen out. Information about PEG tubes added to my medical knowledge bank. If the surgical staff at OU Medical inserts the PEG tube, they use a balloon on the end of it holding it in the stomach. Over time, the gastric juices, which are caustic in order to digest food, can cause the balloon to dissolve. This happened with Jerry's tube, resulting in the tube literally falling out one day. Reinserting the feeding tube necessitated an immediate trip to the ER before the hole for the tube closed. By the time we realized that the tube was out, the hole to the stomach wall had almost closed, making it impossible for the nursing staff at the skilled nursing facility to artificially hold it open.

The decision was mine whether to take him to the ER or let the feeding tube stay out of the body. My incomplete knowledge at that time along with advice from both daughters helped me decide not to have it reinserted. I saw going home without the PEG tube as a positive sign of Jerry's recovery. I did not see the resulting complications of the decision until later. The PEG tube reinserted later was done by the gastroenterology department. They inserted it with a donut on the end. I was told it would never come out on its own. (*Donut* is the exact word used in the explanation to me.)

Jerry would need to take his medications crushed in yogurt, and he would need to drink lots of fluids. The hallucinations and aggressive behavior typically came with the UTIs, but not always. Meal preparation at home was going to be different due to the mechanical soft diet he required. "Mechanical soft" was the term used by the speech therapist for his diet at the skilled nursing facility. Meat was the most difficult food to make soft enough to eat easily.

In preparing our home for Jerry's return, a wonderful friend at church helped me add the grab bars in the bathrooms and a ramp from the garage into the house, modified the bathroom doors (mostly by taking off the doors and extra trim in the middle of the facing to allow for walkers to go through), and added corner guards on the walls to protect them from damage. I added a shower curtain on a tension rod over the bathroom door for others to use the facilities. Near the end of his time in the nursing facility, Jerry said he wanted to go home with me, and he had stopped asking why I couldn't stay there with him. It was sad for me that he accepted this new life as a separation at night. However, that comment was soon to end, and he developed a strong dependence on my presence.

On our last day in skilled nursing, the staff had Jerry ready to be wheeled to the car in his wheelchair. However, he refused and insisted on using the walker to go to the car. We were ending a one-hundred-day chapter of the stroke recovery process and starting a new and totally unknown one—life at home with home health care!

Things I Learned While Caregiving with God!
1. I have learned God is in control—not our healthcare system.

2. I have learned a brain injury really can require twenty hours of sleep a day.
3. I have learned that sacrificial caregiving is not the norm, unfortunately.

4 - Home Alone with Home Health

Daughters, Kara Talley, Kelly Ann Rozmin (adopted), Lynn Herbel

After suffering a major stroke and being away from home for 115 days, it wasn't difficult to understand why Jerry had little memory of our house. We had lived in this house for only eighteen months before the stroke, and short-term memory was typically the first to be affected by brain injuries. Jerry said the home was lovely and seemed to enjoy being in its environment. Learning to live at home was challenging for us both. Jerry still did not want me to do everything for him, and independence was a goal he hung on to as long as he could.

We started out sharing the same king-sized bed as before, with waterproof pads on the mattress and everything else I could come up with for protection. There was a plastic tablecloth over the carpet at night and even an office chair mat beside the bed for additional protection of the carpet by the bed. He was home close to six months before we ordered a hospital bed. Starting out the way we did, sharing our bed was wonderful for us both after being separated at night for so long. Jerry loved having me right beside him while he went to sleep. We held hands a lot. Changing the bed was a true challenge with him in it, for sure, especially with its king size. However, for me it was worth the time we spent together.

Our first week home was not at all what I expected it to be! The very next morning, I was doing a simple transfer from his chair to his recliner but wasn't guiding him correctly. He sat down too early, landing on the floor. He wasn't ready to get on all fours to crawl over to the recliner, and I, being brand-new at this, did what the therapists told me to do at the skilled nursing facility: I called the fire department. They questioned my ability to care for this man, as everyone did. That was the only time I called them.

With no feeding tube in place, I waited until Jerry woke up in the morning to get him to eat his crushed meds in yogurt. Due to waking up as late as he did, often not until 11:00 a.m. or noon, he wasn't getting his blood pressure meds, wake-up narcotics, or anything on time. On top of that, he became very stubborn about taking them for me. One morning, it took an hour for him to finally open up and swallow. Another morning, it took an hour to get him to sit down on the toilet. I was frazzled to say the least, and my patience wasn't as unlimited as I wanted it to be.

The next day, due to strange behavior, I suspected Jerry had another UTI, and using the AZO UTI test strips purchased over the counter confirmed my suspicion. This resulted in my first ER visit with him—and I took him in myself. The ER could not duplicate the results, but I went home with an antibiotic because the physician believed in my testing at home. Thinking back, it could have been dehydration as well causing strange behavior that day.

When the home health agency that was referred to me visited me at the skilled nursing facility, they said, "We will be there to help make your transition smooth." I believed they would be there. An early issue happened when my primary care physician changed his mind about signing off on being the doctor of order for

54

home health. He wanted to see Jerry in the office first, but the first appointment available was not for about three weeks. Yikes! After calling my daughter Lynn to tell her the new development, I felt deserted. One morning that first week, when the medications took me so long to get down Jerry, I cried out, "Lord, I just can't do this. I need help!" Jerry wondered what in the world was wrong with his wife!

Lynn showed up that day as I was struggling to get Jerry on the toilet. She called the doctor's office, let him have it, and contacted a student who was able to come to help me with Jerry. (He didn't work out, but it gave me hope.) Within fifteen minutes of my crying to the Lord, help was there. The doctor signed the orders, and home health was sent out on Thursday after we got in to see the doctor on Wednesday—not exactly there to help with the transition because we had been home since the last Friday!

Jerry was aggressive and belligerent during those early days. The doctor asked him why he was being mean to me, and he told him, "He tells me to." We did not know who "he" was, but it was certainly something to delve into later. Knowing what we experienced later in the stroke, it could have been Satan's first attempt (to my knowledge) to get into Jerry's mind. Of course, I was to learn soon the wake-up medication also caused aggression. (More details on Satan's attacks in future chapters.)

After only one week at home, Jerry suffered a fall, which resulted in an ER visit and a weeklong stay again in the hospital. Coming home was certainly not as easy as I hoped it would be. Falls were common with stroke patients, and the fall occurred during a time of combativeness. I didn't feel totally responsible but felt bad. The stay turned out to be one of our worst hospital experiences. Jerry lost so much ground physically with each hospital stay. That stay was particularly difficult, however we did end up inserting another PEG tube. As much as I wanted the first one gone, I now knew the blessings of having one to get medications in on a timely schedule. He went home on tube feedings after that stay. Another huge blessing of the PEG tube was being able to keep Jerry hydrated by putting water directly into the tube. With my hydrating him, we had only one more UTI during his entire time in my care, and that was a hospital-acquired one! I came to appreciate the PEG tube.

It was obvious with as much ground as was lost, I would need some help at home at first. The hospital actually wouldn't discharge us until I made arrangements. A parent of one of Lynn's students had been a medic in the Navy and agreed to come help. It was wonderful to have him. Not going through an agency meant I could schedule the time I needed, and the cost was less because he wasn't licensed. He was 6'6" and quite capable of bodily picking Jerry up if needed. He was a spiritual man who prayed over Jerry every afternoon or evening when he left for the day. God provided what I needed when I needed it. (See chapter 16 for details on agency nurse aides.)

My daughter Kara also came from Georgia when we came home from that hospital visit. She was a huge support and help with her dad. He got love and attention from her, and she helped me process several needs. In high school, she had trained to become a nurse's aide, and she brought experience to the caregiving.

Every hospitalization we had during the twenty-two months caused a setback—some stays more than others. He was always different in the hospital compared with at home, and staff always questioned me as to whether I could take him home. This was the only stay where I hired help at home because it was such a difficult stay for Jerry. He was anesthetized twice during the stay and went without feedings several days. In his current state, this affected him greatly. I learned with future visits that Jerry was fine once he was back in his home setting. So much more healing happened at home than in the hospital for us. The more positive, less stressed, and more loving environment at home encouraged Jerry to move forward.

With every hospitalization, home health services had to be stopped and restarted again on discharge. Every time he would have to be reevaluated back at home, with services prescribed based on those assessments. As an example, when physical therapy services were ordered, a physical therapist would come to assess the specific goals to be reached. Only then could the therapist schedule the appointments that would be covered by insurance.

Each service period was sixty days with reevaluations at the end of the time. We ended up with almost continual services for the entire time we were at home except for a two-month period in year two. He was discharged several times from physical therapy, occupational therapy, and speech therapy. With each hospital stay, we would usually receive additional services. The nurse visits ranged from three times weekly to only weekly, however I could call the service twenty-four hours a day to talk to a nurse and receive information. I was always supposed to call before taking him to the hospital. If I called and home health thought a nurse needed to check out Jerry, they would send one out at any time, twenty-four seven. It was nice support. However, their marketing sales pitch that they would always be there for a smooth transition wasn't exactly what I felt I received. The therapy sessions were wonderful, but most of the time I was on my own with my sweet guy.

Medical supplies were not supplied by home health care through Medicare, except for a few. I received Foley catheter bags, external catheters, and Calazime cream for (essentially) diaper rash. (Medicaid patients receive much more, including even the incontinence briefs.)

There were a lot of areas of care that were left for me to figure out on my own. When we went home after the second PEG tube insertion (and he was totally on tube feedings), we were told to give him 2,100 calories a day. After researching that number, my younger daughter, Kara, discovered Jerry would gain weight on that many calories with as little activity as he was getting daily. We cut it back to about 1,200 to 1,500 and struggled to find tube feedings heavier on the protein and lighter on the sugar. I slowly started feeding him by mouth again even though I was told not to do so. Who doesn't want to taste his meals as he eats?

Prescription changes were a constant occurrence. His neurologist explained he would never change more than one medication at a time because of the way a stroke patient reacts to medication. When he added a medication to help Jerry sleep more soundly to keep the hallucinations down, he put Jerry on 12.5 milligrams of the medication. He could prescribe up to 800 milligrams of this drug for patients who had not had a stroke. With Jerry's injured brain, it was a tricky job to find the right amounts of the right medications. Home health would always be notified of these changes. A simple medication change could get Jerry renewed for another sixty days of home health services.

We had a difficult time managing Jerry's blood pressure. Finally, we scheduled an appointment with a cardiologist after some scares with very high numbers. Essentially, the cardiologist changed all the amounts of medications the primary care doctor had him on for several years, saying two of the medications did the same thing. I was uncomfortable with the doctor's new or changed doses of prescriptions, and I finally learned to turn to the pharmacist for advice because that was his specialty—not the doctor's.

The reality of Jerry giving up his independence turned out to be a longer conflict than expected. As I evaluated the situation, it was totally understandable. Here was my husband who could no longer get up when he wanted to, had people attending to his personal needs, and telling him he couldn't do this or that, needed to swallow this, or needed to sit down here or there. It was a challenge for him to realize the many things he could no longer do and to learn to appreciate the care being delivered. We worked hard to have only me and his daughters taking care of the private issues. My friend Kelly Ann, who helped so much, would stay back from those jobs unless I really needed her help.

After being home from skilled nursing about four months, I was able to start reasoning with Jerry when he would have his stubborn moments, which often came from him not wanting me to help him. During one of those difficult times, I told him how hard I was trying to be patient and sweet, and that his behavior was not appropriate. He agreed, saying, "You are right." We also had discussed how hard this was for both of us—for him to accept the fact he could no longer be independent, and for me to now have his full-time care as my responsibility. Much later in the stroke, Jerry said, "Thank you," to me after I cleaned him up. I felt so sorry for him. Giving up independence was probably the hardest part for him to do.

After getting off to such a difficult start at home with the fall, hospitalization, and hiring a home health aide for a few months, things started to smooth out quickly. Jerry gained so much strength from his home health physical and occupational therapists that I was soon able to manage him by myself. His mobility was such a blessing and allowed me to manage his care alone so much of the time. The medication changes we made almost totally took away his aggressiveness and hallucinations. He never lost the delusions, but their severity was usually manageable.

The decision to hire an aide after coming home from the second hospitalization was a good one. Not only was he very gentle with Jerry, but he also worked with me to move me to taking total care of Jerry myself. We moved from the aide doing showers totally to working with me to watching me give Jerry a shower without his help. It was a comfort to know he would be there some of the time to help with the care. Gradually over two months, the aide's hours were shortened until I was taking total care of Jerry myself. When the aide left after two months, Jerry gave him a big hug. His time was a true blessing to us in getting me to the point I could manage by myself.

A huge key in the success of caregiving at home was patience. Jerry was always a slow, analytical, methodical person in thought and movement. I would get frustrated with him when he took longer than I thought he should to accomplish a simple task such as turning at the toilet to be lined up to sit down. Everything he had done before the stroke was now a bigger job to tackle.

Gracious words are a honeycomb, sweet to the soul and healing to the bones. (Proverbs 16:24)

I reminded myself every day that Jerry was no longer the same Jerry. He needed my patience, grace, and forgiveness for what he did. Part of his healing was my interaction with him on a daily basis.

Having Jerry at home and now caring for him mostly alone meant there were new challenges every day. The occasional fall would scare me. One time as I was backing him up the ramp from the car in the wheelchair, he got up while I was pulling hard to get him in the house. The force I was using on the chair made me go backward quickly, and Jerry ended up on the floor—thank goodness he fell backward and not forward onto the concrete garage floor. My neighbor was home for that fall and came over to help me get him off the floor and back into the chair. I had practiced my skills getting Jerry off the floor by myself, but this time I needed the neighbor's help.

Time was definitely something we had plenty of at home. Some days were packed full of appointments outside the home to doctor's appointments and inside, with therapists and home health nurse visits. However, there always seemed to be time to hug and cuddle as much as we wanted. I tried hard not to miss an opportunity to hug my sweetie whenever I could. I was blessed that touch was always important to him.

One of the blessings in taking care of Jerry at home was the ability to keep him almost totally rash free. At the skilled nursing facility, he always had a rash of varying degrees of redness and the area covered. At home, at first I assumed it was normal when a patient wore disposable briefs. Not true! It took care and attention, but Jerry was almost always rash free. I understand at the skilled nursing facility, the aides have too many patients to keep them changed in a timely manner, but at home I made it a top priority. One of the nurses who was working also at a nursing home told me one of their night aides' jobs was to put butt paste on every patient before they went to sleep to attempt to prevent rashes from developing.

> I pray that out of his glorious riches he may strengthen you with power through his Spirit in your inner being, so that Christ may dwell in our hearts through faith. (Ephesians 3:16–17a)

Of all the times I needed power in my inner being, it was at home with home health! God daily provided the strength I needed by providing His powerful Spirit living within me. The days I felt powerless were the days I did not call on God and remember the power living within me.

A Charles Stanley devotional addressed discouragement like this:

> Do you ever feel tempted to give up? Perhaps right now you feel overlooked, forgotten, mistreated, and you want to quit. Satan's goal is to get you to do just that—throw in the towel and call it quits. Discouragement is one of his most effective weapons. But remember this: while disappointments are

> inevitable, discouragement is a choice. You do not have to
> yield to the devil's debilitating whispers of doubt and fear or
> be trapped in self-pity. (Stanley 2011, 1317)

With everything going on with Jerry and his care, becoming discouraged was a daily battle, but knowing it was Satan's way to get to me helped me to fight off his arrows.

Close to the end of October of the first year, Jerry's first vomiting episode started at 4:30 a.m. Vomiting is hard for anyone, but it is an even bigger threat for someone with swallowing difficulties. According to all the nurses I had talked to, even the minutest amount of vomit entering the lungs could cause pneumonia. Stroke patients most typically die of pneumonia. After this first vomiting episode, I learned to move fast, propping him up as high as I could get him, grabbing one of the wash basins I brought home from a hospital visit, and helping him hopefully get all the vomit out quickly.

This was a time when the twenty-four-hour nurse hotline was extremely beneficial. I called them several times throughout that day to ask about what to do next. He needed his medications to control his blood pressure, needed liquids to fight off dehydration, and needed some food for strength. It was a very long day getting through the first vomiting episode. It lasted only one day, causing me to assume it was a twenty-four-hour virus.

The second episode of vomiting resulted in a trip to the ER and a hospital stay in early November. The medical team was very hopeful to find reasons for the vomiting, but they did not. It was only an overnight stay. We were to cut his wake-up narcotic in half to try to eliminate some of the side effects. Life was on a roller coaster—lots of ups and downs with some more severe than others.

This short stay in the hospital was followed two days later by taking Jerry to a primary care doctor appointment. I hired our aide to help get him there, only to find out he had a 103.4

temperature. I took him back to the ER, and he was diagnosed with pneumonia from the vomiting episode, as well as hospital-acquired urinary tract infection (UTI). He was immediately admitted and received heavy-duty through the IV. The UTI caused some delusions, as they often do with seniors.

When ready to be discharged this time, I made the decision to go back to a skilled nursing facility to receive some concentrated physical therapy. Once you have not been in the hospital for sixty days (and because during the first visit for vomiting, he stayed in the ER and was not officially admitted), we could now quality for another twenty days paid for by Medicare. I made the decision to go to a different facility, where one of my friends had her mother and was incredibly pleased with their care. It was the beginning of another stay, and I had vowed never to take him back to a skilled nursing facility. However, he was struggling so much, I was not confident in my own abilities at that time.

Deuteronomy 33:25b promised "your strength will equal your days." This was a promise I truly needed to hear after the last week: his aggressiveness, the in and out of the hospital times, decisions for medication changes, and being called back to the hospital one night at 10:30 p.m. (as soon as I fell asleep) because Jerry was being combative. It was only God's strength that kept me going. I managed to get through my days on automatic pilot relying on my strength from above.

After a highly stressful stay in skilled nursing (discussed in-depth later), we were back in the hospital emergency room and waiting to be admitted with more vomiting. The doctor who saw him said they would get to the bottom of this during this stay. Unexplained vomiting for a patient like Jerry meant a danger of aspiration pneumonia was very real. That was the diagnosis this time—aspiration pneumonia again!

Another insight from Charles Stanley encouraged me during this time.

> Perseverance has been defined as accepting difficult situations from God without giving Him a deadline for their removal. We know we need to learn endurance, but we generally shun the process by which it takes root in our lives. (Stanley 2011, 1454)

I found the process was not the least bit enjoyable. Did I really want perseverance in my life, knowing it meant waiting on God totally for answers?

After the third hospital stay during one month and nine days at the other skilled nursing facility, we headed back to the original skilled nursing facility. The hospital stay was to find solutions to his vomiting; however no reason was found. When he arrived at the skilled nursing facility a little after 4:00 p.m., he had thrown up in the transport van—everything from breakfast that morning at 9:30 a.m. We weren't arriving on a weekend, but it was the day before Thanksgiving, which was probably a little worse. With his vomiting on arrival, it meant another night on an air mattress on the floor. There was no way I was going to leave my sweetie with even a chance of throwing up. After his throwing up in the other skilled nursing facility without me by his side holding his hand, it was not going to happen again!

Thanksgiving at the skilled nursing facility when my husband was constantly nauseous was not the most pleasant experience. One of Tim and Lynn's neighbors put out on their neighborhood social media site that they were looking for someone who needed a Thanksgiving meal, and they brought us one. Yes, we could have eaten at skilled nursing, but the food was less than desirable. I spent two nights sleeping beside him to be sure the nausea was gone. No reason was ever found for the vomiting.

God did help me focus on being thankful. I created this list I shared in my journal that day.

Thankful for God's continued love, protection, and strength.

Happy times to be remembered with this sweet man.

A group of family and friends surrounding me with support and prayers.

No reason to doubt God's plan for our lives with the hope of heaven.

Kindness shown to us by so many medical personnel (the majority have been this way).

Spiritual lessons daily from God's Word.

Grandchildren to bring such joy to us.

Insight into scriptures I have never had before.

Very special times with Jerry when he is himself.

Interesting facts learned through this about strokes and the human mind.

Newness of God's love each morning.

God in heaven holding my hand each and every day, providing me with what I need.

Jerry quickly grew stronger with this stay and by day four was asking to go home. He and I were both ready. Being back there brought to my attention the difficult employment situation. So many nurses and aides worked a double shift and often worked eighteen to twenty hours at a time due to staffing issues. Our health-care system has great challenges with the country's aging population.

The decision was made to go home; however because he had already seen a therapist, he couldn't be discharged until the next day. This resulted in Jerry being depressed about having to stay another day. He told me he missed me at night. I agreed to spend the night, and we could go home tomorrow. It was so sweet! We were both ready to get back home, and his returning strength assured me I could handle this again. His blood pressure was high the last few days, and medications were not given in a timely fashion. I needed Jerry back home to care for him as he needed.

The struggle with his blood pressure was a constant battle. The cardiologist would add a medication, and then he would increase another one and have me give extra doses if the numbers were too high around midmorning. Part of my nursing skill included learning to use a stethoscope and a blood pressure cuff rather than the automatic cuffs, which were proven to be unreliable at times. We even had days when the blood pressure was too low, causing dizziness when he got up. The balancing act was never ending.

His PEG feeding tube turned out to be a huge blessing. On the nonverbal days and the days he simply refused to eat, I always had the option of giving him a tube feeding to keep up his strength, providing him with the necessary protein and calories. He fought the tube more some days than others but never pulled it out, though he tried hard at times.

A suspected boil on Jerry's back at the waistline developed in November and December after the stroke. It was annoying for Jerry because the elastic on his pants was irritating. However, it proved to be more trouble than just a boil. A few days after the home health nurse checked it again, we were sent back to the ER not only with the boil, which was diagnosed as a sebaceous cyst, but also because Jerry was experiencing a potential TIA, or mini stroke. The physical therapist had come to work with him that morning. His blood pressure in three readings was very high, then low, and then normal. Next, Jerry opened his mouth and just stared, indicating he was not mentally there. An ambulance was soon there to take him downtown to the hospital.

This was our fourth ER visit in a little over a month. The nurses and doctors greeted us by name and asked how we were doing. It is pretty sad when the ER staff recognizes you! Jerry went in on stroke alert, however a new stroke was not diagnosed. The sebaceous cyst was full of puss and infection and was lanced by the ER physician. They admitted us again for our fourth inpatient stay in thirty-four days.

> The Lord is near to all who call on him, to all who call on
> him in truth. He fulfills the desires of those who fear him;
> he hears their cry and saves them. (Psalm 145:18–19)

After Jerry left in the ambulance, I drove and cried out to God, confessing God must think I was capable of handling more than I thought I could. I knew God would hear my cries, and He always did. It was simply harder sometimes than others. A part of my answer was already on the way because my good friends from Wisconsin were boarding a plane for a visit that weekend, and they would provide great support for me at this time of additional stress.

The neurologist in the ER did not find evidence of another stroke. I would learn later from Jerry's neurologist that when they don't find evidence of another stroke, they go down the list to the next possibility—in this case a seizure. Their decision was to put Jerry on seizure medicine, which caused extreme drowsiness. Wasn't that just what he needed? We were able to go home quickly after only two days because of my friends coming in from Wisconsin to help me care for him at home. Because the sebaceous cyst was full of infection, Jerry required a round of antibiotics.

During this trip, I also talked to the social workers about palliative care (Palliative care is treating the patient for comfort but not aggressively for a cure. Complete definition in a later chapter.) and arranged to have a hospital bed delivered to the house when we got back home. Both of these decisions were partially my giving up and admitting Jerry would not recover from this stroke. I was discussing the possibility of not aggressively treating any health issues moving forward. I would still be able to have home health services. We never were successful in getting the services started, however. Accepting a hospital bed also was admitting Jerry had declined to the point of my needing more help at home with his care. I also hired the nurse aide I used the previous summer to help me with Jerry's lowered physical abilities after the four hospital stays.

The diagnosis of seizures caused Jerry to be on antiseizure medicine, a medication with a side effect of sleepiness. One of the therapists told me during the short time he was on it that she had never seen a patient on this medication, Keppra, who was not a zombie all the time. It sounded like it was definitely not the medicine for Jerry, and this was confirmed by a neurologist visit the next week after discharge. The doctor doubted he had had a seizure, but he also agreed it was not out of the question with a stroke brain. Pretty much anything could happen, however seizures were not typical with his type of stroke. With a change from the Keppra to a newer seizure medicine not as strong, Jerry was again awake for more time. What an adjustment it was working with a brain injury.

I gave him the new medication only once before reading the drug information more thoroughly. It was a time-released medication and therefore did not work when crushed to be administered through a PEG tube, because that took away the time-release properties. Jerry would get the entire dose at one time rather than slowly throughout the day. A call back to the neurologist and pharmacist straightened that out, and a new medication was investigated. One more issue with medications! I was the one to discover this by reading the paperwork with the medication myself. The information clearly said it could not be crushed, but one had to read the material!

A scripture to encourage me during this time was Isaiah 30:20−21.

Although the Lord gives you the bread of diversity and water of affliction, your teachers will be hidden no more; with your own eyes you will see them. Whether you turn to the right or to the left, your ears will hear a voice behind you saying, "This is the way; walk in it."

There were so many decisions to be made for Jerry on my own. It was a daunting task. Even as I filled his pill bottles on a regular basis, I felt the responsibility of getting it right for him. I was waiting for the voice in my ears to help direct me through these dark days. But the darkest was about to change to more light.

Things I Learned While Caregiving with God!

1. I have learned how to put on a condom catheter after Jerry was asleep in the dark, using a flashlight, and how to keep draining catheter bags from stinking.
2. I have learned how valuable good neighbors are.
3. I have learned that home health is one of the best ways Medicare spends our tax money.

Papa and grandchildren Kinsey Herbel, David Manning out for ice cream.

The ending of the thirty-four-day dark season involving four hospital stays and two one-week skilled nursing stays brought a more stable period in caregiving. Home health therapists moved from occupational, speech, and physical to almost totally physical soon after that time. There was even a two-month period when Jerry was completely discharged from home health. Brighter days arrived, and we were settled into a new normal.

With fewer therapy sessions each week, there was more time for Jerry and me to be together just the two of us, go out more afternoons, and enjoy our new life together. The aide I hired for help through the difficult days moved on to other ventures, and our needs for him diminished. Jerry was far from recovered from the stroke but was at a more manageable stage for us both. That did not mean he was easy every day or that the delusions were gone. This Jerry was still not the Jerry I had married, however we moved into a stage of more routine as far as sleep schedules, toileting, and outings. The morning wake-up times never moved to a predictable time, but total awake time for the day did. It settled into being awake for four to six hours each day and normal bedtime at 4:00 p.m. This meant he slept from eighteen to twenty hours each day!

About two weeks after our arrival home after the fourth hospital stay, I knew we must be getting back to a better place with Jerry. One morning as I was kissing on him and telling him I loved him, I asked if he had too much loving. He said, "Yes, it needs to stop." Less than five minutes later he said, "You can start loving me again." I prayed hard this phase would stay, however the home health nurse that day told me these phases come and go with stroke patients.

As I was kissing him goodnight one evening in January, I asked if I was kissing too much. He answered, "Probably, but I like it." Another time when I was kissing him at night, I asked if it was all right. "What kind of numbskull do you think I am? Of course it is," was his response. He was responding to the attention and becoming more spoiled all the time. Still another time, he asked me not to kiss him. I asked him how long I must wait, to which he answered, "Forty minutes." I told him I couldn't wait forty minutes, so how about two? "Okay, sure," he gave in. He liked to tease and liked to be loved on!

As things settled into a new normal around the one-year mark, the time I had with Jerry was so rewarding. Our lives often had been so separate with us working either too many jobs or too many hours in our drive for financial survival. We ran in many different directions for much of our marriage, resulting in often not seeing much of each other. Our move to Wisconsin remedied some of that for a time. With my job in Minnesota going from part-time to full-time to part-time back and forth, I ended up with two jobs, with teaching at the technical college filling in around the high school job schedule. Again, during our years in Wisconsin, we didn't see much of each other.

After the stroke, we spent twenty-four seven together, and what a blessing it turned out to be. Of course, this wasn't the Jerry I had married, but he was the Jerry I had now. Here is a quote from *The Broken Way* that described it better than I could.

Experiencing the whole world will not fill our bucket like experiencing giving yourself and finding the meaning that will fill our soul. (Voskamp 2016, 92)

I received so much more than I gave in caregiving. When I focused totally on the needs of others, my own needs didn't seem as important anymore—just as God always made sure my needs were met as well.

As we neared the one-year anniversary of Jerry's stroke, he had another swallow study. The suggestion was to have him on a Dysphagia II diet, which had some pretty significant changes from the mechanical soft diet he was on. He was now restricted to no breads, cakes, cookies, ice cream, or even milkshakes because the thin liquids posed the danger of aspiration. Ice cream and milkshakes melted in the mouth, turning to thin liquids going down the throat. The speech therapist also said there was a quality of life to maintain. I took that to mean he could still have his favorite ice cream, but not every day. All medical indications said he would not recover from the stroke, which would allow me to continue pampering him from time to time.

The diet changes caused menu changes from my perspective. It was difficult to keep meals healthy when the softest foods were pastas and potatoes—carb overload. Breakfast was the easiest with bananas, as well as scrambled eggs with cheese and sausage ground very small and cooked into them. There were still times when I would feed him pumpkin breads or similar breakfast breads—remember quality of life! The second meal of the day would be lots of baked potatoes, including sweet, mashed potatoes with gravy and meats ground small, and lots of soups. As little as he was awake, we could only get in two meals a day. However, I closely watched the calorie and protein count and maintained his weight throughout the stroke period. He had very few tube feedings in 2017.

The speech therapist watched me feed him breakfast after his swallow test to ensure I was doing it correctly. She praised me for working with Jerry at his speed rather than mine. She also cautioned if an aide was here to help with his care, I should not let the aide feed him. Aides often fed too fast, causing choking issues. The menu changes seemed drastic to us, without full menu choices at our disposal. However, as the therapist noted, Jerry would eat what I offered him, not knowing there could be more. He never complained about his meals, except for Mexican food. He loved Mexican pre-stroke but refused to eat it afterward. Stroke patients often had taste preference changes.

Liquids needed to be kept to medium thick. This meant every drink required adding thickener to it first. His chocolate milk was perfect because it then resembled a milkshake. I stirred in a fiber additive to orange juice, which also helped with regularity and thickening. He loved his coffee and never minded it being thicker as long as it had his sweetened creamers. I kept the thickener in the car for the times we ate out.

Eating out required some planning. Jerry loved eating at Panera Bread and always ordered the same thing. For that reason, it became our most frequented place to eat out for their broccoli cheddar soup. He also had another favorite soup, Zuppa Toscana at Olive Garden. I would ask the kitchen to blend it down to small chunks but not pureed completely, and they complied, offering great customer service. Any restaurant where we could order mashed potatoes, baked potatoes, soups, soft vegetables, and fish broiled instead of fried would be acceptable. Italian dishes such as lasagna and most other pastas also met his dietary requirements.

Another consideration was the wait time to order in a sit-down restaurant as opposed to Panera, where we ordered when we walked in. Any extra time out could create a problem for us with Jerry's limited time awake each day.

When physical therapy sessions moved from three days a week to two or less and then to none, it became important for me to keep him active myself. As hard as I tried to get him to do therapy exercises with me, he almost always refused to cooperate. I wasn't as young and pretty as his normal therapist. He always worked harder for the pretty therapists. However, the therapist told me getting out in the afternoons would be just as much therapy for him. On days he didn't have a doctor's appointment or therapy and he wasn't delusional, we would go out to Panera Bread, Braum's (our local ice cream store), the grocery store (I would push him around in his wheelchair, holding the small basket in his lap), the park for a picnic, the school to visit our daughter's classroom, the coffee shop, or friends' houses. Some days we'd sit in the garden when the weather permitted. These times were great for us both. I loved having him along with me, he loved getting out, and we bonded closer than ever.

One of the times Jerry refused to do assigned physical therapy was truly humorous. The therapist said he should fold small laundry such as wash rags because it would be good for his hand coordination. I proceeded to bring him some laundry after reminding him what she had said. Jerry's response was, "It was a suggestion, not a directive." Once again, I failed to get him to cooperate. About a month later, I asked again if I should get some towels to fold as the therapist suggested. "Yes, that would be fine," he responded. "Will you fold them?" I asked. "No," he said. Just ornery! Again, I asked him one day about the things the therapist suggested he do for himself. His response was she wasn't a soft touch like I was, so he didn't have to for me. He had figured me out!

God continued teaching me the skill of waiting.

Since ancient times no one has heard, no ear has perceived, no eye has seen any God besides you, who acts on behalf of those who wait for him. (Isaiah 64:4)

Waiting was so hard to do, especially when it seemed there was no light at the end of the tunnel. But God had brought us both through the most difficult part of the stroke and was now providing us with a more peaceful, restful time of our twenty-two months. God will act in our behalf if we wait on Him. Our world is one of such instant gratification. Amazon delivers in two days or less. Television provides being there live as it happens, as well as instant replay. Cooking got faster with the newer pressure cookers such as the popular Instant Pot, along with microwaves. Groceries are now delivered to our doors. This makes it harder to wait on anything. God has His own time schedule, which works when it is truly the best for us—not when we think it is best.

Jerry was getting easy to care for most days and nights. One evening when I waited too long to put on his catheter for the night, he was awake and completely wet before I went to bed. I changed the whole bed, sheets, blanket, shirt—everything. I told him, "Now you can go back to sleep nice and dry." Jerry replied, "Bless you, my son." Appreciation from him was so rewarding. Another time when I changed him in bed, he said, "I appreciate all you do for me." Another day he said, "I like the way you treat me." It was so much easier to do these tasks with that kind of response.

I gave Jerry a new nickname after he came home from skilled nursing during our thirty-four-day dark time: sweet guy. My training was as an educator and, part of that training was learning about self-fulfilling prophecy. I decided that calling Jerry sweet guy could potentially convince him he was a sweet guy all the time. He was normally a sweet guy even in the toilet routine, or "emptying his bucket" as he named it during his first skilled nursing stay.

One morning in January, to give me true hope, at breakfast Jerry said as he was looking at me in an admiring way, "You are just so gorgeous." Gorgeous was his nickname for me for years, but it was the first time since the stroke eleven months earlier he had called me that. It made me cry for the memory and the state of normalcy. Not long after that, while drinking his morning coffee, I ran to the bathroom. When I returned, he was walking to the sink to put in his empty cup, scaring me. His balance held, but I told him he was to wait for me. "I can do something by myself," he told me. Oh, how he wanted to be himself again.

The scripture in Philippians 4:19 guided me.

And my God will meet all your needs according to the riches of his glory in Christ Jesus.

The word *all* is a complete word. We came through some struggles, to be sure, however my needs were always met. God helped me get more sleep when I was awake changing Jerry's bed, and He provided calls, visits, and cards on lonely days. He provided just the right morning devotionals and scriptures to meet my spiritual needs and good times with Jerry following difficult times. He truly met all my needs from day to day.

From time to time, starting around February of the second year, Jerry would take off humming or singing the old hymn "Precious Memories." I never focused on finding out why that song, but I wondered whether he was aware of how much he had forgotten. The memories he kept had to be precious to him. I knew we were creating some very precious new memories for me to cherish the rest of my life.

A big part of Jerry's normal life returning was moving to wearing his old underwear. This decision was made for several reasons. Jerry was getting better at using the toilet, especially when

76

I was careful to keep him on a schedule (just like potty-training a child). The other more important reason was the problems incontinence briefs caused. The elastic around the legs started causing issues on Jerry's skin and even at one point bleeding where it rubbed the legs. No matter how much Calazime or other creams I put on the affected areas, I could not keep the area from being irritated. I remembered what helped with babies, open air was a wonderful healing agent. I moved at night to no briefs or underwear of any kind to promote healing. If the condom catheter stayed on, there were no problems. If it came off, he was going to be wet no matter what.

The bowel movements he had in bed were not more difficult to clean up without the briefs on. I used disposable bed pads over the fabric bed pads, which helped considerably with the cleanup process. I think Jerry enjoyed the feel of underwear over diapers. He told the girls and me many years previously that if he were ever to need to wear diapers, we were to take him out and shoot him. Knowing that, I did my best to keep him out of them.

Another contributing factor to skin breakdown was Jerry being on Plavix, an anticlotting drug to fight potential future strokes. It makes the skin fragile and easy to bruise and cut. Just a simple rub of the arm on something on the wall, like a light switch, would cause a bleed that took at least a week to heal.

Once, about a year into the stroke, Jerry's thinking focused. Here was our conversation.

Jerry: I'm going through a metamorphosis. I'm changing into a rag doll—a mirror of what I was. I feel weak today because my body parts are changing. It is hard to say. My legs are definitely not acting the way they used to. My upper arms are sort of different-well different. My brain definitely works differently. I think differently--sort of differently. Hard way to think of what to say. It is frustrating. I remember what happened. I changed in how I thought. [He didn't remember what happened to cause the change.] It is sort of like I changed the way I was thinking.

Me: What do you think about my taking care of you all the time?

Jerry: That was funny, the way you were taking care of me all the time. I've never had anyone taking care of me like that. You were taking care of me like I'm two years old. It doesn't bother me. I like to be treated like I'm two years old, and I like the way you treat me. You were treating me like Kara (our daughter). All of a sudden you were treating me like her—like a kid. But I like that.

Me: Is there something you would like me to do differently?

Jerry: I would like to be treated like a ninth grader. It is a lot like a two-year-old. [All of a sudden, Kara was all grown up.]

Me: What is your future going to be?

Jerry: Don't think about the future—just today.

It was so awesome when God gave me these special moments to keep me going. Jerry was aware of many differences and described them beautifully. It was also great to know he didn't mind my care of him even though he realized I was treating him like a child. This was certainly a change from early in the stroke, when he fought me for his independence. He had accepted his limitations.

78

Jerry's dependence on me became more evident as we went through year two of the stroke. I left him with a neighbor as I went to a doctor appointment and had another one planned. When I mentioned the neighbor would stay with him the next time I went, his response was, "Can't I just go with you?" Another example happened later that fall when he woke up early enough to attend the men's Bible study at church, and I excitedly asked if he wanted to go. At first he said yes. After thinking about it, however, he said, "No, I just want to stay with you." It was a precious dependence on me.

Jerry's singing continued throughout the stroke and brought special delight to me and others. He sang for his speech therapist one day, who was amazed. She said it was unusual for a stroke patient to recover his singing voice. At close to a year post-stroke, he started singing in his sleep. It was both delightful to hear but also kept me awake. It was often very loud. His singing in church or with internet music was wonderful to hear. He kept his bass harmony, which vibrated around him. A side benefit from his singing was his continued high level of oxygen in his system. One nurse was very surprised at this because most patients who sleep so much have difficulty with oxygen levels.

Jerry's therapy sessions improved during this time. The therapist said his mental ability to evaluate was also improving. We were all encouraged by the good days and obvious improvements. When I mentioned to Jerry what a wonderful job God was doing in his recovery, Jerry said, "He sure is!" He realized it as well. One evening after reading from *The Twenty-Third Psalm for Caregivers*, Jerry engaged in a conversation with me over the topics we covered. Then he asked me to pray over him. I prayed with him every night, but he was asking this time. We both prayed. It was so sweet and encouraging for me. He didn't pray often after the stroke because words were so hard to put together for him.

Another evening I was taking off Jerry's shirt and asked if he would give me a hand, and he did. Then he said, "I didn't think you wanted me to applaud you." The thought processes were improving, at least on some days.

The new normal had some disadvantages. As Jerry got stronger and his balance improved, he thought he could do more than he could. We had a hospital stay in March from a fall as a result of this confidence. He was sitting in the sunroom, ready to go to the garden. I told him I was going out to get our lawn chairs and would be right back to get him. This took only minutes, however he decided not to wait for me and got up.

As he fell, he hit his head on the windowsill, which previously was an outside window with a brick edge. It didn't knock him out but scraped the hair off the side of his head, causing pain and bleeding. We checked into the ER, and the triage nurse looked at the bad scrape on his head and asked Jerry if it hurt. He looked at her and then said, "Yeah," in a tone saying, "Duh." It did look nasty.

A side effect of a concussion is vomiting, causing Jerry to have another episode of that as well as the cut. He was admitted due to the vomiting and possible bleeding in the brain. Also, the eye on the side of the fall was very swollen. With the returned vomiting, I stayed the night with him. Nurses don't check often enough to do the necessary suctioning to keep down the possibility of aspiration pneumonia. I told him not to worry about my ever leaving him because I would be there to care for him. He responded, "You don't know how good that makes me feel." He truly wanted me right there all the time. This was a short stay, thankfully, because they did not find a brain bleed or sign of concussion, allowing us to get back home, where the healing really happened.

The short stays were easier to recover from, however the bump on the head gave us some weird days with Jerry before getting back to normal. One of the fun things about the more normal days was talking in fun with our son-in-law, Tim, using a cockney English accent. They were both good at it, and Jerry thoroughly enjoyed the verbal sparring.

I took Jerry back to the eye doctor to attempt to get a prescription to work with his damaged eyes. The doctor kept answering my questions by not answering: this wouldn't work because of that or the other—around in circles. The doctor got up to leave and said goodbye. Jerry, to show the brain was still working, responded, "Thank you for being so obtuse." Jerry's humor was so fun to experience.

When visitors came to see Jerry, he didn't want to miss a minute of their time. Our friends from Wisconsin came for another visit and were getting ready to leave. Jerry said, "I want them to stay." Visitors were welcomed by Jerry and especially by me. It was great to have a break in the day.

April of the second year was when Jerry's brothers from California came for a visit. There originally were seven brothers, and at this time only three were left. Marvin was six years older than Jerry, and Bob was two years younger. They stayed for three days, and Jerry was so uplifted by their visit. They reminisced, and it was almost as if Jerry's brain was functioning normally again. He stayed awake almost their entire first day in his excitement over having them here. Of course, then he slept through almost the whole next day. Their visit did so much for all three of them. The night they were flying back to California, Jerry said a prayer over their travels that was truly precious and well worded. The older brother, Marvin, passed away three and a half months after Jerry's death. Jerry remembered their visit for a few days and basked in the memories.

The Lord has done great things for us, and we are filled with joy. (Psalm 126:3)

Joy didn't wait for things in life to be totally good. The days of the stroke had shown me there was joy in the littlest things and in the magnificent gift of salvation.

Jerry was being such a sweet patient for me. I developed a head cold in April, which would make anyone feel crummy. That morning when he woke up, I explained the cold I had to him. All day, he was concerned for me, watching me and wanting to stay close to me. Even though he knew he couldn't take care of me, his concern was touching and healing for me.

> No one can believe how powerful prayer is and what it can effect, except those who have learned it by experience. Whenever I have prayed earnestly, I have been heard and have obtained more than I prayed for. God sometimes delays, but He always comes. (Martin Luther)

This quote was very meaningful to me as we entered such a peaceful, joyful time in Jerry's care. I went through a year of struggles, adjustments, and drawing closer to God. The response to all my prayers was always heard and answered when God knew it would be best for us both.

One of the mornings we made it to church, after getting Jerry back in the car to go home, he got very angry and insisted we turn around and head back to the church. My daughter met us to help get him back in the foyer. He wanted to see people. Pre-stroke, Jerry had always visited with everyone he could—a true people person. He was also angry with our daughter for helping me take him away too soon from the people he loved.

Back at home, he said he wanted to talk to me. He apologized for jumping all over me and said, "I acted not just belligerently but in a demeaning way. I perceived a wrong and started to right that wrong. I had been inflicted with a wrong—I left too soon. I wanted to see people. I wanted to see that rectified." Not only was the apology so sweet and sincere, but this was my old

Jerry coming out—the one who wanted to stay and visit with everyone before leaving. It was a wonderful happening in the midst of his anger.

Another snippet of Jerry's progress was the day he was saying some strange things when he woke up from his nap. When the physical therapist arrived for his session, she asked how he was today. His response was, "Strange." These times let me know part of his cognitive thinking was still there to recognize his behavior.

Jerry was an avid reader all his life. When his brothers were in high school and reading Shakespeare, it looked interesting to him (in grade school), resulting in him reading the entire works for himself! Now that his eyesight would not allow him to read anything that wasn't projected and very large, I read to him often. Each night I read a devotional to him and prayed with him before bedtime. I would also read to him when he would wake up in the evenings to help him go back to sleep. One night when I asked him if he wanted me to keep reading to him, he said, "I like it when you read anything to me."

Worship at church didn't happen very often due to Jerry's sleep schedule. However, the worship services in our living room became part of our new normal. Often it was just Jerry and I singing with online sites, reading a devotional book, listening to a sermon online, and then having communion. There were also many times when the whole family was involved in the service. The Sundays when David and Kinsey (our grandchildren) were here, I always involved them in the service. It was good to not only hear their thoughts and comments but also have them feel a part of the worship rather than sitting in a big audience. These times became very special to me.

Jerry's analytical mind never quit working after the stroke. When we went to the doctor, he would stare at the acoustic ceiling tiles with the holes in them. One day when I asked if he was looking for patterns, he said yes. Another time when I asked if he was looking for patterns, he said he was looking for bilateral patterns. This was less than two weeks before he died. His mind was amazing. One night after I read the evening devotional to him on joy in suffering, we discussed it. He said he was content but not content. "I don't have all the pieces of my thinking but am content," he said. How sad his brain was so damaged, but how amazing he could find contentment in that state.

The new normal did not mean there would be no more hospital visits for him, unfortunately. In May he somehow caught a virus, causing more vomiting and taking us right back to the hospital. There were so many nights I spent sleeping in the ER either in a side chair or with my head on his bed while sitting in a chair. Jerry was always aware of my presence, and I never wanted him to be alone in the ER. I would have loved to stay in the room with him when he was hospitalized, however I knew I needed to be as rested as possible when we returned home.

God took care of us in many different ways during our twenty-two months after the stroke. After moving back to Oklahoma in July 2014, we installed a safe room in our garage in 2015 in case a tornado hit our area. This shelter sat above ground, resulting in much more comfort for Jerry if we needed it. There was never a tornado warning requiring us to go to the safe room. Tornadoes typically come after three in the afternoon, which would necessitate waking up Jerry from his sleep to get him to a safe room. This would have been extremely difficult even with Tim and Lynn's help to get Jerry awake, into the wheelchair, out to the safe room in the garage, and propped up so he could go back to sleep. God protected us from ever needing to go there during the twenty-two months.

A new understanding of Genesis 2:24 came to me one Sunday in June.

That is why a man leaves his father and mother and is united to his wife, and they become one flesh.

This is a very well-known verse used in most wedding ceremonies. The thought of being brought together made me think of the marriage union. At our wedding, Jerry and I said "I do" and vowed to live together until death do us part. However, the stroke months made that commitment very real. We had a stroke February 24, 2016. We had physical limitations. We had a limiting sleep schedule. We had a new life. We limited our activities to what fit our new awake times. We had doctor appointments. We had a new diet. We had the same responsibilities but shifted who did what. We stayed home most of the time. We decided where to go out in the afternoon. We had become one flesh! More than ever before in our marriage, we were truly one. Jerry was so dependent on me, however when I was out away from him, my mind never quit wondering what he was doing and how he was getting along.

As closely connected as we were, however, Jerry was still insecure at times. He never wanted me to be away from him, as I mentioned previously. One day in June, our daughter Lynn was staying with him while I was out doing a little shopping. While I was out, he told her he didn't think I was coming back. This comment of his made me not ever want to leave him, but it also made him very happy to see me on my return.

Things I Learned While Caregiving with God!

1. I have learned the tear ducts never run dry.
2. I have learned a loving home environment is therapeutic.
3. I have learned people are what is important in life. Possessions require money, repair, cleaning, and storage; often have to be moved; and eventually have to be sold or given away.

Good friends Mara and Paul May from Wisconsin

The caregiver's journey is one needing support of all kinds. Throughout Jerry's stroke, my God was my strong tower, my refuge, my strength, my Father who listened and answered, and my companion each and every day. My morning quiet time was essential to the day going well. I learned that my evening prayers—especially in my garden, weather permitting, and during days of longer sunlight—were critical as well. I called out to God many times through my advocate of the Holy Spirit during the day and asked for the strength of His Spirit to help me accomplish my caregiving duties.

The second support network that I could not have survived without was my daily journaling on CaringBridge. Writing my thoughts, activities, and concerns; sharing a scripture and thought; creating my thankful list; and asking my readers to pray for specific needs became a true lifeline for me. Each comment left by my readers was read and was an encouragement to me. The prayers were a strength and brought answers from my heavenly Father, and I felt I was being lifted up daily.

> But encourage one another daily, as long as it is Today. (Hebrews 3:13a)

This was a good foundation verse for having a CaringBridge site. The daily encouragement from my readers was invaluable.

Facebook provided a connection for so many family and friends who weren't following CaringBridge to be kept up to date. Prayer requests were shared on the site, and additional prayers were lifted to the Father. People who knew my children but not me were also praying for us through that connection. Comments would be posted on CaringBridge from people I didn't know, but I was thankful for everyone.

Very early in the stroke (on day thirty-five), one of my cofacilitators from Bible Study Fellowship presented me with a prayer quilt made by the ladies at her church. It was lap size and had ribbons stitched on it with knots tied in it. Each knot indicated a person who was praying for us both. As visitors came to see Jerry, they would add a knot, indicating they were going to pray. To this day, the quilt serves as a precious reminder of the prayer support during the twenty-two months.

Proverbs 12:25 says, "Anxiety weighs down the heart, but a kind word cheers it up." Friends do that—they lighten the load you are carrying. Proverbs 18:24 states, "One who has unreliable friends soon comes to ruin, but there is a friend who sticks closer than a brother." The friends who reached out to me during the twenty-two months were precious. We lived back in Oklahoma eighteen months before Jerry had his stroke. Strong friendships had not had time to be formed and closely bonded. There were a few who jumped in to support me as they could.

When Jerry first had his stroke, a neighbor called and said if there was anything he could do, I should let him know. About six months before the stroke, Jerry had started to put a gate in the fence on the east side of our house. We were getting a garden shed built, and not only would it be easier for the workman to carry in supplies on the side the shed would be on, but it would also be easier for me getting the mower from the shed to the front yard. He got as far as cutting the fence to allow for the middle section to be posted as a gate. After I thought about my neighbor's request, I called back and told him that the fence was something he could do. I asked if he could please hang the gate in the fence. He was thrilled to have a job he could accomplish, and I was thrilled to have the gate finally installed. The neighbor's significant other mowed my lawn until I got home from the nursing home. Great neighbors are a treasure! People simply need to be told how to help.

As mentioned previously, a friend from church helped make the house handicapped accessible. He also made some repairs for me at the house. Another friend from church picked up the recliner I ordered for Jerry to use at home for his naps. A third friend worked on a side walkway at the house I had started but had been unable to finish after the stroke. All I did was ask for the help.

My friends back in our Wisconsin church set up a schedule to call me on a regular basis. There were weeks I would receive several calls a week, and other weeks I received just one or two. The calls were always an encouragement to me. The stack of cards sent to me was amazing. I tried to read each one to Jerry and show him the colorful card. He seemed to recognize the names of those who sent them, but I will never know for certain.

Some special friends sent me good books to read to help me get through the days. These were very encouraging, and I have sent several to friends of mine who would get into caregiving situations after mine started and even since Jerry passed away. Others would email me a song they found especially meaningful. All these helped tremendously.

I posted often on CaringBridge about our many trips to Panera. Jerry loved Panera, and in all the years we ate there, he always ordered the same thing: broccoli cheddar soup and a sierra turkey sandwich. I could always be sure he would want what I ordered for him. During our twenty-two months, I received over seven hundred dollars in gift cards from friends all over the country to Panera alone, along with others to our local ice cream shop and an occasional one to Olive Garden or Red Lobster. We used every one of them. What a blessing to me! Often dark chocolate was on my thankful list as a major comfort food. I also received dark chocolate from friends and through the mail.

Kelly Ann's mom worked at Olive Garden. Anyone who knew Jerry knew he loved the Zuppa Toscana soup from Olive Garden. She would call from time to time to see if it was a good time to drop off some soup for Jerry. He loved it, and I appreciated the thought so much.

During the skilled nursing days, I didn't feel comfortable leaving Jerry during the day because of his poor eyesight and the time between staff checking on him. Several of the people we knew at church, especially from the men's Bible study Jerry had attended, would volunteer to sit with him. One even came to sing with him. The nursing home was close to our church, and we received several visits from staff and the Praise Team, who came to sing with him. Older women came to sit with him so I could go get a haircut or run needed errands. They could turn on the call light if they needed help.

Once home, getting people to stay with Jerry was not practical, and I totally understood. Staying with Jerry at home meant taking him to the bathroom if needed, knowing how to get him up from a seated position, walking with him, feeding him, keeping him from falling, and always realizing the possibility of delusion. This was more than I could ask anyone to do, cutting down drastically on who could relieve me outside of a paid nurse from an agency.

Several of my lady friends would occasionally come and bring lunch to eat with me or with us if Jerry was awake. Those were special visits to brighten my day. As the newness wore off, people tended to get busier with their own schedules, which I understood. My good neighbors Bert and Wanda kept up their support to the very end. Bert didn't mind learning how to get Jerry up and down, and because he was a man, he could help him with the bathroom if needed. Bert was a tall man, which gave him the height needed to help Jerry. I called them several times for help. If Wanda was going to the store, she would text to see if I needed anything, which I often did.

Because of what I learned from the speech therapist about feeding Jerry, each meal took up to forty-five minutes to feed him because of the slow process of chewing and swallowing with his compromised abilities. This encouraged me to stay home with him during mealtimes unless my daughter, Kelly Ann, or others who were trained were available.

The next-door neighbor was a very sweet woman of eighty-two years of age during the time she was helping. Once I got comfortable with how long Jerry would nap, when he went down, I would call to see if she could come, and she would zip right over. I could get to the closest Walmart Neighborhood Market and back within about thirty-five minutes. There was only one time he woke up while she was here, when a delivery man rang the doorbell. That time, I found Jerry sitting at the table. He had gotten out of his chair, and she managed to help him sit down at the table.

Once he was home and the stroke care continued, much of the interest from others slowed down or stopped. The staff from church did not make visits after we came home. Most hospital stays were without many visitors other than close family and friends. I was settling into a time of being on my own with my sweet guy. There were times this made me feel deserted and forgotten. I also realized my own actions in the past with similar situations lasting into months and years and forgetting these people still needed prayers, cards, and visits. God truly filled the gap, helping me to know He never left me. I relied on the promise He made to Joshua in Deuteronomy 31:6, when Moses told him, "Be strong and courageous ... the Lord your God goes with you; he will never leave you nor forsake you."

Home health provided therapists, and nurses came regularly during our time at home except for two months. We kept the same physical therapist, Jenny, during the entire time in home health services. We saw her from one to three times a week during the times services were approved, causing us to get to know each other very well. She would come for an hour, and if I was desperate for something at the store, I could leave her with Jerry when she came and have an hour to return home. Nursing visits were also from one to three times a week. These visits from people provided us both with a contact from the outside world.

When we moved back to Oklahoma City eighteen months before the stroke, it put me closer to my family, who lived mostly in Texas. I was blessed with visits from several of my cousins during the stroke days, some from Dallas and others from the Houston area. My sister also got to come twice to see me. Jerry's two remaining brothers were in California. They made one trip together, and the younger one came another time, plus he came for Jerry's memorial service. Several friends from our Wisconsin family also made some encouraging trips to see us. Some were from our small group, and others were adopted family from there. Each visit was a bright spot in our days of the stroke.

One special friend, Linda, lives in Hereford, Texas. I was on the path from her home to see relatives in Missouri. She would take the time to stop and spend the night with me on one or both ways. Linda had cared for her mother for over five years until she passed away. Because of her caregiving times with her mother, Linda's insight was precious as I cared for Jerry, and each visit was a great encouragement to me. She was one of those friends I could tell everything to, knowing she understood my heart and kept things in confidence.

> But God, who comforts the downcast, comforted us by the arrival of Titus, and not only by his arrival, but also by the comfort he had received from you. He told us about your longing, your mourning, and your zeal for me, so that I rejoiced all the more. (2 Corinthians 7:6–7)

Comfort, encouragement, strength, courage, and endurance all come from God. But as this scripture says, we can also be comforted by those who visit us. Any time you visit someone who needs it, God is using you. When you send a card or write a journal comment on the CaringBridge of anyone you follow, God is using you. When you put people on your prayer list and hold them up in prayer, God is using you. How wonderful we can be God's hands, feet, and voice.

My immediate family is both here in Oklahoma and in Georgia. Our oldest daughter and her husband live about ten minutes from our house. It is a blended family, with my grandson living here but splitting his time between mom and dad. My step granddaughter lives in Dallas and is here every other weekend, plus holiday time, being split between the two homes. My daughter Lynn, who lives here, is a high school teacher, giving her the most availability during school breaks and summer. The reality of our children's support was that their lives were extremely busy. Lynn is a high school choir teacher, giving her the responsibility of concerts, musicals, and many after-school and weekend contests and choir trips. She also conducts the Norman Children's Chorus, requiring more time during the week. My son-in-law is an entrepreneur, spending many hours getting a business started plus several side jobs to keep earnings coming in during the business growth period.

I learned to accept their lives were full to overflowing. Lynn loved her dad very much but also had a family and a job to take care of, requiring most of her time. Sundays became the time when we almost always saw them. They would come for breakfast at times and join in our living room worship. When they became involved in a new church, they would come for lunch after church. Their Sunday schedules were as busy as their schedules during the week, and twice a month they had to leave by 1:30 p.m. for choir practice with Windsong Chamber Choir. The grandkids stayed here during that time and were picked up for the 4:30 p.m. class my son-in-law taught at church.

Jerry genuinely enjoyed seeing them for their weekly visits. He adored the grandchildren even when he couldn't remember who they were. Lynn and our son-in-law sang with Jerry. On some Sundays, part or all of the family were here for our worship service in the living room. Jerry loved having them around for whatever time they could be here. Their presence added to the loving environment for Jerry's healing.

For me, this was great family time but not great support time. I ended up planning and often cooking a big part of the meal for the week. Because getting to the grocery store was such a challenge to schedule, it was difficult. I learned to accept the fact they were doing what they saw as support by working us into their busy lives. I appreciated that fact. There were times I needed to call on Lynn for an emergency situation, but I tried to keep those to a minimum. When the grandkids were here, they were willing to run the vacuum, clean the bathrooms, or do anything else I asked them.

In order for me to be able to maintain contact with my grandson David, who lived here, Lynn either brought him over on Tuesday afternoons or had a student drop him off after school. David saw very little of Jerry because Jerry was going down for the night about the time David arrived, but it gave us a time to be together. We ate dinner together and enjoyed fun activities once his homework was done. This was precious to me because my time was so limited to be with the grandkids. After Jerry's death, Tuesdays with David have continued. We love our time together.

My other daughter, Kara, living in Georgia, was miles away throughout the twenty-two months. She and her family work in the film industry, and every job is a contract one for a specific movie. Because of this, they can't schedule vacation time—or sick time for that matter. Her time was quite limited to visit. She was here the first summer for a week when Jerry and I really needed her help. The second summer, she came with our other two grandchildren for our golden wedding anniversary and stayed for a week. Jerry loved her presence and attention. Then she was here the first week after Jerry passed away to help me get some things organized.

There were many calls to Georgia for Jerry to talk with them. When he was delusional, one of the best ways to get him back to reality was to distract him. Calling someone we knew often helped a lot to change Jerry's thinking. There were days when I called everyone I knew who might be available to talk to get him to a better place.

Caregiving for working moms and dads with families is a tough one for sure. As the population ages, this will become a greater challenge for them. Parents will still need to be cared for, but it won't be an easy task. In years past, parents moved in with their children, and everyone took care of grandma and grandpa. Today's society lives apart from families, and support systems have been created by our healthcare system. Today's nursing homes are a response to those needs. However, with decreasing availability of staff, the challenges could increase as the aging population increases.

Out of my friends' support, the most consistent was Kelly Ann, Lynn's best friend. She and Lynn became friends four years before Lynn had any children and remained in a strong friendship through the years. She is the family hairdresser, and she loves to serve others. Early on, she came to the hospital and the skilled nursing facility to keep Jerry's beard and mustache trimmed, as well as trimming and cleaning his finger and toenails. This service was invaluable because I would have eventually learned the process, but she was already a pro. We settled into a routine of her coming every Wednesday and Saturday morning for about two hours of time. She learned the caregiving duties and was comfortable being left with Jerry if I needed to get out to an appointment or pick up things at the store.

Kelly Ann lost her sister to cancer four months prior to Jerry's stroke. All the unpleasantries of home nursing care did not bother her, and she developed a good sense of how to take care of things. Jerry endeared himself to her during her time of caring for her sister, and now she wanted to return the love. Jerry included her as one of his daughters, which she accepted with love. Kelly Ann was always willing to get something for me, stay with Jerry at the hospital while I ran home to shower, or sit and talk with me. She has no children of her own, and her husband often works strange hours, giving her an availability not many have. Kelly Ann's support was a true blessing and helped me get through long days and weeks.

This chapter needs to end as it began: with the support from the Father, Son, and Holy Spirit. When other friends and family could not be here, I was never alone. God would give me scriptures to help me through each day. It ever ceased to amaze me how I would read a scripture perfectly fitting how I felt that day or filling a void.

Here are just a few of the meaningful scriptures.

Why, my soul, are you downcast? Why so disturbed within me? Put your hope in God, for I will yet praise him, my Savior and my God. (Psalm 42:11)

God was the reason I could face each day without my soul downcast. He was there when I woke up in the morning and through the night. He was the reason I could sleep so well knowing I needed restful sleep.

Ask and you will receive, and your joy will be complete. (John 16:24b)

I questioned having joy as we began this journey; however God kept showing me joy. He would give me precious moments with my Jerry from time to time. He gave me hugs and kisses from my sweet guy. He gave me the joy in Jerry's future life in heaven after he struggled with his physical body after the stroke. I don't believe I ever experienced complete joy like I did during our twenty-two months together.

Weeping may stay for the night, but rejoicing comes in the morning. (Psalm 30:5b)

Some nights after a long difficult day, it seemed my joy was gone. However, God always refreshed me by morning and returned my joy to me. This happened over and over, with God never allowing me to stay in the depths too long.

I can do all this through him who gives me strength. (Philippians 4:13)

So many days I would question my ability to keep going day after day. However, promises such as this (and the next one) affirmed to me that, yes, I could keep going. My strength didn't come from me but from above.

To this end I strenuously contend with all the energy Christ so powerfully works in me. (Colossians 1:29)

Energy was a constant need. Jerry slept a lot, but then he also needed assistance a lot during the night. There were mornings when I had already done three loads of laundry by 8:00 a.m. It seemed on those days, God always provided additional morning sleep time to catch up for what I missed at night.

He gives strength to the weary and increases the power of the weak. (Isaiah 40:29)

But those who hope in the Lord will renew their strength. They will soar on wings like eagles; they will run and not grow weary, they will walk and not be faint. (Isaiah 40:31)

I knew the strength I needed physically could not come from me. I was thankful I had kept my body in good shape for age seventy, when the stroke happened. However, I was being called on to do physically demanding jobs in my care for Jerry. Physical therapy trains you how to transfer the patient without lifting. Jerry weighed 175 pounds, so lifting was totally out of the question. I was up and down on the floor while dressing and bathing Jerry. Changing the bed completely at night required rolling Jerry back and forth while changing the bed half at a time. God kept providing strength to my often weary body.

God is our refuge and strength, an ever-present help in trouble. (Psalm 46:1)

God was ever present in good times and times of trouble. We seem to be more aware of His presence during the troubled times. We often forget about our need for Him when things are going well and we can "handle it" ourselves. God answered every prayer, every need, and every situation that arose. He was my refuge, my safe place to run to and cry out for help.

The Lord is my strength and my defense; he has become my salvation. (Psalm 118:14)

Being my defense meant He was fighting for me—I could sit back and let Him handle it. He became my salvation not just in the way we normally think of salvation, the saving us from our sins. My Lord was my salvation throughout the long days and nights, the delusions and hallucinations, the hospitalizations and nights spent in the ER. He saved me daily.

> If any of you lacks wisdom, you should ask God, who gives generously to all without finding fault, and it will be given to you. (James 1:5)

Wisdom was something I suddenly needed mega doses of when it came to making decisions for Jerry. I had always gone to Jerry for wisdom because he was such a wise man who drew his wisdom from God. Now I was making decisions about repairs in the house, paying taxes, paying bills, investing in my son-in-law's business, and managing the household completely alone, not to mention making decisions about Jerry's care. How much was I to feed him? What medicines was I to give him? What care did he need or was unnecessary? How was I to plan for my future financially? How was I to plan for Jerry's and my inevitable end of life?

I came to the realization one day I had replaced asking God for wisdom by asking Jerry for his wisdom. Jerry already seemed a mature man of God when I had met him. He was twenty-five as compared to my twenty. Not only had he worked and lived on his own for several years, but he was known for his knowledge of the scriptures. God always gave me answers and a feeling of security knowing I was relying on God. There was a security I felt in Jerry's presence, believing he could take care of anything I needed. He was adept at making financial and career decisions, and I saw him as a man with tremendous spiritual maturity.

It is tempting to read a good book, listen to an inspiring sermon, draw close to a Christian friend, attend an enriching conference, and put faith in our mother or father or any number of other sources of wisdom. Proverbs 27:17 tells us, "As iron sharpens iron, so one person sharpens another." Although these are all sources of thought-provoking ideas and even advice, true wisdom does come from God. Keep reading those books, listening to Bible class teachers and pastors, attending conference, sharing with friends, and taking advice from parents and spouses, but seek God for the wisdom that can only come from Him.

From the day we married in 1967, I put my faith in Jerry as the head of the household in all ways including spiritual. We became very active in our local church and in hospitality. We went on a mission trip together. Eventually Jerry served as a deacon and then an elder at church. Everyone looked up to him for his spiritual wisdom. He became my go-to for advice, knowing his source of wisdom was his foundation of faith and knowledge of God. I never thought about the fact I was replacing my asking God for wisdom with asking Jerry for wisdom until Jerry was no longer there. The security I always found in Jerry was now found in God, who always gave me answers and a true security in reliance on Him.

Your eyes saw my unformed body; all the days ordained for me were written in your book before one of them came to be. (Psalm 139:16)

The first time I read this one after the stroke, my first thought was, "Wow. God knew all about the stroke and my caregiving." This gave me great comfort because now I could look back and see how He had prepared me through experiences in my life to be able to do this work. He knew the day I was born, I would marry Jerry, and our lives would reach its highest point in the twenty-two months at the end. He knew all He was going to teach me through the time. It was all written in His book.

My soul is weary with sorrow; strengthen me according to your word. (Psalm 119:28)

My grieving started the day of the stroke because I had lost my Jerry that day. There were many days I cried because of what I had lost and what Jerry was going through. I had a wall-hanging over our bed that said, "Grow old with me. The best is yet to come." It hurt so much to read that until God worked through the true meaning with me. I was grieving because we would never grow any older together. Yet heaven was the best and was yet to come. It came sooner for Jerry, but what a blessing for him to be home with a whole body again. God continued to strengthen me in my sorrow after Jerry's passing on to sing in the heavenly choir.

> You keep track of all my sorrows. You have collected all my tears in your bottle. You have recorded each one in your book. (Psalm 56:8 NLT)

God keeps quite a journal. He had my life written down before I was born, and He also kept track of every time I cried. I found a wall plaque shortly after Jerry passed away that held three bottles. I had a friend letter it with the previous verse to hang over my bed.

As you can tell, the Psalms became my go-to for comfort and strength. I read Psalm 23 as if I had never read it before.

> The Lord is my shepherd, I lack nothing. He makes me lie down in green pastures, he leads me beside quiet waters, he refreshes my soul. He guides me along the right paths for his name's sake. Even though I walk through the darkest valley, I will fear no evil, for you are with me; your rod and your staff, they comfort me. You prepare a table before me in the presence of my enemies. You anoint my head with oil; my cup overflows. Surely your goodness and love will follow me all the days of my life; and I will dwell in the house of the Lord forever.

This psalm was packed with comfort for me. My garden became my green pastures, with my pond and its running fountain as my quiet waters. Many evenings, God refreshed my soul while I worked in His beauty. The stroke days could certainly be perceived as the darkest valley of my life, but God took away my fear with His presence. We were in the presence of evil and enemies when Satan tried to get into Jerry's head on several occasions. The promise of dwelling in heaven forever was more real with Jerry's life coming to an end. I truly lacked nothing, and my cup was overflowing. I was living the abundant life.

> The thief comes only to steal and kill and destroy; I have come that they may have life, and have it to the full. (John 10:10)

> Precious in the sight of the Lord is the death of his saints. (Psalm 116:15)

I have held onto these two verses since Jerry passed away. I remembered back to the days when I was pregnant with our girls. Once I knew a baby was in the making, I made many plans. The nursery was set up, and I bought necessary items to bring our child home. Family celebrated with us, and we all waited in great anticipation of the birth of each child. On the day of each birth, there was great joy in receiving this precious child into our lives. Love was abounding over our new family member.

How much more must the joy be at God's receiving one of His faithful home forever? I could almost hear God saying to His Son and Spirit, "My kingdom there has enjoyed this sweet servant of ours for seventy-seven years now. He has suffered long enough. Let's bring him home!"

Understanding those scriptures in this way doesn't make me miss Jerry any less, but it gives me a different perspective on his death. It is God's plan all along to take his children home to live with Him forever. My job is to rejoice over his new life in heaven, and to let God give me back my joy in this life.

Even with all the people who rallied around me at different times during the twenty-two months, there were many days and hours when it was just Jerry, me, and my heavenly support team. I soon learned that was enough! God was helping me live the abundant life by taking care of all my needs and giving me joy and peace in the midst of my husband's stroke.

I found support in many different places. Sometimes I had to ask for the support, and other times the support found me. People generally wanted to help but often didn't know how. Suggesting something they could do was appreciated. Once your caregiving is over, either through recovery or death, you are trained and prepared to offer support to others in similar situations.

Things I Learned While Caregiving with God!

1. I have learned how journaling through CaringBridge is a great way to create a community of support while creating a place to transparently share the struggles of a dependent patient.
2. I have learned how important it is to have family support, and how much it hurts when I don't have it.
3. I have learned how valuable a phone call or visit from a friend is.

7 - Fighting for the One You Love--Put on Those Boxing Gloves

Out to dinner with my sweet guy

My training to be Jerry's advocate started in skilled nursing. I grew up in America in the 1950s and 1960s, so I had been trained to respect the medical profession and accept doctors and nurses as authorities. By coming from that background of trusting authority without question, it was a shift in my thinking to ask more questions and demand good care for Jerry.

Comparing the hospital setting where Jerry and I had constant attention on the acute stroke unit and moving to a skilled nursing facility setting was quite an adjustment. In the hospital, we had a call light connecting us audibly with the nurse's station. Call lights were answered in a timely fashion. At the skilled nursing facility, the call light turned on a light outside the door and on the desk monitor, but nothing audible was turned on at the nurse's station. The nursing assistants had to see the light to know we needed help.

Once, after waiting two hours early in our stay in skilled nursing for a call light to be answered, I discovered there had to be a better way to get attention for Jerry. Because Jerry slept so much and was seeing double during his stay there (as far as we could tell), turning on the call light by himself was not possible. If I wasn't there, it didn't happen.

As time went on, I learned to walk down to the nurse's station to seek help, learned where the supplies were and often got my own, and essentially squeaked loudly to be heard and taken care of (hopefully quickly). Also, Jerry had been left up to two hours wet or needing a messy brief changed. I didn't learn to change them at first but needed to voice my frustration.

As mentioned before, Kelly Ann had a client who was a patient advocate and was willing to come help me learn to fight. She arrived and immediately asked to talk with the head nurse for the facility. When she arrived, she asked questions about what a reasonable time was to expect certain things to happen like a brief to be changed and a call light to be answered. The information was good for me to start becoming bolder in speaking up for Jerry's care. This was not to say the one conversation took care of everything and the response time was remedied as I wanted. However, it did empower me to step up to the plate for Jerry.

As a result of that first meeting, Jerry was given an air mattress to help with the possibility of bed sores. On several occasions after that meeting, I contacted the building administrator, who always immediately contacted the shift manager, who would then check on me. But it wasn't a one-time talk that took care of the situation. The administrator informed me they were staffed above Medicare standards for their type of nursing facilities. Unfortunately, those standards meant there was never enough staff to care adequately for the number of patients they had.

Many times, nurses and nurse aides would end up working a double shift because of inadequate staff available. For some, this would mean they worked eighteen or more hours straight. No one could give adequate care with that kind of demand on them. I believed I had to be there as much as possible to make sure things happened. The longer I was there, the more care I gave. They didn't tell me I couldn't and often welcomed the help.

Once home, the advocacy did not end. One of the early ER visits was due to Jerry's blood pressure being too high. If the diastolic (the bottom number) was over 100, it was more of a problem than the systolic (the top number) being over 160. I learned how to take the blood pressure at home, first using an automatic machine and then moving to a stethoscope and blood pressure cuff for a more accurate reading. If the diastolic number was too high when I first took it early morning, I had to wait a couple of hours and take it again. On this occasion, it was still too high when the home health nurse came, who suggested a trip to the ER.

Of course, they did all the necessary blood work and prescribed a medicine to bring down his blood pressure. I highly recommend that you talk to the pharmacist when you fill a prescription like this one. The physician's training is in diagnosing health issues. The pharmacist's training is in how medications work and the contraindications of taking medications in combination. The pharmacist advised this one definitely brought down the blood pressure but often had a negative rebound effect. This episode was the beginning of taking many questions to the doctor and deciding what to do with new medications. Questions to the home health nurse often gave me a different perspective on blood pressure medications, along with other medical practices.

During a hospital stay in November, about nine months into the stroke, it was a battle from the beginning of our time there. No orders were put in for food or water. Can you imagine? I had to ask questions, move to the next level of command, and keep asking until action happened. It was so frustrating when I was giving him care at home and knew what he needed on a daily basis. At the hospital, my hands were often tied, causing me to look for the scissors to untie them!

Following the hospital stay just mentioned, Jerry was taken to a different skilled nursing facility to get some intensive physical, occupational, and speech therapy sessions. Upon arriving at the new facility, I was impressed with how beautiful it was from the decor and seeming cleanliness. However, an indication of what was to come immediately was the lack of a recliner in the room. There was one side chair in the room, telling me I was not welcome to spend the night if needed. I don't think they wanted me around throughout the night.

We arrived there Friday evening—typically not a good time to arrive at a skilled nursing facility. Weekends were sparse with staff other than the regular nurses. The admitting nurse saw his PEG tube and assumed he was on tube feedings. as was indicated on his chart. I started my advocacy by asking for an upgrade from that or pureed meals to a soft mechanical diet. Next, I asked for the director's number to call and discuss the change with her. The nurse came back reporting she had called the director to let her know the wife "was not happy" and the orders were changed. I was also able to get the orders for water through the tube changed. This was just the beginning of the director hearing from me during this short stay.

On Saturday, my daughter came in, and we asked about the shower schedule for the facility. For Jerry, it had been almost a week since his last shower, and I had found him in bed messy from a bowel movement. I asked the nurse if we could give him a shower. This facility had showers in each room. The weekend staff was normally a little easier to work with, and she agreed. My advocacy paid off, and Jerry got a very relaxing and needed shower with my daughter's help.

On my arrival the third morning, Jerry was extremely wet and had a bowel movement overnight. When I saw how wet he was and then saw the horrible rash that had developed from sleeping in the feces, I immediately called the nurse, and I also discussed it with the associate director of nursing. Upon changing him again later that day, I found more dried fecal matter, indicating it had been there quite some time. The nurse aide agreed the rash had not been red the night before confirming my concerns.

This was the third day he now had extremely runny bowel movements (which resulted in two showers not on the schedule). The nurse said she would stop giving him his stool softener. Oh, my—why would one give a stool softener given what was going on? I ended up in a very long meeting with the associate director discussing this and a few other things. There was no stool softener ordered, and she assured me none had been given. I thought, *Then why did the nurse admit she had given him one?* More issues for me to deal with.

While I was still struggling to get the water orders set, the nurse who came in that evening was going to make up for the water missed throughout the day by giving him sixteen ounces of water then. As she gave him the water, I asked if his meds would also be given in eight ounces of water. Well, yes, they would. When I stopped her after giving sixteen ounces of water, she was very abrupt with me, saying, "I thought you wanted the sixteen ounces of water." Perhaps this nurse didn't take basic math, but we were already at sixteen ounces of water, with another eight to come later. Hmm, were we trying to float him away? Her attitude was what disturbed me: she acted like I was causing extreme problems when she was doing what I wanted. This attitude was replicated over the next few days.

I wrote in my journal on the day this happened:

As my advocacy for Jerry today often feels like I am getting too bold, I think of the Holy Spirit taking our requests to God and translating for us. He is our advocate, and I must be Jerry's. I want to be bold but also want to be kind and understanding. I was with the associate director of nursing today, but the way the nurses look at me, they probably see me as another grouchy wife! One of the times Jerry woke up on Saturday, I asked if he knew who I was. He said, "Yes, you are my advocate." He knows I am here advocating for him every day.

On day five of our stay in the facility, the physician came to see us, and the associate director of nursing was with him. When he asked why I had not gone back to the first skilled nursing facility, I told him this one was highly recommended. When he said he hoped they had met our expectations, I bluntly said no, explaining the issues I had experienced. He told the associate director it was unacceptable, and because I had cared for Jerry at home for five months successfully, "We need to listen to her. She has done well." As thrilled as I was to hear that, his statement didn't last through the stay.

There is a scripture in Ezekiel 22:30 (CSB) applicable to this situation: "I searched for a man among them who would build up the wall and stand in the gap before Me for the land, so that I would not destroy it; but I found no one." There would have been a huge gap in Jerry's care if I was not serving as his advocate and standing in the gap for him. So much would be missed in his care. An advocate stands in the gap, for sure!

The next day, following the encouraging physician meeting, it was quite apparent the message had not gone down the chain of command. Jerry was on half the dosage of his wake-up meds (trying to control the combative side effect), and that caused him to be much sleepier than even two weeks previously. When the nurse came in to get him up on her schedule, I asked if there was any concession for those with a bilateral thalamic stroke, explaining that he had little ability to awaken and was being given less wake-up stimulant. Her response in a rather snippy tone of voice was, "Well, if you don't want him up, we will let him sleep all day. This is a rehab facility, so we thought you wanted him up." It was 8:00 a.m., which was a time he was rarely awake on any kind of stimulant.

Before she came back, he was super wet. I turned on the call light to get her back. When she arrived, I told her he was very wet and asked if we could change him now. "I thought you didn't want him up," was her snippy response. So far that morning, he had not gotten his ordered water through the tube, causing me to administer eight ounces myself before his scheduled therapy session.

That got an immediate visit from the director of nursing— we moved up from the associate director. I was informed I was not to give water to the patient even though the weekend staff told me I could. What communication problems! One would have thought I had tried to sabotage their nursing efforts when I was simply making sure Jerry got what he needed. The next I heard from her was wondering why he hadn't eaten his lunch at noon despite the fact he hadn't eaten breakfast until 10:00 a.m. An aide was there to wake him up from a deep sleep to ask if he wanted a shake to make up for it. My first reaction was to ask why such ridiculous rules were in place and why was there no consideration for differing patient needs. However, I refused to let her wake him up.

This facility had a policy against using bed alarms to alert the nurse's station if Jerry got out of bed on his own or fell out of bed. When I discussed it with the social worker and told her what I thought of this policy, she agreed with me. She went to the long-term side of the facility and brought me an alarm to use. Another advocacy battle won.

On day seven of our stay, when I came in for the day, the empty catheter bag and catheter were lying on the floor, obviously having come off during the night. When I checked, he was swimming in a pool of urine. His meds were given at 6:00 a.m., indicating a nurse had been in at that time. It was hard to imagine all this had happened after 6:00 a.m. The nurses also did not attach the catheters correctly because he had some extremely irritated red skin. The administrator who caught me in the hall and asked how things were probably was not happy to hear today's report.

The final straw with this skilled nursing stay came on day nine of the stay. I arrived at my usual 7:30 a.m. to find Jerry with the bed elevated and bed pads all around. The trash can was on the floor close to the bed. I headed to the nurse's station and asked what was going on, however it was easy to tell. He had been throwing up since 3:00 or 4:00 a.m., and his blood pressure was elevated to 167 over 130. Of course, my first question was, "Why wasn't I called?" I never wanted him throwing up without my being there to sit beside him every minute. Their policy was not to call the family until the patient had thrown up three or four times.

The nurse then told me she had called the doctor, who had ordered a dose of Clonidine. He'd previously had a bad reaction to that drug, and I was told by his cardiologist to never give it to him again. When I told her both his cardiologist and neurologist advised against that medication, she responded, "You can leave him here without the Clonidine and let him have a heart attack, or you can take him to the ER." After clearing my head briefly and talking to Kelly Ann, I asked an ambulance to be called. While I was at the ER that day, Lynn and Kelly Ann cleaned out his room, and we decided he was not going back there. I sent a seven-page letter to the director of nursing with my complaints.

After a four-day hospital stay, Jerry still needed more skilled nursing time before we could go back home. I made the decision to go back to the first skilled facility despite all the issues we had had there. I now felt more prepared to advocate for his needed care. The nurses were told of how I kept the rash off his bottom with my care at home, causing them to be more attentive. I was also insistent on the forty ounces of water a day, but I must admit I gave him most of it myself, or else he would have had only eight ounces the first full day there. I made it clear I wanted no medication changes during our stay.

On our third day back at this facility, another issue came up with feeding him breakfast, previously discussed when they did not put in his dentures first. They also had not combed his hair—he looked like no one cared for him. There was no question why I spent so much time there to ensure he was cared for properly. This was my husband, and I wanted him to look like he was truly loved because he was!

I received some validation my advocacy was bold from the doctor we had seen at the hospital the last three stays. He questioned me as to why we were returning to the first facility rather than going back to the second and more recent one. After sharing some of the problems at the second one, I told him I was now bolder as Jerry's advocate, so believed I could demand the care he needed. To that, the doctor responded, "I didn't think you had a problem with being bold." I thought to myself, *I have arrived as a patient advocate.*

When Jerry went to the ER, I always printed the current medication list before I went. If he went by ambulance, they also wanted a copy of his DNR. One visit in March, the medication list was taken by the admitting ER nurse, causing me to assume she put it in as listed. However, the next morning when they came to give his meds and she read them (as I always requested), it wasn't the updated list. I had to refuse some of the medications and correct it with the doctor. Jerry needed me there all day (and night too, when I could give up the sleep).

During this same visit, I had another conflict with the nurse over his condom catheters. When she brought it in, I asked what size it was and was told 29 millimeters. When I informed her he wore 35 millimeters, she said I could bring some from home. I also informed her she was putting it on incorrectly, which would cause irritation for him. I was using my nicest voice, but this nurse was not happy and told me she had never put one on—it was her first. I guess she didn't want to hear the experience of a wife who put them on at night, under the sheet, either using a flashlight or just by feel (after I warmed my hands with a microwaved rice bag). The things I learned as a caregiver!

A hospital visit about six months later had the staff finally listening to me more. When I offered advice to a nurse putting on the condom catheter, she listened and corrected what she was doing. Another staff person during that visit did not give a medication they wanted to give because it would have made him so much sleepier. I found over and over, however, how unusual my care was from the normal spouse or significant other. They learned to trust me more due to the success I had with my sweet patient.

As I got more vocal in my questions and concerns, my daughter noticed they seemed to listen better. I learned not to be afraid of saying anything of concern and took it to the nursing manager for the floor. They want to make patients and families happy and offered gift baskets a couple of times, as well as cafeteria gift cards. Of course, I wasn't complaining to receive gifts but to ensure Jerry had the care he deserved—as do all patients.

> But very truly I tell you, it is for your good that I am going away. Unless I go away, the Advocate will not come to you; but if I go, I will send him to you. (John 16:7)

As I read this verse again, I realized how much the Holy Spirit does for us as our advocate. My thoughts were constantly on what they were doing to and for Jerry—and the consequences of what they were not doing. I never stopped asking for what he needed and interceded on his behalf whenever needed. My place was by his side to be sure the care was right. What an awesome thought to know the Spirit living within me was advocating for me with even more strength and perfect wisdom as to what I needed in every situation.

One of the funniest times I received affirmation from Jerry about my role as advocate was when the family was here from Georgia for our fiftieth anniversary. We discussed how he enjoyed all the attention he was getting. Then I asked Jerry if I was his advocate. His response was, "You're darn tootin!"

Jerry's last hospital stay in August of year two resulted in my having to be the most forceful yet. Jerry was almost comatose and staring at the ceiling. After doing a CAT scan that showed nothing, the OU family medicine team ordered an MRI. The nurse asked if he would need something for calming him down for the MRI. Memories of the last one when he woke up in the MRI and went ballistic came to mind. He was in restraints a week after that one in June of the previous year.

"Yes, he will need meds to do that," was my response, especially considering his lowered mental state. They kept paging family medicine to get an order of one of two meds. I refused one of them because the neurologist had told me it could cause hallucinations and delusions. As they were getting close to taking him down, the nurse said they still hadn't gotten a call back and that I needed to sign a consent form down there for the MRI to be done. "So, if I don't sign it because he hasn't gotten meds, they won't do it, right?" was my response to her.

She looked horrified and asked, "You wouldn't do that, would you?" Lynn and I assured her I would—she didn't know who she was dealing with here.

After getting into a room at 1:30 a.m. with Jerry having scary hallucinations, I realized I would not be able to go home that night. Throughout the night, there were several issues, which I addressed with the nurse manager the next morning. The nurse manager listened well to my concerns. She agreed it made no sense to have only one size condom catheter (the first issue), and I shouldn't have to bring in my own as the nurse suggested. When I asked about the Nystatin powder (on his med list) for the yeast infection I had been treating, they said I should bring mine from home—they didn't have it here (another issue). The nurse manager said that was not right and promised to address the issues. I received another gift basket for voicing my concerns. Of course, I did it for Jerry's care to be what it should be, but the gift baskets were a nice touch. Being a patient advocate was a constant battle but one I was willing to continue to fight. Where would Jerry have been without me?

On a side note, please remember to be empathetic and gentle with your comments to the nursing staff. The nurse hearing your complaint could have just come from another room where either the patient or advocate brought something to his or her attention in a less than nice way. Everyone has a day when things go wrong. Your nurse could be having one of those.

The LORD will fight for you; you need only to be still. (Exodus 14:14)

When I read this verse, I thought this described Jerry and me. Jerry was totally still through all my fighting. He lay there, and I fought—and hard! I knew what he needed and advocated until he got it. I knew my patient and how he reacted to good care and not-so-good care. Jerry didn't have to ask me to go to battle for him; it was my job. I researched to find out what I needed to know to be his advocate. I asked questions. I didn't quit fighting until I got resolution! As a medical team, you probably didn't want to go up against me!

The comparison to God fighting for me was crystal clear after my advocacy experience. God fights for me while I sleep. He knows what I need and when I need it. The Holy Spirit advocates for me to the Father on a day-by-day basis. How fortunate I am to have such a perfect advocate.

Things I Learned While Caregiving with God!

1. I have learned how much I truly miss Jerry's gorgeous bass voice singing every day.
2. I have learned no matter how attentive my caregiving was, I still missed things, and he still had ER visits and hospital stays.
3. I have learned you have to fight for your loved ones as an advocate to get the care they need and deserve.

8 - Finding a Sanctuary for Survival While Being a Captive in Your Own Home

The survival of the caregiver depended on many things. One of the most important, I believed, was to create my own sanctuary for a retreat when possible. God met me in the sanctuaries of my garden and my prayer corner in my sunroom. I couldn't leave the house without great planning and willing volunteers who were trained to help with Jerry's care to come to stay with him, so it was best for me to find a haven at home.

My little time away from the house was not enough to replenish my soul to continue going the next day, the next month, the next year. It was critical to have a sanctuary and a prayer place. Yours may be a comfortable chair with a stack of books you want to read. My sister found great comfort when she had knitting needles in her hand and was busy creating something. Some like to be involved in various hobbies such as stamping, scrapbooking, woodworking, painting, quilting, or sewing. Every caregiver needs to find that perfect getaway to have even thirty minutes to oneself to build oneself back up.

Another survival tip is to take care of your physical body needs. For me, it was finding a massage therapist who would come to the house for monthly massages to ensure my back would stay in shape. The price for me was worth it. This was a more valuable expense for me than paying an aide to stay with Jerry while I got out of the house for alone time.

Exercise is difficult to get at home. However, YouTube and many channels on Amazon Prime, Netflix, or other video streaming services will provide you with the opportunity to work out in your living room. You can also purchase exercise DVDs in many forms of exercise. As important as it was for Jerry to be awake every day to keep up his strength, I needed to keep mine up as well.

We have a great example of Jesus going to gardens many times during His ministry. The ones recorded are the times when He was under great stress from what was coming or a decision He needed to make. The times when He just got away by himself, He sought nature. Jesus felt closer to God when He was closer to nature.

There are many reasons I love my garden so much—seeing God's creation and beauty, as well as the many lessons He teaches me. The daily lessons helped me see beauty, creation, serenity, faithfulness, the power of rest, patience, and more. The more I dig in the dirt, the more God seems to speak to me.

> I John, who also am your brother, and companion in tribulation, and in the kingdom and patience of Jesus Christ, was in the isle that is called Patmos, for the word of God, and for the testimony of Jesus Christ. (Revelation 1:9 KJV)

This was the verse in my *Streams in the Desert* devotional book early in the second year of Jerry's stroke. Of course, history tells us John was exiled to the Isle of Patmos, but I never thought about what this would have meant to John at the time. He was involved in ministry, and being exiled was definitely a kink in his plans. Here is a section of the devotional.

It might have been thought that John in dreary exile was terribly isolated. Someone has said not isolated, but insulated, and there is a world of difference between the two. True, the island was small and his confines narrow, but that was only the outer circumstance of his life, his daily environment.

Nothing to see! Alone! Ah, but John found it not so! The overwhelming glory of sight of his risen Lord robbed him of his strength until he felt the gracious gentle pressure of the pierced hand resting upon him. Again and again he tells us that he heard a voice speaking to him. Whilst these things were so he could never feel that there was nothing to see! He could never feel alone! And the Spirit so insulated John that God's messages might pass through him to the entire world! (Cowman 2016, 305)

I was exiled on the isle of caring for Jerry in southeast Oklahoma City. I went through many different phases on this journey. I felt isolated from the world at times. I felt like a prisoner trapped in my house with my husband, who couldn't be left alone. And yet God worked through me and insulated me as I turned to Him for more and more for support. This season of exile had its moments—I can't deny that. There were times when I wanted to go shopping and spend as much time as I wanted wandering up and down the aisles, go out to dinner and not feed someone, go to dinner later than 2:00 p.m., or go to a movie or the theater. But God satisfied my needs every time I turned to Him; it was when I didn't turn to God that I got into trouble.

There are other examples of exile in the Bible. Abraham was seventy-five years old when God told him to leave his country because God was going to bless him, to make him the father of a great nation. He had to wait another twenty-four years before the promise came true after trying to "help" God out by having a child by Hagar. He had a long wait for God to bring his promises to fulfillment. (Genesis 12–17)

Joseph was forced into exile by his jealous brothers selling him into slavery in Egypt. If that wasn't bad enough, he ended up in prison after being falsely accused by scorned Potiphar's wife. Finally, interpreting the Pharaoh's dream allowed him to be put into a position of authority to save the people of the land from the impending drought. When he was finally reconnected with his brothers who had sold him years previously, Joseph's understanding of his exile was clear to him. In Genesis 45:7, Joseph revealed to his brothers they were part of God's plan to provide food during the drought. As difficult as the exile was for Joseph, he could see God's providence in preparing him for the great task at hand.

Moses was in exile in the land of Midian for forty years after he killed the Egyptian and had to flee for his life. He settled there, married a wife, had children, and had a quiet life working as a shepherd. Don't you wonder what Moses thought about God calling to him after those forty years of a life of solitude and telling him he was going back to Egypt to free His people? We know he tried to get out of it with several excuses of not being the one for the job. God used those forty years to bring Moses to leadership (Exodus 3).

Elijah the prophet was directed by God to leave where he was and go to the Kerith Ravine east of Jordan, where God provided a stream to drink from and ravens to bring him food. He stayed there until the brook dried up (1 Kings 17:2–8). Don't you wonder what God taught him in this nature retreat? After the great victory at Mt.

Carmel (1 Kings 18), Elijah had to flee for his life. He ended up in a cave in Mt. Horeb after traveling forty days and nights. Elijah felt very depressed and thought he was the only servant of God left, so he had a pity party. However, God told Elijah He was going to pass by. There was a great wind shattering the rocks, an earthquake, and a fire, but God was not in any of these. I love that God chose to pass by in a gentle whisper (1 Kings 19:12). God assured him there were seven thousand who still served Him, and Elijah needed to get back to work.

I think God needs to get us in exile where we are away from the busyness of the world to get our attention enough to hear the gentle whisper. God has all the strength to be able to speak to us any way He wishes, but He wants us quiet to listen to His loving messages.

After Paul's conversion, he spent three years in Arabia (Galatians 1:17–18). It is conjecture what Paul did for three years, however it would make sense he needed to study the life of Christ and his teachings after so fervently attempting to kill Christians. Whatever the reason, Paul spent some time away preparing for the ministry he had, establishing churches around the known world.

During my exile of twenty-two months, I enjoyed the luxury of my garden. It was the perfect sanctuary for God to come to me, hold me, speak to me, have me still enough to listen to His gentle whisper, learn to wait on Him, and mature in my faith. The garden exile was just what I needed.

The garden was also a sanctuary for Jerry. One day in our last October together, we were sitting in the garden in the afternoon. It was a little cool, but sitting in partial sunshine covered with a blanket made Jerry comfortable. At one point I said, "Isn't it wonderful out here?"

"It is one of God's mysteries," he responded. When asked why, he said, "How can God create in one place—create so much beauty?" I felt the same way as Jerry. It was not only my sanctuary but also Jerry's sanctuary. The serenity and beauty of my small backyard was a true gift to us both.

Nature and gardens have been considered valuable throughout history. This quote from Cicero says it all: "If you have a garden and a library, you have everything you need."

You will seek me and find me when you seek me with all your heart. (Jeremiah 29:13)

As I get older, this verse is especially meaningful. How many times do you go through the house looking for something you just had yesterday? Or an hour ago? Our seeking of God will not be in vain but will always produce a find. Perhaps this is because God wants to be found. He wants us to seek Him because He wants to be our refuge, our helper. I called out to him consistently for Jerry's mind to clear and for my strength, wisdom, and patience. I sought God in my garden, and He was there waiting for me every day! My backyard isn't very big, but it was and is a true sanctuary for me.

I am reminded of a song I loved to sing while growing up, "I Come to the Garden Alone." Here are the lyrics.

> I come to the garden alone,
> While the dew is still on the roses,
> And the voice I hear falling on my ear,
> The Son of God discloses.
>
> And He walks with me, and He talks with me,
> And He tells me I am His own,
> And the joy we share as we tarry there,
> None other, has ever, known!
>
> He speaks and the sound of His voice,
> Is so sweet the birds hush their singing,

And the melody that he gave to me,
Within my heart is ringing.

And He walks with me, and He talks with me,
And He tells me I am His own,
And the joy we share as we tarry there,
None other, has ever, known!

I'd stay in the garden with Him,
Though the night around me be falling,
But He bids me go; through the voice of woe;
His voice to me is calling.

And He walks with me, and He talks with me,
And He tells me I am His own,
And the joy we share as we tarry there,
None other, has ever, known!

—Words and Music by C. Austin Miles, 1912

I sang this hymn as a child and adult, and it was simply a pretty song. The harmony is good, and the song is serene and reverent. Now that I have experienced firsthand walking with God in my garden, holding His hand, listening to His sweet voice, and feeling the love He showered on me every day, the song is very precious to me. It was a true joy to be in the garden with Him during the stroke months. My garden therapy is still a critical part of my continuing life in my relationship with my Father.

Therefore let us draw near with confidence to the throne of grace, so that we may receive mercy and find grace to help in time of need. (Hebrews 4:16 ESV)

Prayer means we are coming close to God's throne! How awesome is that thought? As far as I was concerned, His throne room was within the privacy fence of my backyard by the pond and my prayer bench. I could approach that throne any time, no matter how dirty I was from all the garden work of the evening.

Florence Williams is a researcher discovering the benefits of nature for a variety of health issues. She discovered that the Japanese go "forest bathing," spending time in the forests for the calming and relaxing effect it has on their mental state (Williams 2012). Japan has forty-eight official forest therapy trails, with more in the planning. Because the Japanese work long hours and feel the pressure of competition, the government has put a lot of research into this type of therapy. Nature is now being looked at as medicine by many researching this idea of forest bathing.

Dr. Mercola discussed a malady called nature deficit disorder. This is an increasing field of science called ecotherapy that has been shown to decrease anxiety and depression, improve self-esteem and social connection, decrease fatigue in cancer patients, and improve blood pressure (Mercola 2018). Americans spend between 80 to 99 percent of their time indoors and usually looking at a computer screen, phone screen, or TV screen. This creates the disorder of being deficient in spending time in nature. The benefits are proven effective, so why stay indoors? My garden is the perfect place to cure my nature deficit disorder.

Gardening became a huge part of my life when we moved to Onalaska, Wisconsin, in 1997. Until that time, my children were at home, and I often worked multiple jobs to make financial means meet our needs. As I began this chapter of life with an empty nest, the garden called to me. Within a few years, I became a master gardener and transformed my yard of grass into a sanctuary garden of flowers, a large pond, and places to sit and meditate. I was hooked on creating my garden space.

When we moved to Oklahoma City in 2014, I had a much smaller yard, which fit my aging body. The second summer there, I put in a retaining wall, brought in fresh dirt, and created the beginning of my sanctuary garden in my new home. The timing was wonderful because the garden was in place when Jerry had his stroke. Time in my garden helped to connect me with God in a way I didn't find any place else. My pond was smaller but still had the all-important waterfall giving the sound I so loved to hear. Adding my prayer bench the following year created a place to pray in the evenings for needed strength.

Using a baby monitor, I could spend time after Jerry went to sleep in the evenings digging in my garden, talking and listening to God, and replenishing myself for the next day. With our high privacy fencing, it was a totally private space full of birds, butterflies, and flowers everywhere. It wasn't long before I was gathering swallowtail and monarch caterpillars to put in my butterfly house and watch their transformation into beautiful butterflies.

A favorite lesson from my garden comes from my compost bins. I have five, three of which are the current year's composting materials, and the other two are cooking over the winter to be spread out the next spring (or late winter if ready). Fresh vegetable cuttings from my cooking, grass clippings, weeds, shredded paper, chopped leaves, and trimmings from flowers (especially after they freeze in the fall) go into the compost bin. These are the items most people put in their trash because nobody wants them. It is the trash to be discarded. And yet as it sits and cooks, God turns it into rich soil full of nutrients for the garden—free of charge!

God takes us with all our trash of sin in the same way. We are worth nothing until His grace is given to cover the sins of our lives. God composts us into holy and perfect Christians worthy of living eternally with Him in heaven. It is nothing we can do for ourselves. but as we turn our lives over to God, He transforms us.

In Psalm 90:14, we see why a sanctuary is so important.

Satisfy us in the morning with your unfailing love, that we may sing for joy and be glad all our days.

The sanctuary of my rocking chair was another critical place for me. The rocking chair was in my sunroom, which allowed me to sit about ten feet from Jerry's bed. I could keep an eye on him while I satisfied myself with God's love each morning. Being reassured of His love every day helped me through the more challenging days. I was filled with joy knowing His love followed me all day and would take Jerry home to a fully healed body.

Psalm 92:1–3 gives us another reason for morning time with God.

It is good to praise the Lord and make music to your name, O Most High, proclaiming your love in the morning and your faithfulness at night, to the music of the ten-stringed lyre and the melody of the harp.

I was struck one morning by this verse separating our praises to God by morning and evening. It makes sense to praise God for His love in the morning. What a better way to start the day than to realize the powerful God of heaven loves each one of us dearly. Then at night, once God has brought us through the day, we can praise Him for his faithfulness in getting us to the night safe and sound. Of course, I often praise Him for both on both ends of the day, but I sure liked this idea.

Just as our bodies need to be fed every day with nutrients to keep them working at peak performance, our souls need to be fed daily with spiritual nutrients. Unlike our physical bodies, we can't "eat" too much spiritual food. The more time you spend with God, the more time you want to spend with God.

Nature is full of genius, full of divinity; so that not a snowflake escapes its fashioning hand.

—Henry David Thoreau

The simplicity of nature is a lesson for our lives. Its beauty, consistency, and total dependence on God give us an example to follow.

Often our lives easily become too busy with our church activities. We can get involved with every ministry the church sponsors: food bank, weekly ladies' lunches, prayer groups, midweek Bible study, hospital visits, cooking for shut-ins, doing cleanup around the building, participating in a small group, teaching classes, singing on praise team, sending out cards, working in Bible hour with the kids, organizing baby and wedding showers, planning pot lucks, working with the media team, and on and on. These are all extremely important and a critical part of the church's outreach to the community. However, if we are so busy that we do not take time to build a relationship with God and Jesus and to feel the power of the indwelling Holy Spirit, have we missed the boat? Do we stay so busy doing the church's activities that we don't take time for God?

A devotional recently made me stop and think.

Jesus said, "Have the people sit down." (John 6:10a)

Read what Gari Meacham said about that thought.

Sometimes in our pursuit to be godly; work hard; raise a good family; be a good spouse, friend, and church member ... we forget to sit down. We forget it's not about what we do; it's about who we become. To sit down means we relax our posture. We forgo all temptation to "help" Jesus perform His miracles of provision in our lives and lives of others. We simply sit and wait to be filled by the miraculous hands of our Savior. When we sit down we allow God to work on our behalf, filling us with the nourishment we need in order to go back to our lives and flourish. (Aughtmon et al. 2017, 328)

How often do we measure our religious commitment by our activity? God wants us to develop a relationship with Him first and foremost, followed by relationships with those we serve with and are trying to teach about the love of God and salvation. We need to sit and let God come into our hearts through His Word, prayer, and His presence. We need to sit and watch God work His miracles. Only after our relationship with God is in place can we effectively serve Him as we interact with others.

That is what a quiet time will do for you. In your special place in your home, simply sit and allow God to work with you. Allow Him to come close to you. Allow Jesus to hold your hand and pray with you. Allow the Holy Spirit and His power to abide in your soul. Sit and be filled. Only after that can you be effective in whatever God has for you to do that day. This is not a one-time filling either. We can't have quiet time with God tomorrow morning and then be good for the week. It is a daily communion with our Lord, a daily filling of our spiritual cup, a daily seeking God's help for the day, and a daily singing praises to God thanking Him for His goodness.

Things I Learned While Caregiving with God!
1. I have learned there is no better way to start the day than with God.
2. I have learned a garden is a place of God's beauty and a solace for the gardener.
3. I have learned how much I miss corporate worship when I can't attend but also how meaningful worship in my living room could be with just Jerry and God.

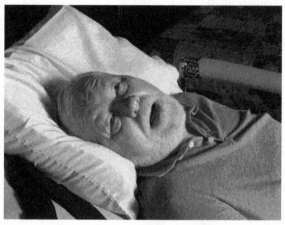

Hallucinations and delusions can be caused by many factors with a stroke patient. Deciphering the real cause was a shot in the dark. Jerry's hallucinations started in skilled nursing. As the doctor would tell us, causes can be the stroke itself, side effects from medications, an allergic reaction to a medicine, loss of eyesight (remembering things he used to see), a urinary tract infection, or dehydration. We later attributed the hallucinations to the higher dose of his wake-up narcotic.

For those who don't know the difference between the hallucinations and delusions (as I didn't), the neurologist explained it as hallucinations being imaginary images seen and heard. Delusions are imaginary images you only see. According to the website PsychCentral.com, "Delusions are false or erroneous beliefs that usually involve a misinterpretation of perceptions or experiences" (American Psychiatric Association 2018, para. 2). Hallucinations are defined by the same website as follows.

Hallucinations may occur in any sensory modality (e.g., auditory, visual, olfactory, gustatory, and tactile), but auditory hallucinations are by far the most common. Auditory hallucinations are usually experienced as voices, whether familiar or unfamiliar, that are perceived as distinct from the person's own thoughts. (American Psychiatric Association 2018, para. 7)

The first indication Jerry was hallucinating occurred in skilled nursing when a nurse aide told me she saw Jerry late at night staring at the ceiling and speaking aloud. Not too long after that, while I was waiting for Jerry to go to sleep so I could go home, he started staring at the ceiling but with total fear in his eyes. As I questioned him, he finally told me there were dead bodies on the ceiling, and they were saying, "Eat me." No wonder he was scared. We had some long nights with my praying over him, trying to get him to sing with me, and casting out the evil spirits in the room by calling on God's help. I wouldn't leave until he went to sleep, but it was hard to leave, not knowing whether he would wake again in the night with no one there.

During the first week home after the second hospitalization, our youngest daughter, Kara, was here visiting from Savannah, Georgia. Either the hallucinations got more frequent, or I was simply there more to witness them. Kara and I would take turns trying to get his mind back into a better place so he could calm down to sleep.

One evening during her visit, Jerry woke up an hour after going to sleep and was reaching for the ceiling and talking. He was scared and said we all needed to get out quickly as he tried to get out of bed. He saw dead people and warned we would all be dead by morning. Kara started singing silly songs, which eventually got him to change from scary to vivid, and he saw a wonderful girl named Nikki on the ceiling. In trying to bring him back to reality, we suggested we go on a picnic the next day. He liked the idea but started trying to get up to go. He didn't know either of us. We decided to give him the antianxiety medicine he was prescribed while in the skilled nursing facility. We would later learn from the neurologist that many medications can cause hallucinations, including the one prescribed and we had given him. It was such a puzzle to find out what was the right solution for the situation.

The hallucinations were finally brought under control with a medication called Seroquel, given at night to help Jerry sleep more soundly. His wake-up narcotics, Provigil and later Nuvigil, both had the side effect of hallucinations, delusions, and aggression. The decision was made to have Jerry awake less during the day, which also cut down on the frequency of the delusions. The aggression almost totally disappeared.

The delusions, and at times very strange thinking, never did go away throughout the stroke days, but they varied from day to day. Some days he was lucid, and other days nothing he said made a lot of sense. One night, I found him trying to get out of bed at 9:00 p.m. When I asked where he was going, he informed me he had to go to work in the neighbor's attic. This one did have some logic to it from his experiences that day. We had workmen blowing in additional insulation into the attic, and our neighbor had come over with his jumper cables. His mind was thinking and trying to process information of the neighbor and work being done in the attic, but not correctly.

Convincing him he did not need to go to work was another story. His reality was needing to get up for work. It took a lot of talking to get him back to sleep and hopefully forgetting about going to work in the morning. There was no sense in trying to convince him he didn't need to go to work.

Other brain-processing deficiencies would show up from time to time. One evening when Jerry was asleep and Kelly Ann was there, I ran to the store to grab a few things. Jerry slept only twenty minutes and was awake when I arrived home. Kelly Ann had talked about a flower girl whose hair she was doing for the coming weekend. After Kelly Ann left, Jerry was convinced I was not his wife because "she left in the car," which was probably what Kelly Ann had told him. Then he was looking for the five-year-old girl she had left in his care. This shows his mind was working but not clearly enough to process properly the data coming in.

There were different names he called me when he couldn't remember who I was, including his mom, Molly, and our daughters Aimee Lynn and Kara. Also, he called me April, Veronica, his wife's woman, a very good friend but not his wife, Sally, Hazel, Dick Robey (his good friend in Tulsa), and his wife that he used to be married to. Then there was Alice, Sandy, Jenny (our neighbor in Wisconsin), Rhonda, his general manager, Jane, Carol, Hilda, Sophia, Amos, or his brother. Hearing the names he chose was comical in some ways.

There was even one night when he didn't recognize me and told me I needed to sleep in the guest room because it wouldn't work for me to sleep in his bed! (This was right before we got the hospital bed in our room.) When he thought I was Jenny, our neighbor, he said it would be inappropriate for me to sleep in his room. At least his moral character was still there—sort of. Later in the stroke, he said he did not know me. However, when I had him stand up and give me a kiss and a hug, he happily obliged. Then I asked if he always kissed and hugged women he did not know. "Just the pretty ones," was his response. At least he did have his boundaries.

One evening when David (our grandson) and Paula (the exchange student from Germany) were here, I asked him if he ever remembered who I was. He said, "It is a long name." No, I told him it was the shortest of the four of us and then whispered "Lois" to him. He took his hand and put it to his forehead like you do when you finally remember something! He didn't say it out loud, but I could almost hear, "Oh, yeah," in his head. It was pretty funny. There is a story in our history of his not being able to remember my name. When we were dating, I lived in the dormitory at the college we attended. He had to go to the desk and have them call me down. As he left his dormitory room, he would have to ask his roommate, who knew me, what my name was because he would forget from one date to the next.

Another day he said, "I wish I knew who you were." It was also rare for him not to remember his name, however one day when I asked who he was, he answered, "Juan Montoya." Another time I was on the phone trying to set up his online patient portal. Because I was calling for Jerry, she asked Jerry over the phone what his name was. He responded was, "Jose Jimenez." What a hoot! Needless to say, I couldn't set up the account. One day later, he was George. When I told him he was Jerry, he looked truly confused and even a little scared. In late November, he thought he was Santa Claus. We had been listening to Christmas music, which could have given him the idea. This could also have been a memory. During the Christmas season, he would wear a Santa hat every day. With his white hair and beard in his later years, children were always pointing him out to their parents and whispering. If he noticed, he would play the part and ask what they wanted for Christmas.

During our last hospital stay when he didn't know my name, I told him my name was Lois, his wife. He said, "That is a common name, and you are not a common person. Your name is Sophia— that is not common." I mentioned that to the neuro team, and one of them said, "Lois was not a common name." Jerry replied, "It was in my time." He was still thinking!

Only one time during the twenty-two months, Jerry said to me, "Good morning, gorgeous." This was so very special because that was the way he had addressed me during our entire marriage. About nine months after his death, I found a wall plaque that said, "Good morning, gorgeous." It now hangs in my bathroom as a greeting from Jerry each morning.

Isaiah 43:1 helped keep all this in perspective.

But now, this is what the Lord says—he who created you, Jacob, he who formed you, Israel: "Do not fear, for I have redeemed you; I have summoned you by name; you are mine."

Even if Jerry couldn't always remember who I was, God always knew my name because I am His! How awesome is that?

One night after our first Christmas home, I went to check on Jerry, and his eyes were open. He looked at me and said, "Hello, my name is Jerry Cox." I said hi and asked if he knew who I was. No, he didn't. I told him Lois Cox, and he asked how we were connected. Then I told him we were husband and wife, to which he said, "You are tied to an awesome guy!" Lynn went in to visit a little later, and then I went back in. When I got ready to leave, I asked if this strange lady could kiss him good night. He said, "Yes, but my wife is coming in soon." Later, I went in to check, and his eyes were open again. I asked if he knew me this time. He said, "Are you someone different than the last time you came in?" I loved the days when the humor was there but sure wish he knew his wife of fifty years.

God was always there in the tough times to remind me of His presence. One morning as Jerry was practicing being contrary, I looked out the window. It was September, and I hadn't seen my hummingbirds in several days. According to Google (the expert), they were supposed to be around until October before migrating to Mexico. Out loud I said, "I miss my hummers." God, being the magnificent God He is, decided to show me His presence. At that moment, a hummer flew close by my window and stopped briefly for me to see him up close. Then off he flew—he didn't even stop in my garden. I thanked God that morning for showing me His presence that day as things were getting tough!

Jerry's delusions took a different turn one morning in October. My friend Kelly Ann was taking Jerry to the bathroom while I attempted to get some garden work done. When I came back in the house, I heard the call for help. She couldn't get Jerry to sit down because Jerry kept saying it was the "other guy" who needed to go but not him. After he refused to go, we walked around the house looking for the other guy, and he accused me of sending him away. Of course, we never found him, and Jerry finally gave up. Because he refused to sit for the bathroom stop he needed, we had an accident to clean up after his nap.

The "other guy" showed up another time. Early on when we returned from the nursing home, Jerry had an appointment with his primary care physician. Jerry had been mean to me since coming home, as was discussed in chapter 4, and I told the doctor about that. During the exam, he asked Jerry why he had been mean to his wife. Jerry's response was, "He told me to." There was no explanation as to who the "other guy" was. The explanation, I believe, came later.

These later delusions happened on two separate occasions and were very real to Jerry, and I believe were the work of the expert deceiver, Satan. Jerry had been a devoted child of God all his life. We served in full-time ministry seven years of our marriage. He served churches as a deacon and elder through the years, went on several mission trips, and taught many classes. This was a man Satan had not been successful in trying to sway away from his Savior—until Jerry had a brain injury. Satan now took his chance.

One day I was walking him from the kitchen back to the bedroom when Jerry looked at the ceiling, which was totally normal for him. However, this day he said, "Beelzebub." I stopped Jerry and asked if he knew whose name he was saying, to which he repeated again, "Beelzebub." At this point, I figured out what was happening. Satan thought he finally had a chance to get into Jerry's mind. This made me furious at this master deceiver. Knowing scripture as I did, I began to denounce Satan. I told him he was not welcome in this house because we served God. I reminded him of God's power over him and demanded he leave this house and us alone. Jerry was then content to go on to the bedroom.

The last and most intense situation was on a Sunday. Jerry and I often had our worship service alone. We sang hymns using the recorded hymns on the Oklahoma Christian University website. Jerry knew these old hymns. Each Sunday, I would either play a recorded sermon or pick something to read as our thought for the communion service we would have next. For several weeks, I had been reading a chapter from 3:16, *The Numbers of Hope* by Max Lucado (2012). The author dug deeply into the well-known scripture John 3:16. We had gotten to chapter 10 that day, "Hell's Supreme Surprise," corresponding with the part of the scripture that says, "Whoever believes in him shall not perish."

Jerry was in his recliner, and I was in my rocking chair only a few feet away. I read the chapter, looking only at the text as I read. When I finished, I looked up to see fear in Jerry's eyes. I knew immediately what was going on. I went to him and said, "Satan is here, isn't he?" Jerry stared at the ceiling with terror in his eyes as he nodded his head yes. As I had done before, I told Satan, "Jerry has served God all his life, and Satan is not going to get into this man's head now." I told Satan the scriptures said if I fled from Satan, he would leave. Again I demanded he leave in the name of God. Then I watched Jerry's eyes follow Satan from the ceiling out the window. It was truly awesome to remind Satan his powers were limited!

Of course, I could chalk up these experiences with Satan as total delusions. However, I chose to take them as literal encounters with this demon whose job it is to get Christians off course. Our aging population has many with dementia, Alzheimer's, and other brain-related diseases. Could it be Satan's effort to get into their minds to give them fear and cause their personalities to move from calm and sweet to one full of malice toward those they love?

A huge lesson I learned early on was to make no attempt to reason Jerry out of the wrong thinking he was having. When he said the "other guy" needed to use to bathroom, it was much easier to look for the "other guy" than to try to convince Jerry there was no one else in the house. If he was convinced I had asked him to leave the house, the simplest way was to apologize for doing that in order for Jerry to accept that and move on. There was a day in January when he saw police cars and trucks in the backyard. It was easiest to ask what color they were or how many.

The following verse propped me up many days.

Come to me, all you who are weary and heavy burdened, and I will give you rest. (Matthew 11:28)

I needed physical, emotional, and spiritual rest on many days throughout my caregiving. God always came through, providing me a good night's sleep after a difficult day or a calmer time with Jerry after an upsetting situation.

A definite delusion one night was being on a battleship. I got into bed beside him, but he asked me why I was in his bed. I got out, and then he wanted to know why I wasn't in bed with him. I was told I couldn't go to sleep because we were on a battleship, he was the captain, and there were yeomen behind me. Never a dull moment with a stroke patient!

In November, we were again on a battleship one evening. Next, he wanted to call our son-in-law, Tim, on my voice communicator (my cell). I also had to write down some numbers for someone else to call. His message to Tim was to warn him the battleship he was on was about to have an explosion, so he was to get off. Tim played along and agreed to get off the ship. Finally, Jerry told me I was scatterbrained and gullible. When I asked why, he said because I actually believed the explosion story. It was quite an interesting conversation with humor scattered throughout.

We experienced a repeat of the ship, a pirate ship, the next afternoon after dinner. He was up walking around the living room and not allowing me to touch him. This time he wasn't aggressive, but he was definitely going from place to place on the ship. Thankfully, my daughter Lynn called, and I asked her to come by immediately. With the two of us together, we were able to convince him to go to his "bunk" for the night.

Urinary tract infections can also cause delusions in the elderly. We had only one more UTI after I started taking care of him and monitoring his water intake, however he had a hospital-acquired UTI, causing some monsters to be in his room. He also insisted on talking on the phone (I gave him the nurse call phone), and he used it several times that day. I have no idea why seniors are affected so severely by a UTI, but they certainly are. Many seniors do not drink enough water, adding to the possibility of a UTI.

I also experienced episodes of paranoia with Jerry, which often accompanied being delusional. One afternoon, we decided to head out to Panera for dinner. When we got to the car, however, he suggested we take his car (which he had not thought of until this day). I explained it was at our daughter's house because they needed to borrow it. He thought I was trying to trick him. Even after getting our daughter on the phone to explain it further, he was not convinced. Upon taking him to the bedroom that evening, he stopped at the door and wouldn't go in, saying he was afraid of me; I was behind him. We backed up and sat down in his recliner, called our daughter again, and she talked to him. Finally, he either forgot about it, or everything was once again back to normal.

Other times he was in another place, like when he was looking for someone to take him in, but he had just parked the car in temporary parking. He was very relieved when I told him he could spend the night here. He went right to sleep.

Then there were the nights when sleep was delayed due to delusions. One evening after he went to sleep, I went to check on him before a planned trip out to attend a class that evening and found him awake. He started out knowing me, but it wasn't long before we were on a ship again and taking on water. He sent me to look for help once. When I asked him if he couldn't just go downstairs, sleep in his bunk, and face this tomorrow, he said he was assigned to this ship—it wasn't his normal one, so didn't have a bunk here. Finally, at 8:30 I was exhausted and so told him I was going to my bunk, and he should too. He said he was on watch and couldn't go to sleep, but I could go to sleep; he would protect me. He was finally asleep a little after 9:00. I knew it was delusions because he only saw things; with hallucinations, he heard things too, as mentioned before.

One night before the one-year anniversary of the stroke in February, my friend Linda from Texas was here visiting. Jerry had been asleep, but at 8:45 that evening, he decided he had to get up. We walked to the living room where Linda was. He told us he needed to price the merchandise. He cautioned us we couldn't price it too low or we would lose money, and we should not price it too high either. I convinced him he could go to bed, and my friend and I would do the pricing in the morning because we had lots of markers. That seemed to satisfy him, and he went back to bed. The only connection we could figure out for that one was that Linda had once owned a Christian bookstore, and Jerry had helped her a few times.

Jerry even had pleasant delusions at times. One evening close to a year in, he was having delusions at night but was laughing at them. Another night, he saw a black carousel on the ceiling. I was playing soft music for him that night and asked if I

138

should turn it off to let him go to sleep. He replied, "No, it is running the carousel." Other times, he was not sure about where he was. Friends from Wisconsin called one night, and he told them he was in New York City and had been in Boston the day before. When I tried to correct him by saying we had gone to church the day before, he said, "Yes. We went to church in Boston yesterday."

Although these were very trying times for me, God promises relief to all afflictions at some point.

> Although I have afflicted you, Judah, I will afflict you no more. Now I will break their yoke from your neck and tear your shackles away. (Nahum 1:12b–13)

For me, my future was in this affliction with Jerry, but I knew at some point, it would be over. The sad part to think about was how the affliction would end because I knew death was a strong possibility.

One delusion even carried over to morning. Before going to sleep one night, Jerry talked about getting on a plane. When he woke up the next morning, he must have thought about it through the night. He was trying to crawl out of bed over the bed rails, talking about finding the plane. He wanted me to stay away from him and was almost combative. I guessed, as discussed earlier, it was Satan playing with his mind again. Prayer and rebuking Satan took care of it this time. I often wondered if many of the delusions were caused by this master of all deceivers, Satan.

The periods of delusions would come and go. Home health told me there would be better and more difficult times through his care. After some very good times during spring of the second year, a different delusion came one night. He woke up about 8:30 at night after going to bed at 3:30. This delusion was of a family who had gotten out of a car in Rogers, Arkansas, because a little boy was drowning in the water. Jerry was very upset about the little boy and was determined to help. I found him in bed on his hands and knees, reaching out and trying to help. Prayers for God to keep Satan from infiltrating Jerry's mind worked to calm him down.

The morning following this incident, Jerry informed me we were different now. He wasn't sure how but said we were. He was having a discussion with "him," who was telling Jerry what to do. When Jerry was delusional, his speech was different, childlike. He could never identify the guy he was talking to in these situations. This time, he wasn't being told to do anything mean, but it was keeping him from his normal eating schedule and making the care less easy for me. I was quite sure Satan was involved when someone was talking to Jerry.

One morning before a difficult day, God gave me this scripture.

A person's wisdom yields patience; it is to one's glory to overlook an offense. (Proverbs 19:11)

God knew I would have offenses to overlook even if it was because of an injured brain. Jerry would never offend me intentionally when in his right mind. Now, however, it was easy to get offended by the person he sometimes was.

I was tested one day in our second June during the stroke months. It was an unusually sleepy day for Jerry but also very cantankerous. He needed to go to the bathroom but told me, "No pee." He said he wanted to go to Braum's, our local ice cream store, but stopped at the garage door, refused to go any farther, and said, "No Braum's." I walked him back to the kitchen to feed him dinner, but he said, "No eat." I tried singing questions to him, which would often encourage him to sing an answer back to me. This day, however, he would sing a phrase back to me over and over and over. I tried calling our daughters and grandchildren to try to distract him, but nothing worked. Finally, in his fatigue, I put him to bed at 3:00 p.m., and he stared at something on the ceiling until 4:00 p.m.

After a quick run to the store while my neighbor stayed with him, he was once again awake by 6:00 p.m. I went in and asked how he was. He responded, "I'm much better now." He knew he had been difficult but had not been able to control it earlier in the day. Something had definitely been wrong, and now things were better. He thought the pictures of our daughters were beautiful but only said, "Wow," rather than recognizing who they were.

An ER visit during the second June followed a strange few days, including the events in the previous couple of paragraphs. When we were discharged, Jerry was still confused. When the nurse got us to the car with Jerry in the wheelchair, he said he needed to get the other car he arrived in. I convinced him we would come back later for it, and he got in. When we were getting on the highway, he said we had to turn around and go back. He insisted on getting the car he left there.

Finally, I convinced him that because Kelly Ann was meeting us at the house, we could get her to go back and get it. "Okay, that's a good idea," he said. Success. I asked him color, make, and model. It was a red and white Ford Ranger. We decided he parked it in the valet parking because he didn't have the keys and also didn't have his parking ticket. I had an extra parking validation ticket and so handed it to him and said, "This must be it." He held onto it and gave it to Kelly Ann when we arrived at the house. We also discussed how we could get our neighbor Bert to go get the car if Kelly Ann couldn't.

We were not finished with the paranoid delusional activities for the night, however. He said there were some men trying to get our money. I had called Lynn and then Tim. We decided Tim would take care of the men wanting the money. But that didn't work for long. Jerry wanted up. At this point, he was so tired, I was afraid I wouldn't be able to get him back to bed. I texted Wanda to send over Bert because they had offered to help. Bert is a neighbor who has a house key to use when I can't get to the door. One of the first things he asked Bert was, "Do you know where our car is?"

Bert didn't know our earlier conversation and said, "Yes, it is in the garage."

"Well, God really does take care of things," Jerry said.

I couldn't get the money out of his mind. I finally got him to agree that I would take our money and put it in the tornado safe room in the garage, where the guys couldn't get to it. With this solved, we were heading to bed. Bert helped me get him back in bed and also helped me reason with him. Another strange scenario was over.

> The Lord your God who goes before you will himself fight for you, just as he did for you in Egypt before your eyes, and in the wilderness, where you have seen how the Lord your God carried you, as a man carries his son, all the way that you went until you came to this place. (Deuteronomy 1:30–31 ESV)

God fights for me daily, but more important, He carries me through these tough times in His arms to the final destination of heaven. I have the feeling of being carried so many times and know it is God's strength—it certainly isn't mine! Isn't God amazing?

The ship days came back in the second July when Jerry was still awake late one evening. We were to stay on board the ship because it could get tough any time. We weren't getting a signal out right now! The alarm had sounded for all hands on deck. He was working on a system off the main system to replace the signal system that was broken. (Maybe this went back to his computer programming days.) The boat must have docked at 7:40 because he was back asleep! With no background in maritime, I was not sure where all the ship delusions came from. They may have resulted from his love of reading history, especially about war.

There were so many days we were on the verge of disruptive delusions. There were as many days when I was able successfully to cause a distraction to stop his delusional thinking and bring him back to reality. The constant redirecting on my part was emotionally and mentally exhausting. It seemed I was always trying to come up with someone to call, some place to go, or some redirection of the conversation to keep things from getting out of hand.

First Peter 5:8–9 comes to mind here.

Be alert and of sober mind. Your enemy the devil prowls around like a roaring lion looking for someone to devour. Resist him, standing firm in the faith, because you know that the family of believers throughout the world is undergoing the same kind of sufferings.

Satan was always on the lookout to cause Jerry any discomfort he could, whether mental or physical. After the stroke, Jerry was no longer able to fight off Satan himself. It became my job to be aware of the attacks and fight them off with prayer and my gentle, calm responses to Jerry. Satan also used my fatigue against my caregiving efforts. My mother would have said, "Satan only attacks those he doesn't already have." He wasn't going to get to my sweet husband as long as I was on task to be watchful.

Often Jerry was very different when he woke up from his afternoon naps. It seemed he dreamed a lot. Even at night, I observed restless sleep. One afternoon later in the stroke, he woke up saying I owed him twenty dollars, and I should pay him right now. I had no idea where he got twenty dollars or how he was going to use it. I put a twenty-dollar bill in his hand, and he put it in his pocket. He was obsessed with the money. It went back and forth a few times. He finally gave it back to me and told me he had paid me, so "Get out! I don't like the way you look." He was close to getting combative. I called Kara, and she talked to him on the phone for a while. It helped reconnect some of the wires in his thinking. He didn't know any of us at first but was coming back before we hung up the phone. Distraction was the best plan of attack—when it worked.

On another afternoon, I woke Jerry up after two and a half hours of his nap. Going to three hours always meant trouble. This time, two and a half was either too long, or the dream he was having was too vivid. He started by telling me he needed to go to school. I was trying to get him up and go to the bathroom, as usual. He kept being confused, would start to get up, but then would sit back down. Finally, because he delayed getting up, when he did get up, he was very wet. On top of that, he did not want to cooperate to get his clothes changed. I finally talked him into the bathroom, where he could hold the handles for me to change him. But he got worse, telling me to get out of his way. I texted "Help" to Lynn and kept trying to talk and reason with him. We called our granddaughter in Savannah, but he didn't know her and wouldn't say anything to her. At one point he started crying and saying, "I don't want to grow up. I want to go home." I hurt for him in his confusion. Lynn arrived, and together we talked him down.

Bathrooms seemed to cause strange behavior. One afternoon as I was walking him to the bathroom to get ready for bed, he headed toward the front door. When I tried to redirect him to the back, he said the bathroom was outside. I convinced him if it was, it wouldn't be in the front yard, so let's look in the back. We walked around the garden because he was sure it was in the back corner. He pointed to the fence as the bathroom. After convincing him it was a fence and the neighbor's yard was on the other side, we went back in.

He gave me little trouble in the bathroom until I tried to get him to take off his pants and shoes. "No, I will keep them on." I pulled them back up, and we walked to bed. Then he said he had to protect me because our lives were in danger. I asked him what the source of the danger was. He said I was trying to kill him. After hugging him and reminding him of all the things I had done for him that day, I convinced him that was not true. He finally stood up and let me pull off his pants. Once his head was on the pillow, he was out cold. What a difficult afternoon it had been! No wonder I slept soundly most nights. I was exhausted from the mental challenges of delusional thinking.

A milder but strange delusion occurred on a day when we were trying to leave the house to run an errand. He said, "What do I do with him?" In questioning, "him" was apparently a baby. I assured him the baby could go with us. Jerry kept one hand close to his chest or in his vest pocket, holding the baby when we were in the car, in the store, and on the way home. By the time we finished dinner, he finally had forgotten about the baby. The delusion was again manageable for me.

Delusions and hallucinations kept my caregiving days from being boring for sure. They were times of great stress for us both. I had such pain in my heart for what Jerry was going through and how helpless I often felt in the situations we found ourselves. His delusions are now over. The pirate ship has docked for good!

Things I Learned While Caregiving with God!
1. I have learned patience.
2. I have learned that the Bible has the answer to every problem and concern, and it is the source of joy and peace that cannot be understood.
3. I have learned to experience delusions and hallucinations through Jerry.

So many days (and even weeks), it was difficult to go on. I thought of 2 Corinthians 12:10 (ESV), "For the sake of Christ, then, I am content with weaknesses, insults, hardships, persecutions, and calamities. For when I am weak, then I am strong." Yes, I had my daily quiet time with God every morning and talked to Him throughout the day. However, so many times when the situation was tough, Jerry was delusional, he didn't know who I was, we were making another trip back to the ER, and many other things that made for tough days, I would cry out to God in prayer.

I worked toward being content with my weaknesses, hardships, and calamities but always realized when I totally depended on God, my strength was there because it was His strength. Particularly tough times were always followed by better days, hugs, and smiles from Jerry, as well as a hope things would get better. I also knew that "better" could mean Jerry's going home to heaven to a fully recovered body. God always came through for me. He even gave me the delight of intimacy with Jerry following depressing times.

The role of caregiver twenty-four seven had never been on my resume, and I did not feel competent to tackle the task now. However, I had this promise from God:

> Now may the God of peace... equip you with everything good for doing his will, and may he work in us what is pleasing to him, through Jesus Christ, to whom be glory for ever and ever. (Hebrews 13:20a–21)

He would be the one to equip me with the skills I needed for this most challenging job of my life. He would be the one to work in me to hold me up, give me strength, give me skills, give me patience, and give me empathy to keep going as long as it took.

The attacks from Satan started early and continued throughout much of the stroke. During these highly stressful times, my only respite from his attacks was God's intervention and His overarching power over Satan. Every time Jerry had a scary hallucination, I wondered whether this was an attempt from Satan to make life even more miserable for Jerry and for me. Some of the ones he described to me were terrifying in the characters and what he was hearing.

I know Satan is the supreme deceiver and will do anything to pull those saved by the blood of Christ away from the fold, so his attacks should not have surprised me. When Jerry would hallucinate, one of my main tools to fight it off was playing Christian music. Distraction during hallucinations was the goal of anything we said, sang, or tried to do with touch. I kept a cross close to his bed wherever we were—in the skilled nursing facility or at home. Through experience, I had found distraction to be the most effective way to get Jerry's mind back to reality. What he saw and heard were real to him; hence, it was counterproductive to try to convince him otherwise.

As mentioned already, the trip to the primary care physician soon after Jerry was home from the skilled nursing facility pointed out one of the ways Satan was trying to get into his head. Jerry was never mean to me until his brain wasn't functioning properly. I saw signs of dementia starting prior to the stroke; the most significant was Jerry's lashing out at me in anger. This was so unlike this loving, compassionate husband of mine.

When Jerry told the doctor he was mean to his wife because "he" tells me to, I later decided that must have been Satan trying to change his Christian conscience from one of love to one of purposefully wanting to cause pain to those around him. We had days throughout the next five months when I saw Satan at work, particularly when Jerry was working hard to make my life miserable; I alluded to this in other chapters. When I would "bribe" Jerry with coffee or something else if he would stop giving me grief, he would sometimes control himself. This told me his brain, although injured, was still able to make judgments. Yes, the medications also affected this a great deal, but we never completely moved to all sweet days—they were interspersed with days of refusing to talk, refusing to eat, refusing to get in the car, refusing to get in the shower, and on and on.

As I discussed previously, the first time I knew Jerry was visually seeing Satan in the room was early December, nearly ten months after the stroke. This was the time he was looking at the ceiling and calling out the name Beelzebub. It required more strength of faith from me to be able to protect us than ever before. I reminded Jerry we served God and Jesus in this house and had no room for Beelzebub. An injured brain was an open invitation for Satan to try to move in.

My first reaction was anger. Out loud I said, "How dare you! This man has served God all his life, and you couldn't get into his mind. Now that he has a brain injury, you are going to try to sneak in!" Knowing the scriptures as I did, I knew if we told Satan to get behind us, he would (Matthew 16:23). I was appalled and frightened, and then as bold as I could, in all confidence, I told Beelzebub he was not welcome here. God's strength was with me that day.

God gave me a scripture that day for my journal devotional.

When I called, you answered me; you greatly emboldened me. (Psalm 138:3)

The New King James version says, "And made me bold with strength in my soul." There would be no way we could fight off Satan on our own. He is too powerful, but God always holds the upper hand. With God on our side and the power of the Holy Spirit living in me, Satan had no choice but to do as he was told and leave us alone!

One night I believed Satan was working him again; this was only a few days after the Beelzebub incident. Jerry woke up because he was wet. As I started trying to change him, he was pointing to a guy who kept telling him to get rid of me. He would not let me work with him and kept holding my hands tightly. I called my daughter to come help, however by the time she arrived, he had calmed down. It was clear in rereading my journal that this was another attempt by Satan.

Typically, when Jerry got into bed, his hallucinations were crazy characters—at least the ones he described. One night, however, in the first December when he was staring at the ceiling, I asked what he was seeing. His response was, "Demons." With friends there that night, we were able to pray around Jerry and alleviate the demons.

An afternoon delusion at the end of February brought in a conversation from Satan. Jerry was seeing a battle in the Vietnam War for some reason. The battle went on for almost an hour as he stared at the ceiling in fear. When I asked what was going, he said, "They say there is no heaven."

Out loud I said, "Satan, you get out of this house. We serve God here, and you are not welcome." Then Jerry began singing "Low in the Grave He Lay," and Satan had to leave. Jerry was still afraid that night as I put him to bed. Hugging him close, I assured him God was here and he was safe. Finally, he settled down and slept.

In March, Jerry recognized there was a force working in him. One morning when I found him extremely wet because he had pulled off the catheter, I gathered the necessary supplies and tried to start the process. However, he did not want me to touch him. When I came back about twenty minutes later, he was even more adamant about not touching him. He was totally saturated. This time he even used profanity with me—a very rare happening. I went to my prayer rocking chair across from him and sent out an urgent plea to Kelly Ann and Lynn to pray. I also rebuked Satan, knowing he was behind this. An hour and a half after this started, he was ready for me to change him. Once on dry sheets and dry shirt, he said, "It feels heavenly." I asked him later why he didn't want me to change him that morning. He said, "That wasn't me." His perception was correct that someone was working through him.

The last attack by Satan I was aware of was close to the end of our last August together, also discussed in the last chapter. We were reading in Max Lucado's 3:16 book, which talked a lot about punishment and people making a choice as to where they will spend eternity.

All the reading about hell gave Satan a narrow entry portal into Jerry's mind. He was seeing Satan, and I don't know what else, on the ceiling. How scary to know Satan was in our sunroom working on Jerry's mind. I called on God to put a hedge around us for protection and told Satan to get out. Jerry said he was still there. Next, Jerry and I both confessed our belief in Jesus and stated that our hearts belonged to Him. Again, I verbally told Satan to get out, that Jerry's heart belonged to Jesus, and there was no room for him. I saw Jerry's head move and look toward the window, indicating Satan had left. It was so scary, and I was shaken from it, but I believed I kept Jerry calm through it. I had never dealt with Satan in such an in-your-face manner as with Jerry's delusional mind. Then we sang several hymns and received peace and calm.

During the period from November 6 through December 10 of 2016, Jerry had four emergency room and inpatient hospital stays, plus two one-week stays in a skilled nursing facility, to get him through a very stressful time of unexplained vomiting and pneumonia. In writing this book and rereading this section of my journal, I truly wondered how I got through that extremely difficult time; see chapters 4 and 7 for more details. It would be easy to ask where God was during this time of repeated vomiting, repeated hospital stays with no answers, and the difficult skilled nursing stays.

I continued to read scripture and be held up by my CaringBridge prayer warriors, who took my requests to God. A Bible Study Fellowship topic in the fall of 2018 helped answer some of my questions. The study of the Promised Land started with Joshua conquering the land of Canaan. God seemed to use two methods to help Joshua accomplish this overwhelming task. In conquering the Southern kings, God intervened with some miraculous help. Five kings had banded together to attempt to overtake the Israelites (Joshua 10). When Joshua went to battle, God confused the opposing army, and He sent down hail stones so large they killed more of the enemy than did the Israelites. Then when Joshua asked for a longer day to finish the victory, God stopped the sun to allow for that.

Amazing what God did to give them the victory, wasn't it? The Israelites still were required to go to battle, but the victory was assured even before they began to fight. The army certainly went into battle with the confidence of knowing they would be victorious over their enemy. God could have easily won the battle for them without their having to go into battle. However, they were put into action as God worked alongside them.

Joshua 11 told of Joshua's victories over Northern Canaan. God assured Joshua of their victory, however again they had to go to battle and do the work. They listened to God and followed His instructions for the victory, but they had to fight. An important fact about defeating the Northern kings was the inclusion of the Anakites in the enemy who were overcome. The Anakites were the giants living in the Promised Land who terrified ten of the twelve spies sent to scope out the land before they entered. Their size caused these ten spies to say there was no way the Israelites could take the Promised Land. Yet now they were following God's instructions and were able to destroy them and their towns.

How does this relate to my time of the multiple hospital and skilled nursing stays? I never felt alone when things seemed so dark. I kept in the Word, prayed hard, and maintained my daily quiet time. My friends, family, and prayer warriors continued their prayers and words of encouragement. It did seem things were not progressing as they should. Every time we would get home from one hospital stay, another one would come along and hit Jerry hard again. Before we went home from the last stay, I contacted palliative care to work with Jerry.

Palliative care (pronounced pal-lee-uh-tiv) is specialized medical care for people with serious illness. This type of care is focused on providing relief from the symptoms and stress of a serious illness. The goal is to improve quality of life for both the patient and the family.

Palliative care is provided by a specially trained team of doctors, nurses and other specialists who work together with a patient's other doctors to

152

provide an extra layer of support. It is appropriate at
any age and at any stage in a serious illness, and it
can be provided along with curative treatment. (Get
Palliative Care 2018)

Was this the end of his life coming quickly now? I had no
idea but was not sure about continuing aggressive care for health
issues when I wasn't sure how much more his struggling body
could take. Was my weakness giving in without counting on God as
I should? I was making difficult decisions. Pharmaceuticals had
drastic effects on Jerry; which ones should I start or stop? Jerry
could no longer assist me in making these decisions.

However, God was at work behind the scenes. The victory
was guaranteed with a home in heaven at some date unknown. As I
leaned on God through the darkest days of the stroke, He came
through, giving us the best days during the stroke and leading up to
his final departure date to heaven just over a year later. There were
some truly miraculous days to come in Jerry's life.

Shout and be glad, Daughter Zion for I am coming, and I will
live among you,' declares the Lord. (Zechariah 2:10)

This is an amazing thought. God resided in my house with
my caregiving problems, concerns, lack of faith from time to time,
loneliness, and down days. He not only never left me, but He also
lived with me! It's an awesome thought to have my heavenly
support team move in and take residence.

Martin Luther's wife gave insight from her experiences long
ago in the following quote.

I would never have known the meaning of various psalms,
come to appreciate certain difficulties, or known the inner
workings of the soul, I would never have understood the
practice of the Christian life and work, if God had never
brought afflictions to my life. (Cowman 2016, 67)

I could relate to her insight! I was raised in a Christian home, never had a time of rebellion, went to a Christian college, married a Christian man, and always was part of a church community, but nothing grew my faith and understanding of God as the twenty-two months of caring for my husband with a stroke. I was truly blessed.

> This is the deal we all get: guaranteed suffering. We all get it. It is coming, unstoppable, like time.

> There are graves coming, there is dark coming, there is heartbreak coming. We are not in control, and we never were ... Why are we afraid of suffering? What if the abundance of communion is only found there in the brokenness of suffering—because suffering is where God lives? Suffering is where God gives the most healing intimacy. (Voskamp 2016, 17)

When I read this, I realized I wanted the most healing intimacy God could give me, but once again, I was not in control. There was no way to escape this life without suffering. God promised, however, healing was possible through Him. The healing intimacy with God did not end with Jerry's healing in this life but in total and complete healing in a new body in heaven. The healing intimacy God brought to me was so special and also brought healing to me spiritually and emotionally. It was a healing that continued into the grieving journey I started on December 30, 2017, with Jerry's arrival in heaven.

> A man's heart plans his way, but the Lord directs his steps. (Proverbs 16:9 NKJV)

This was another one of the well-known verses with different meaning to me now. My retirement was planned; caregiving was not worked into those plans at all. Corrie ten Boom had this quote about my new life:

> The Lord never makes a mistake. One day, when we are in heaven, I'm sure we shall see the answers to all the whys.

My, how often I have asked, "Why?" In heaven, we shall see God's side of the embroidery.

God turned my life upside down. Now it was time to trust in Him, depending on Him for my every step along the way. I was looking at all the knots I saw on my side of the embroidery, but at the same time I was living a joyful, fulfilling life serving my husband.

With thoughtless and
Impatient hands
We tangle up
The plans
The Lord hath wrought.

And when we cry
In pain, He saith,
"Be quiet, dear,
While I untie the knot." (Cowman 2016, 126–127)

Dependence on God also meant He would provide the rest I needed as promised to Moses in Exodus 33:14.

The Lord replied, "My presence will go with you, and I will give you rest."

In the situation I found myself, I would never have thought there would be adequate rest. However, when the nights involved lots of getting up to change Jerry's bed, he would sleep a little longer the next morning or take a longer nap that afternoon. God always saw to it I received adequate rest for my weary body to keep going.

During the twenty-two months, I read many devotional books and other inspirational books; many were sent as gifts by others and some were recommended readings for me. Here is a quote from one of them that was particularly meaningful.

> Lord, help me to cherish these precious days of total dependency on you. It is easy to forget that they are a gift, that you are, day by day, teaching me to awaken every morning with this request on my heart: that you would grant me your perfect portion for whatever the day holds. (Woolsey 2014, 8)

They were precious days because as I learned, the more I depended on God, the more capable I was at doing the job of caregiving. This was validated repeatedly in scriptures, but especially in one place.

> But the Lord stood at my side and gave me strength. (2 Timothy 4:17a)

My strength was truly in my weakness. When I cried out to God for help, He filled in the gaps. When I leaned on His strength, I found mine. When I admitted I needed His help, He provided more than I asked for. The indwelling Spirit helped me up, gave me wisdom to make decisions, and made me strong. Days of total dependency were truly precious!

And then there was peace even in the center of everything going on with Jerry's care. It was true peace, as talked about in Psalm 4:8.

> In peace I will both lie down and sleep. For You alone, O Lord, make me to dwell in safety.

The peace was difficult to understand. How I could have peace with Jerry suffering from a terrible stroke and my life upside down? But still there was peace. As an unknown author said, "Peace does not mean to be in a place where there is no noise, trouble, or hard work. It means to be in the midst of all those things and still be calm in our heart." During a particularly stressful hospital visit, the social worker was visiting with me in our room. After I answered all the questions about Jerry's care, he commented on how calm I was through all this. It was the supreme compliment! God had moved into my heart with peace.

There was joy also in the center of everything going on with his care.

> You become imitators of us and of the Lord, for you welcomed the message in the midst of severe suffering with the joy given by the Holy Spirit. (1 Thessalonians 1:6)

I didn't have to wait until the time the stroke was over because my source of joy was not in anything going on around us but came from the Holy Spirit. Happiness is an emotion depending on what is surrounding us. However, joy is an internal emotion dependent on the Holy Spirit. I was filled with joy each day, knowing I was right where God wanted me to be. And yes, I was filled with joy when Jerry finally passed, knowing he was now fully capable of moving and thinking feely in a new body and was at the feet of Jesus.

Depending on God also gave us strength to do what needed to be done with Jerry. Of course, because he slept as much as he did, making appointments was extremely difficult. On one such occasion, he had a particularly early appointment, 9:30 a.m. So many mornings, he was nowhere near awake at that time, much less sitting in a waiting room for an appointment. However, I had my CaringBridge prayer warriors praying for these appointments. My thinking was if he was up by 8:00, we could possibly make it. That morning, I would almost hear God saying, "You wanted Jerry up by 8:00? I can do one better than that." Jerry was awake at 7:00, had breakfast, went to the bathroom, was back down for a nap by 8:10, slept twenty minutes, and then was ready to go!

Another even earlier lab appointment was scheduled at 8:00 a.m. This appointment was discussed previously. When my daughter arrived at 7:15, Jerry was sitting on the bed dressed. That morning, he already had his bowel movement and urinated in bed—not the best thing for me, but it saved us tremendous time getting out the door. On the way to these early appointments, I would always sing, "God Is So Good." It is difficult now to sing that song without many tears of joy in remembering those God strengthened days! I was also reminded of the following verses.

> Now to him who is able to do immeasurably more than all we ask or imagine, according to his power that is at work within us. (Ephesians 3:20)
> Since we live by the Spirit, let us keep in step with the Spirit. (Galatians 5:25)

I must have read the Galatians verse many times, but the words never struck me as they did during the stroke. The King James version says, "let us also walk in the Spirit."

This statement gave a little different slant on the verse. To me, keeping step with the Spirit indicated a higher level of relationship. If you take a walk with friends, and they walk faster than you, it requires you pick up the pace to keep up. For this to happen with the Spirit, you would have to have His power to help you keep in step! This verse should be a picture of our individual walk with the Spirit day by day. His power is available for us to keep in step and turn our weakness into His strength! Praise God for that.

> Here is a devotional thought I read to Jerry one night:
> God's greatest gifts come through great pain. Can we find anything of value in the spiritual or the natural realm that has come about without tremendous toil and tears? (Cowman 2016, 388)

Without the pain, toil, and tears, we might not ever turn to God for the help He is offering. If we never seek God for strength, we could go through this life truly weak. The struggles turn us to the one who can help us get the strength we need to endure through the hard times and come out victorious on the other side.

Though I walk in the midst of trouble, You will revive me; You will stretch forth your hand against the wrath of my enemies, and your right hand will save me. The Lord will accomplish what concerns me; Your loving kindness, O Lord is everlasting. Do not forsake the works of your hands. (Psalm 138:7–8)

So many verses tell of the strength we receive when we go through struggles—not through good times. A quote from Nathaniel William Taylor, who was a Protestant theologian in the early nineteenth century, affirms this.

The strength of a ship is only fully demonstrated when it faces a hurricane, and the power of the gospel can only be fully exhibited when a Christian is subjected to some fiery trial. We must understand that for God to give "songs in the night," He must make it night.

Jerry sang a lot! During the later days of the stroke, he also sang at night. He wasn't awake when he did it, and the music wasn't recognizable and had no words, but he would sing for up to an hour at a time. Perhaps God was giving him songs in the night for his soul.

I found out quickly after the stroke that any strength I had came from God. He revived me day after day to keep going. The dark nights force one to turn to the light of God for His warmth and guidance. The scripture in Colossians 1:10–11 talks about that idea.

So that you may live a life worthy of the Lord and please him in every way: bearing fruit in every good work, growing in the knowledge of God, being strengthened with all power according to his glorious might so that you may have great endurance and patience.

We are promised to have strength according to God's power. Wow—that should be enough to help us get through any situation. Joyce Meyer talked about struggle in one of her devotional books.

God does not allow us to go through difficult times because He likes to see us suffer; He uses them for us to recognize our need for Him. Everything you go through ultimately does work out for your good because it makes you stronger and builds your endurance; it develops godly character; it helps you to know yourself and to be able to deal with things at an honest level with God and take care of those things so you can reach spiritual maturity. (Meyer 2012, 374)

God knows we will grow when we need to go outside our own abilities for the strength, wisdom, and character to accomplish the task. As long as we can keep going on our own efforts using Google to find whatever knowledge we need, we may not ever find the need to call on a higher power. God wants us to recognize our need for Him and call for help. That is when our strength grows, and we gain spiritual maturity.

Another day, Joyce Meyer discussed the idea of a testimony beginning with a test (Meyer 2012, 345). After reading this, I knew why I have felt so passionate about sharing my experiences during our twenty-two months. God gave me a test but didn't leave me alone to take the test. He was with me every day with every new situation, every new challenge, every new delusion, every new decision, and every new question on the test. It was an open-book test with God providing the answers in His Word each day, having prayer as a direct line to seeking more help, Jesus holding my hand through each difficulty, and the strength of the Holy Spirit living within me. And beyond that, He provided peace and joy while enduring the test. What an awesome God we serve!

But as for me, I will look to the Lord; I will wait for the God of my salvation; my God will hear me. (Micah 7:7 ESV)

There is encouragement knowing God will hear me in our struggles. It is such a frustration to be visiting with someone, and they aren't listening (thinking of their next response), checking their phone, tuned in to other conversations in the room, or generally not interested in what you are saying. With God, that never happens. Whenever you pray to Him, He hears you! It is easier to wait on Him when you know He hears.

Casting all your care upon him; for he careth for you. (1 Peter 5:7 KJV)

There were days when everything seemed to go poorly. One of those days when I had to cast my cares to God was following a weekend of dealing with my UTI. Because I had so many that were false alarms, the doctor didn't want me to take antibiotics until I was tested. It was a Saturday, and the urologist preferred I go to their lab, so I had to wait until Monday. After suffering the symptoms all weekend, I was already on edge. My daughter came to stay with Jerry in order to let me run downtown to the lab, and it took about an hour longer than it should have.

Jerry's blood pressure was pretty high that morning and was still high when the physical therapist came for his session. She called and made an appointment with the cardiologist for the next afternoon. I called back to the urologist and convinced them I needed something to take care of the symptoms while waiting on the culture. Then a trip to the mailbox brought a rejection letter from the insurance company for the wake-up narcotic Jerry had been taking since the stroke had happened eighteen months earlier. Without insurance, it would cost over five hundred dollars a month at Walmart. The tears flowed easily all day with everything going on. My body was requiring sleep every minute I could get it. At bedtime, I was ready to cast my cares on my heavenly Father to handle for me!

Of course, God always comes through with solutions. One of my readers on CaringBridge told me of a pharmacy close that did not take insurance. There I was able to get a three-month supply of what I needed for $108—a savings of approximately $1,500 every three months out of pocket. And this time I did have a UTI, and antibiotics took care of it quickly. God always came through with what I needed to keep going. In my human weakness, I immediately assumed I would have to spend the extra money for Jerry's medicine and was not leaning on God to solve the problem for me.

> Woe to those who go down to Egypt for help, who rely on horses, who trust in the multitude of their chariots and in the great strength of their horsemen, but do not look to the Holy One of Israel, or seek help from the Lord. (Isaiah 31:1)

Where would I have been if I had depended on the strength of my state's social services? Or what if I had trusted the medical profession to take care of Jerry? Our country needs to be ready to protect its citizens, however our strength is not in our local or federal government to take care of us. My strength came from the Holy One. I needed to seek help from the Lord, not anyone else! And He provided all I needed.

> It was good for me to be afflicted so that I might learn your decrees. (Psalm 119:71)

So many scriptures talk about the benefits of affliction and struggles. This one specifically indicates affliction causes us to turn to God's Word and study it more deeply. A morning quiet time has always been a part of my days. However, after the stroke, the time was lengthened and became more meaningful. Scriptures I read all my life took on different meanings. They spoke to me when I needed them the most. God seemed to arrange what I was going to read each day to give me a lesson for that day and that struggle.

My strength also came from God's protection.

> As the mountains surround Jerusalem, so the Lord surrounds His people from this time forth and forever. (Psalm 125:2)

At the same time God was allowing me to go through the struggles of the stroke, he was also surrounding me on all sides. He was working hard to keep out depression, loneliness, fatigue, physical illness, and feeling like a prisoner. God was protecting me on all sides every day, encouraging me along the way.

> I pray that out of his glorious riches he may strengthen you with power through his Spirit in your inner being. (Ephesians 3:16)

I don't know about you, but I want and need power in my inner being! I certainly can't make it through a day without extra strength from somewhere outside my own strength. Knowing I don't have to have to rely on my own strength to make it through each day is such a comforting thought. There is no way I could have done this job without the strength of God through His Spirit living within me each and every day.

> He said, "Look! I see four men walking around in the fire, unbound and unharmed, and the fourth looks like a son of the gods." (Daniel 3:25)

As a child, I learned the story of Shadrach, Meshach, and Abednego in the fiery furnace. It was truly an amazing story of God's protection of His followers. The cool thing for me in caregiving was the fourth man in the furnace with the other three. He was described as a heavenly body; we would think of him as an angel. There were so many days when I know we had a third body in our home with us to help us get through whatever was going on. The three Hebrews who refused to bow down to a golden idol were put in an impossible situation when they were thrown tied up into a furnace heated seven times hotter than normal. When my situation seems impossible, God was there, and often our guardian angel was too! There was a third one here to give me the strength I needed to get through each day.

> This is the confidence we have in approaching God: that if we ask anything according to his will, he hears us. And if we

know that he hears us—whatever we ask—we know that we have what we asked of him. (1 John 5:14–15)

What a tremendous promise this is from our heavenly Father. God always hears us when we ask according to His will. Not only does He hear us, but He responds to our request, granting us what we need from Him. I never have to worry about my weakness because I have God's strength.

Many nations will come and say, "Come let us go up to the mountain of the LORD, to the temple of the God of Jacob. He will teach us his ways, so that we may walk in his path." The law will go out from Zion, the word of the LORD from Jerusalem. (Micah 4:2)

This scripture tells how to know God's will for our lives. When I worship Him, whether on the mountain, in the temple, in a church building, or in my sunroom at home sitting in my rocking chair, God will teach me His ways. He doesn't keep me in the dark about how to serve Him. If I follow Him, I will know how to serve Him.

God uses our weakness more if we admit our weakness to Him rather than trying to use our strengths. Recognizing our weaknesses will encourage us to follow Him and gain His strength. What a great blessing for the caregiver! No, you can't do this job by yourself! You need God guiding you, Jesus walking beside you holding your hand, and the Holy Spirit living within you and giving you strength from day to day.

Things I Learned While Caregiving with God!

1. I have learned that the promises in the Bible are true—every one of them!
2. I have learned Satan will take any opportunity to try to move in on a dedicated Christian because he has a brain injury.
3. I have learned that when you give up your life for someone, God gives you a new life.

11 - Thank You for The Struggles!

Visit by daughter, Kara Talley, and grandchildren Cassidy and Alexander

In difficult times, seek God.
In quiet times, worship God.
In painful times, trust God.
In all times, thank God.
—From a coaster

What a strange title for this chapter! How could I thank God for the struggles I was going through? How could thankfulness even be a part of my day, my week, or my life? This was the most difficult time in my life, and I needed to be thankful?

However, there were many scriptures telling me just that. These are not in any particular order.

So then, just as you received Christ Jesus as Lord, continue to live your lives in him, rooted and built up in him, strengthened in the faith as you were taught, and overflowing with thankfulness. (Colossians 2:6–7)

A key word in this scripture is *overflowing*. We have all had the experience of pouring too much of a drink into a glass, causing it to flow over the top. The glass is so full, there is no place to go but over the edge. Our thankfulness should be completely filling our hearts to the point it overflows into every area of our lives, not just during the Thanksgiving season.

> For everything God created is good, and nothing is to be rejected if it is received with thanksgiving, because it is consecrated by the word of God and prayer. (I Timothy 4:4–5)

I am reminded of the very sweet times of the stroke days and know they were consecrated by God. My caregiving was consecrated by God—even the difficult times. I needed to receive my new task with thanksgiving—not regret, anger, resentment, but with thanks.

> Let the peace of Christ rule in your hearts, since as members of one body you were called to peace. And be thankful … And whatever you do, whether in word or deed, do it all in the name of the Lord Jesus, giving thanks to God the Father through him. (Colossians 3:15, 17)

My caregiving was the way I was serving God for those months of staying home and by Jerry's side. There were so many things day to day I found to give thanks to God for in the never-ending strength He gave me. Even the days when I never left the house provided blessings to send up my thanks to God.

> Do not be anxious about anything, but in every situation, by prayer and petition, with thanksgiving, present your requests to God. And the peace of God, which surpasses all understanding, will guard your hearts and your minds in Christ Jesus. (Philippians 4:6–7)

As I thanked God daily, peace was given to me even in the most stressful days and hospital stays. Jerry was a winner whether he lived or died and went home to God. There were days when taking my requests to God with thanksgiving first was challenging, however God was always there to listen, and that alone was enough to praise Him.

> I always thank my God for you because of his grace given you in Christ Jesus. (1 Corinthians 1:4)

The ultimate thanksgiving is for the grace extended to me each and every day promising me salvation. Thanking God for my support people in prayer was an easy task. By the grace of God, we were connected through our salvation.

> Enter his gates with thanksgiving and his courts with praise; give thanks to him and praise his name. (Psalm 100:4)

> The Message translation of this scripture puts it into today's lingo.

> Enter with the password: "Thank you!" Make yourselves at home, talking praise. Thank him. Worship him.

We have passwords for almost everything we need to access. Now we know how to access the throne of God—with the password of thanks for all He has done and will continue to do for us. This one we don't have to write down to remember.

> Devote yourselves to prayer, being watchful and thankful. (Colossians 4:2)

> It is difficult not to come to God's throne in prayer with our list of wants and needs. God knows our list and does want to hear us ask Him. However, there are so many more things to be thankful for in our prayer life than to ask for from our magnificent God. Some days when I get through with my thanks to God, I have forgotten what I needed to ask Him.

> Give thanks to the LORD, for he is good; his love endures forever. (1 Chronicles 16:34)

> Praise the LORD. Give thanks to the LORD, for he is good; his love endures forever. (Psalm 106:1)

There is no one in this life who can be completely depended on for never-ending love. Even with spouses whom we love the most, there are days when we don't feel particularly loving. Mentally I loved Jerry, but emotionally not so much on difficult days. With God, His love for us is never-ending. What a blessing!

Of course, I should be thankful to God because of all He has done for us. God blesses us with the material things we need to sustain life. He gives us health and blesses us with families. He gives us the beauty of nature with all its magnificence in the mountains, oceans, rivers, flowers, birds, butterflies, and animals—such a beautiful world. God had blessed my life before the stroke with a good career, beautiful daughters, a Christian husband, and wonderful grandchildren, to name a few. Those blessings continued after the stroke, but I didn't anticipate the new ones. God continued to give me scriptures on being thankful even when things didn't go so well.

> Give thanks in all circumstances; for this is God's will for you in Christ Jesus. (1 Thessalonians 5:18)

Close to our second Thanksgiving after the stroke, I asked Jerry what he was thankful for that year. His first response was, "I'm thankful for you." After a few tears of joy, I asked what else. He said, "There are so many." I thought, *Wow! If I were in his place after having a serious stroke, would I have lots to be thankful for myself?* The passage does say in all circumstances! Even in a stroke, there were things to be thankful for in his life. I learned to be thankful for every day God gave me with Jerry after the stroke.

> Count it all joy, my brothers, when you meet trials of various kinds, for you know that the testing of your faith produces steadfastness. And let steadfastness have its full effect, that you may be perfect and complete, lacking in nothing. (James 1:2–4 ESV)

It is easy to look back on the twenty-two months and see how the trials were beneficial to my Christian maturity. In the midst of them, it was more difficult to experience yet another hospital stay and be thankful for the stressful situation. However, the blessings came on the worst days. Strength came when I needed it. Kisses and hugs from my sweetie were always there pushing me forward.

> Giving thanks always and for everything to God the Father in the name of our Lord Jesus Christ. (Ephesians 5:20 ESV)

Going through Jesus Christ in my prayers reminded me of the friend Jesus was to me as well. There were so many days I could feel the closeness of Jesus beside me, holding my hand and at times carrying me. It was much to be thankful for not to have to take this journey alone.

> I have said these things to you, that in me you may have peace. In the world you will have tribulation. But take heart; I have overcome the world. (John 16:33 ESV)

Peace was there when there was no reason for me to have peace. We will never live in this world without tribulation—God states this as a fact; however, knowing God is the winner gives us great peace. We know how the book ends.

> And we know that for those who love God all things work together for good, for those who are called according to his purpose. (Romans 8:28 ESV)

The days of the stroke were used by God in a variety of ways to work for our benefit and that of others. Sharing my journal with so many online gave them strength and encouragement. We were a witness to the healthcare professionals at the doctor's offices, the hospital, or the home health personnel. And God is working it for the good of others by being able to share our story through this book.

The scriptures were overpoweringly clear. I was to be thankful all day every day. But was God not seeing what was going on? Did God not see the horrific stroke that happened on February 24? Was God not aware of how our lives changed in an instant? Was God not watching me struggle through delusional thinking on the difficult days? Did God not see how Jerry was so different and at times hard to take care of from day to day?

Of course God was seeing everything, yet the scriptures remained. I was to be thankful in all circumstances every day, no matter what was going on during that day. It didn't matter Jerry had a stroke that would eventually take his life. It didn't matter my life was now on hold, and everything I planned to do was no longer feasible. It didn't matter we would not make it to our fifty-first anniversary. I was to be thankful!

I found this quote by Elie Wiesel about thankfulness: "When a person doesn't have gratitude, something is missing in his or her humanity. A person can almost be defined by his or her attitude toward gratitude."

Here is a quote by Melody Beattie outside of God's law stating how crucial gratitude is for humanity: "Gratitude makes sense of your past, brings peace for today, and creates a vision for tomorrow." (Beattie, 2001)

On Day 233 of the caregiving experience, I read an article in *Reader's Digest*, "The Goodness of Gratitude" by Lisa Fields. In the article, she said, "Gratitude is among the top five predictors of happiness" according to research (Fields 2016). She suggested keeping a journal of what you are thankful for to help you focus on the positive. I started adding ten things I was thankful for on day 236 of the twenty-two months.

This was such a blessing to my life and to several of my readers, who started a journal of thankfulness for themselves. There were days when I would get to number four or five and get stuck. I could always add things like air conditioning, a washer and dryer, and air to breathe, but I tried hard each day to focus on what I truly had been blessed with during that day. I continued my thankful list into my grieving blog after Jerry passed. This has been a big part of my grieving process. In our marriage, I had so much to be thankful for, creating long lists. Of course, I still grieve over not having Jerry beside me, but the thankful list helps me focus on what I have to be thankful for in over fifty years of marriage to a sweet Christian man.

God is the supreme counselor and psychiatrist who knows what is best for us. Colossians 2:7 ends with "overflowing with thankfulness." The word *overflowing* indicates a Christian is already full of thankfulness but then has so much more, one can't help but overflow. Before the stroke, I had a lot to be thankful for. Now the challenge was to continue my thankfulness with the addition of a handicapped husband.

First Timothy 4:4 states how God created all things and for us and "nothing is to be rejected if it is received with thanksgiving." This one hit me hard because I had some pretty difficult days with Jerry. Could God really have created all things, and I was to receive them only with thanksgiving? Early on, I was not ready to be thankful for the stroke. However, there were so many factors of the stroke God was turning into blessing for us. Jerry suffered from erosive osteoarthritis before the stroke and was in tremendous pain. After the stroke, he had no joint pain. And after about a year, Jerry did not remember his life before the stroke. He had no regret for those things he didn't remember being able to do.

> Whatever you do, whether in word or deed, do it all in the name of the Lord Jesus, giving thanks to God. (Colossians 3:17)

My new twenty-four seven job was caregiver for my husband. I had to learn to be thankful I was able to take care of

Jerry, had him at home most of the time, and had the strength to keep going from day to day, and that Jerry was as mobile as he was because it allowed him to be at home. I didn't have to look far to see how blessed I was with my patient.

Philippians 4:6 encouraged me not even to be anxious, but all my requests to God needed to include thanksgiving. That meant my prayers for recovery from the stroke must be coupled with thanksgiving if God chose not to give him healing. I was encouraged not to be anxious in praying for recovery. Anxious is defined as "experiencing worry, unease, or nervousness, typically about an imminent event or something with an uncertain outcome" (Google Dictionary 2018). What a challenge for me to release my worry and uneasiness over not knowing when the stroke would take Jerry or whether another one was on the horizon. I had to look for thanksgiving in the life surrounding the stroke and not in the life inside the stroke. God was sending blessings daily—I simply needed to recognize them.

The reward for following verse 6—not to be anxious and to be thankful—is the promise of peace in our lives in verse 7. It truly was a peace beyond all understanding. How could there possibly be peace in the situation we found ourselves? And yet our days were often peaceful. One of the hospital social workers even asked me how I could be so calm and peaceful during one of the hospital stays. God's peace was there when humans thought it impossible.

The last part of verse 7 gives us still another promise. The peace coming from God will guard our hearts and minds. There were so many fears and feelings I needed to be guarded from: depression, loneliness, the future, losing my wise husband, finances, household management, and more. But God's peace protected my heart and mind from those thoughts taking over. And then God gave me this verse:

I always thank my God for you because of his grace given you in Christ Jesus. (1 Corinthians 1:4)

The thanksgiving wasn't in the stroke but the reason we look forward to a home in heaven after the stroke. I can be thankful because God promised us forgiveness in this life to take us home to the next one for eternity. Every day I have my salvation to be thankful for, no matter what else is going on that day!

I recently saw a saying on a plaque with a thought-provoking message. "What if you only had today what you had thanked the Lord for yesterday?" I fear most of us would be sitting in a large, empty space with nothing to eat, no place to sleep, and perhaps not even air to breathe. We take so much for granted that is provided by God each day to sustain our lives.

Enter his gates with thanksgiving and his courts with praise. (Psalm 100:4a)

When I think about how I enter my prayer time with God each day, I have to say my first words are not always thanksgiving and praise. There are days when *help* is all I can utter. Those times are okay as well. But God wants to be praised and thanked for the countless blessings He gives us each and every day. As a parent, I can still remember the wonderful feeling I got from one of my daughters saying thanks or telling me I did a good job on something!

On our first Christmas day after the stroke, we had come through the darkest time of our journey. Our four hospital stays as well as two one-week skilled nursing facility stays were behind us, and God had given us glimmers of hope of better days. Here was the thankful list I posted on Christmas:

Many good times even through ten months of the stroke.

Every hug I receive from Jerry—they are wonderful.

Rest I receive each night because Jerry sleeps such long hours.

Relaxing times in my rocking chair in my sunroom.

Your comments and hearts each day (liking my post with hearts).

Chocolate—any day of the year. And is there any kind other than dark?

Hearing Jerry sing from time to time.

Rare times when my old Jerry comes through to me.

Inspiring devotional and Bible reading time in the mornings.

Special people in my life who visit and help me out in so many ways—even prayers and encouraging thoughts from far away.

Time each morning with my God before starting the day.

My sweet husband who is a joy to care for, even on difficult days.

Any smiles I get from Jerry—they are so special.

Sources of strength from God, scriptures, and people every day.

There was never a day without something to be for thankful for in our lives. Whether it was just the fact God had brought us to this point or the lessons I was learning, it was a thankful praise. And all days the joy of salvation was there to hold me up.

Give thanks to the LORD, for he is good; his love endures forever. (1 Chronicles 16:34)

Here is another reason always to be thankful to our God. He is good! His love for us never fails! Those are two very great characteristics of God we need in our lives. We will never know a human being in our lives who is consistently, 100 percent of the time good and always loving. That is the human part of us—full of shortcomings. But we will never have a day when God is not good and does not love us no matter how bad a day we are having.

First Thessalonians 5:18a told me to "give thanks in all circumstances." No matter what was going on during the day, how serious the hallucinations, how many times I called 911, how big a mess I had to clean up, or how little Jerry talked to me some days, I was commanded to give thanks in that day's circumstances. And I did, and God helped to change my attitude and perspective that day!

Some days I could get angry reading James 1:2a (ESV), "Count it all joy, my brothers, when you meet trials of various kinds." Joy did not come in having strokes, in my thinking. Joy would come from healing from the stroke—complete healing. I had to learn to accept God's definition of joy, knowing His grace saved me from this world for a better world someday. Jerry's complete healing was his death to this life and rebirth to his new life. Along with the peace that passes understanding, this was a joy from the Lord.

Then there is the great promise in Romans 8:28.

And we know that for those who love God all things work together for good, for those who are called according to his purpose.

Please notice this scripture does not say all things are good but work together for good. God did not send Jerry's stroke but used it for much good. Jerry's life encouraged so many others with his smile, hugs, and songs. What I learned and wrote about in my journals helped others as it helped me to write it. There was and still is much good coming from our twenty-two months of caregiving and eventual death of Jerry.

Here is a scripture emphasizing our need for God.

Be we have this treasure in jars of clay, to show that the surpassing power belongs to God and not to us. We are afflicted in every way; but not crushed; perplexed, but not driven to despair; persecuted, but not forsaken; struck down, but not destroyed; always carrying in the body the death of

Jesus so that the life of Jesus may also be manifested in our bodies. (2 Corinthians 4:7–10)

The total power comes from God, however I am so thankful He chose to use jars of clay here to do His will. My life needs to show God's power in order to be afflicted by the stroke but not crushed by the caregiving; perplexed by the enormity of the task before me but not despondent over my limitations; persecuted by all the fighting I had to do to ensure Jerry's care but not left alone by God; struck down in my retirement plans, but those plans were just on hold and not completely gone. This verse says I am carrying in my body the death of Christ—that is powerful because his death didn't end in the grave!

On January 1, 2017, at the beginning of our second calendar with the stroke, I wrote these New Year's Resolutions in my journal.

1. I resolve to start and end each day with thanksgiving to the Lord.
2. I resolve to not complain about the job I have been given to do. That will only make both of us miserable.
3. I resolve to be more purposeful about my praying and sticking to my list of prayer needs rather than trying to remember them each day.
4. I resolve to take one day at a time knowing the future is in God's hands. If I take care of today, He can take care of all the tomorrows.
5. I resolve not to live in the past of if only, and what if, and I wish I had.
6. I resolve to make worship to God a part of each day whether in just scripture or song or both.
7. I resolve to appreciate Jerry every day, whoever he is that day. I don't know how many more days I have.
8. I resolve to read my daily scriptures with more attention rather than letting my mind wander.

9. I resolve to try to get some purposeful exercise in each day.

10. I resolve to allow God to direct my days.

God brought us through a very difficult year but stood beside us all the way. We both experienced ups and downs during the year. My poor sweetie suffered more in the past year than he should have in his entire life. Still, I resolved to work again with his caregiving until he was taken home.

This quote by Charles Spurgeon was sent to me during my caregiving days: "I have learned to kiss the wave that slams me against the Rock of Ages." It was difficult to get to the point in my faith journey where I was ready to thank God for the stroke, however it was what slammed me full body into the Rock of Ages. Never had I relied on God with the intensity I did now. Never had I felt His presence more than I did now. Never before had I created a daily thankful list giving God the praise as I should have been doing my whole life.

The story of the ten lepers healed by Jesus in Luke 17:11–19 always made one wonder where the other nine were, didn't it? Being healed from leprosy in that society meant they could return into public life again after being shunned their whole lives. And yet only one returned to thank the Lord for the healing. I need to always be the one!

How should this change your life? Everyone needs to keep a thankful journal, especially on bad days. Those "oh-woe is me" days can be turned around by stopping to pray thanksgiving to God at that moment. Blessings abound daily. Wake up in the morning asking God to give you thankful eyes throughout the day. It will change your life!

Max Lucado said about gratitude, "Gratitude lifts our eyes off the things we lack so we might see the blessings we possess"

(Lucado 2012, 23). It would have been easy each day to focus on things I had lost with Jerry's stroke—there were so many. I could forget any plans we had for a future together as a couple, or for my encore career, or even the freedom to leave my own house when I wanted. Instead, I was choosing to focus on the countless blessings God was showering on me each day through a close relationship with Him, prayers answered, Jerry's miracles through the stroke, his hugs and kisses, the songs I continued to hear from his bass voice, discovering my true friends, my garden, having the financial means to take care of Jerry, God's wisdom in tough decisions, and being able to keep going in Jerry's care. How amazingly blessed I was when I focused on what I did have rather than what I didn't have.

My biggest challenge to being thankful every day of Jerry's care came close to the end of his life. One morning as I was having my quiet time, I noticed Jerry was already awake. I always preferred to complete my time with God before I started my day with Jerry. When I went in to check why he was awake, he was extremely messy. I cleaned it all up, bemoaning the fact of the future of this with Jerry. He would not grow out of this as a baby would. However, once back to my quiet time after all the time required to get him settled again, the first scripture I read was Ephesians 5:20.

Always giving thanks to God the Father for everything, in the name of our Lord Jesus Christ.

My first thought to God was that this wasn't funny! However, the scripture spoke to me, and my challenge was to meet it. This is the thank-you list I came up with for that morning's activities.

1. I still have Jerry at home under my care.
2. If Jerry were in a skilled nursing facility, he would stay dirty for thirty minutes to two hours.

3. Jerry isn't combative when I clean him up but is very cooperative.
4. His body functions are working well.
5. He has no constipation to irritate his hemorrhoids.
6. I have lovely candles to dissipate the smell.
7. I have disposable bed pads that I just throw away to cover the fabric bed pads.
8. I have medical gloves to cover my hands while cleaning him up; I didn't have that with our children.
9. Because I was a mother first, this doesn't bother me.
10. Jerry is still alive to make a mess.

It was an excellent experience for me to realize there truly were things to be thankful for in every situation.

The value of struggles is shown in nature. One of my morning devotionals spoke of this to me. This story is from Pastor Joyce.

Two years ago, I set out a rosebush in the corner of my garden. It was to bear yellow roses. And it was to bear them profusely. Yet, during those two years, it had not produced a blossom!

I asked the florist from whom I bought the bush why it was so barren of flowers. I had cultivated it carefully; had watered it often; had made the soil around it as rich as possible. And it had grown well.

"That's just why," said the florist. "That kind of rose needs the poorest soil in the garden. Sandy soil would be best, and never a bit of fertilizer. Take away the rich soil and put gravelly earth in its place. Cut the bush back severely. Then it will bloom."

I did—and the bush blossomed forth in the most gorgeous yellow known to nature. Then I moralized: that yellow rose is just like many lives. Hardships develop beauty and the soul thrives on troubles; trials bring out all the best in them; ease and comfort and applause only leave them barren. (Cowman 1999, 86)

There you have it! If your life is running too smoothly, you won't blossom in your faith and relationship with Jesus. You need adversity in your life to provide the spiritual growth. I wasn't sure I wanted to bloom! And yet the adversity I endured was causing growth in my faith I had never experienced before. "The school of suffering graduates exceptional scholars" (Cowman 1999, 501).

And giving joyful thanks to the Father, who has qualified you to share in the inheritance of his holy people in the kingdom of light. (Colossians 1:12)

Our daily practice of giving thanks should not be because we know we will grow through the struggles. It says with joyful thanks to the Father. It reminds me of our children when they were learning to thank someone for a gift or doing something nice. We had to prompt them to say thanks. Their heart was certainly not in it when they gave their thanks, and it certainly was not full of joy. Our thanks to our heavenly Father cannot be just because we were commanded to be thankful. Our joy goes along with it even in the midst of struggles.

The struggles taught me so much about God as my strength, Jesus as my friend, the Holy Spirit indwelling me, and why my dependence on Him made me strong. As Isaiah 40:31b says, "They will soar on wings like eagles." This is a very familiar verse to most of us. A devotional I read during the end of the twenty-two months explained the eagles' flight like this:

One of the flight dynamics of which eagles often take advantage is obstruction currents. These form when moving air runs into an obstacle—a cliff or mountain. Air is forced up and over the object. Where we would see a barrier, eagles see an advantage. They ride the obstacle currents high into

181

the air where they can soar for long stretches of time. That high position gives them a better vantage point from which to watch life, stay informed, and find ways to meet their nutritional needs.

The parallel is striking. What if we saw obstacles as gifts to boost our ability to fly higher? What if we appreciated rather than resented the new perspective we gain? (Aughtmon 2016, 307)

Reading the description of this magnificent bird gave me an even greater understanding of the struggles and their purpose. I need to thank God for the struggles because each one gives me the current to ride up high above the struggle to see Him at work in my life. When I climb to God's level through prayer, reading His Word and drawing on the strength of the Holy Spirit, I can be truly thankful for the obstacles He provided to help me mature past my wildest dreams. My faith in God would never have grown to this height without Jerry's stroke and my twenty-two months of caregiving.

I will give thanks to you, Lord, with all my heart; I will tell of all your wonderful deeds. (Psalm 9:1)

Not only was I to give thanks to my God from the bottom of my heart each day, but I also need to tell others about my marvelous God. This book and speaking engagements help me to do just that. God's greatness pushes me to shout it from the highest mountain and from every speaker's podium I get asked to fill. I plan to spend the rest of my life here telling as many as I can about God's greatness, care, protection, love, and concern, as well as the lessons learned. I am truly thankful for the life Jerry and I had, and also in my new life!

Things I Learned While Caregiving with God!

1. I have learned that grieving doesn't wait until the end but is a process day to day.
2. I have learned God will weave the threads of your life, positive and negative, into a beautiful tapestry if you allow Him to do so.
3. I have learned that every day has more to be thankful for than it has problems.

12 - Caring for the Man Who is No Longer the Same

The day of Jerry's stroke, he was changed into a different man. One of our dear friends, Mara, a stroke nurse in Wisconsin, came to visit when Jerry was still in the hospital. With all her experience, she explained to the whole family that the Jerry we all knew and loved was not coming back to us. That man was gone, and if Jerry survived the severity of this stroke, he would be different. How different, we did not know at that time.

What did change? It would take months for Jerry to settle into who he was from the stroke. At first, the constant sleeping was an obvious change. A similarity was his affection for kissing. When I would get close, even during those early hospital days when he seemed soundly asleep, he would pucker up and take all the kisses I would give him. I was more than willing to continue kissing to keep that part of Jerry with me.

Once at the skilled nursing facility, the staff would tell me things I could expect. Often, stroke patients who never used profanity before would become very foulmouthed. I was so thankful

Jerry was not one of those patients. He continued to be gracious in his language even though he lost his filter of etiquette.

As I mentioned in an earlier chapter, early on I started calling Jerry my sweet guy. He truly became my sweet guy while giving me trouble at the same time. There were days his stubborn streak broke through, causing him to refuse to get in the tub, sit down on the toilet, open his mouth to eat or to talk, and other annoying things for the caregiver. However, most of the time he was only troublesome when he was delusional.

In August after the stroke, he was sitting on the back patio in the glider and watching me do garden work. I could always see him while I worked. One of the times I checked on him, he said, "I need to be able to do things like you." His mind was watching me but also wishing he could get off the glider and do something.

The longer the caregiving went on, the more dependent Jerry became on me and the less he wanted to be separated from me. There were two days in a row in August when I was out of the room thinking he was asleep but then heard noises. When I checked, Jerry was sitting on the bed. I asked him what the matter was, and he said, "I thought you left me." His dependence on me created a fear of being left by me.

One of the reasons he developed the dependence on me was the realization he was not able to do things as he used to do. Another evening in that first August, after he had fallen, I got him up using the technique I was taught by the occupational therapists at the skilled nursing facility. I was able to get him off the floor with only rug burns and put him back in bed. When I asked him how he felt, his response was, "Helpless." I knew that was difficult, especially for this man who had helped me throughout our marriage with anything I was unable to accomplish without assistance. Now he depended on me and other caregivers for everything.

Then there was a day when he was frustrated with me as I tried to clean up a wet brief. I am sure embarrassment was also a part of it. He told me to leave him alone and said, "Why don't you just leave town and leave me alone?"

After a few minutes of thinking about it, I asked him, "What would happen to you if I did leave town and leave you alone?"

He got quiet as he thought about that question and replied, "I would die." As much as he wanted his independence, he was realizing his limitations and need for my care.

There was an instance when Kelly Ann was here helping me, and we were trying to get Jerry to the toilet. It was a strange day for him; he objected to everything we tried. The trip was unsuccessful and resulted later in the morning with an accident while he was in his recliner. It was such a mess that we decided to take him to the shower to clean him up. Neither of us was embarrassed but ready to take care of the problem at hand. When the therapist came to work with him and he was still sitting in the shower because he wouldn't let us get him up, he indicated to her he was embarrassed because of his diarrhea. Kelly Ann and I felt badly because we had not been sensitive to his feelings. We simply expected him to allow us to take care of his physical needs, and we were not being sensitive to his emotional needs. What a good lesson this was for a caregiver. Even when his mind was not functioning at top capacity, his emotional side still felt embarrassment.

The therapists reminded us he couldn't help the way he was now and couldn't remember what he had done to be sorry for later. He would occasionally say he was sorry. On the day after the shower experience, he woke up in an agitated mood. After playing praise and worship music for him and continuing to be as sweet and gentle as I could, he eventually hugged me tight. I took that as "I am sorry" without his needing to say it. I knew down inside, his sweet personality was still there, but I couldn't always see it coming out.

In early August, Jerry started making moves like he was getting sexually fresh with me. My first thought was this man had just had a stroke, and I wondered how this could be happening. However, research confirmed stroke patients do still have their sexual desires. Some male patients even develop hypersexuality and try to grab any woman who walks by. Thankfully, Jerry displayed his sexual advances only toward me.

This behavior would come and go as well. There would be months without any advances by Jerry, and then we would have a streak of several weeks when he was always grabbing me. As surprising as this was for me, it was also a delight to know he still desired our relationship as husband and wife. Schedules throughout our lives never allowed for lots of extra time for ourselves and our relationship. Now we had all the time in the world at our disposal. At the same time, his filters were gone, taking away any shyness he had before the stroke.

During our twenty-two months together, we had lots of time together to enjoy each other's company. This time was certainly a serendipity of the stroke time I never expected. The relationship we developed was truly special for us both. I never turned down the sexual advances unless we had company in the house.

His compromised eyesight was a continual problem, at least for me. Because Jerry had little memory of anything in the past, he didn't remember what he used to be able to see. He tended to look up at the ceiling. I only have guesses as to why he did that. One is that when he had the double vision in the first few months of the stroke, there was only one ceiling even if he was seeing double. Once that stopped (at least I think it did), he probably had blurry vision, but this was another guess. He was uncomfortable wearing his old glasses, and the eye doctor said there would be no way to do an accurate eye exam on him.

The therapist worked with him to look down, to keep him from running into things. I can't say it really was very effective. He never did get proficient at using a walker because of his eyesight. I learned early on it was easier to walk beside him guiding him myself. I joked with Jerry, telling him I was his seeing-eye dog without fleas. He also learned he had to have me help him get up, which helped with fewer falls. Of course, there were times he forgot and got up anyway.

Because his eyesight was extremely compromised by the stroke, it was difficult to tell exactly what he could and could not see. There were times he would be reaching in the direction of something, making me assume he couldn't see clearly what was there. He could still read if the letters were up high and larger, such as when we would make it to church. He could read the words for songs on the screen overhead.

With his limited activity, however, and not really needing to see, it didn't seem to bother him. One day I was discussing with him an eye doctor's appointment and praying we would get some answers, a new lens prescription, or something to help his eyesight. His response was, "It bothers you more than it does me." I would find out later he couldn't remember he loved to read before the stroke and certainly wouldn't be able to focus on a screen of any kind after the stroke.

In September, six months after the stroke, Jerry asked me one morning, "What am I supposed to be doing?" I was not sure what prompted that question. He could have been trying to remember what he used to do. After watching me busily working around him to bathe, dress, feed, and toilet him, he may have wondered what his part was in all this. I tried several activities with him without success. Once after the therapist worked with him to lower his head to look down, we watched a TV show. He could hear it, but I am not sure about what he actually saw.

I also tried reading books to him. He did enjoy it when I read, but he would quickly tire of listening. The therapist told me with the brain injury, Jerry would process data much more slowly. For this reason, playing a book on tape or even listening to too much music would quickly overload his brain. I tried one day to put earbuds in his ears to play a book. He pulled them out after only a few minutes because of the overload of information. What a difference for my genius husband who read voraciously all his life. It was so sad to watch.

The snippets of the pre-stroke Jerry I would receive as a gift from time to time kept me going. One day due to his eyesight, he ran into a table, knocking it over. I explained it was his limited eyesight, so he should not feel badly. However, he turned around, hugged me, and said, "I am sorry." I was always encouraged to know my sweetheart was still in there, and the times he would be mean were truly not him.

During the fall season following the stroke, I had our patio enclosed to construct a sunroom. It connected the master bedroom with the kitchen, making the many trips back and forth much easier while allowing me a greater view of Jerry. I sat in the sunroom most evenings after dark with Jerry's bed in full view. During the construction, Jerry watched the workmen intently. His father had been in construction, so Jerry grew up with that skill and knowledge. One day as he was watching, I asked him if they were doing it right. He said, "No, but they are doing it the way they think is right." His analytical mind was at work watching, processing, evaluating, and assessing their work.

Of course, there were plenty of times when he was nothing like himself. Several ER visits and nurse evaluations diagnosed that Jerry also had dementia along with the stroke. At times, that seemed totally possible when he would have discussions making absolutely no sense whatsoever. Other times he would be insistent on getting rid of the feeding tube, and I could not convince him how important it was or that pulling on it would be very painful and require another trip to the ER. However, his neurologist thought it was the effects of the brain injury from the stroke. Either way, it made life at times difficult in caring for Jerry.

> The eternal God is your refuge, and underneath are the everlasting arms. He will drive out your enemies before you saying, "Destroy them!" (Deuteronomy 33:27)

There are many enemies to the caregiver: depression, worry, loneliness, fatigue, lack of patience, taking care of the house, finances, and illness. All these would be present at one time or another, especially as I thought about this man being so different than the man I lived with forty-eight years before the stroke. Now I turned over each enemy to God, and He would take care of them for me!

For Jerry, there were serendipities of his stroke and needing so much care. After breakfast one morning when Kelly Ann was here, she and I were commenting to Jerry on how spoiled he was with us doing everything for him. I asked if he enjoyed being spoiled, to which he responded, "Yes, I do." He knew the treatment he was getting and was thrilled with it!

In the fall of our first year, we went to visit someone I had gotten to know because her husband had had a stroke a month before Jerry's. She was a friend of a friend. We messaged each other on Facebook to encourage each other, but I wanted us to meet. I got Jerry in the car, and we drove to their house about twenty minutes away. Her husband could only say yes and no due to being paralyzed on one side. Before we left, however, the two men shook hands, and the bond was unmistakable. My Jerry was still the caring man he had always been—interested in others with a concerned love. It was an awesome moment.

Other days he was ornery just to be ornery. One day when he insisted on getting out in the car, I loaded some donations in the car for the thrift shop while he sat in the garage and watched. When I opened the door and took him close, however, he gave me trouble getting in the car. On the way back, we stopped at the gas station to fill up and get him coffee. I told him he could go in if he would not give me any trouble getting back in the car to come home. He agreed and complied with my request. This let me know he could choose to be ornery or not.

On another occasion, however, after waiting several minutes for him to get in the car and him not making any effort to do so, he told me he didn't remember how to get in the car. At our next neurologist appointment, I mentioned that to him. The doctor confirmed Jerry was correct. With the brain injury, he could actually not remember that day what the process was for getting in the car. It encouraged me to have more patience with him on those days and reteach again and again if necessary.

Some days my patience wore extremely thin with this man who did not act like mine. One day in our first October, it was shower time. However, when we got to the shower, he refused to get in. I did everything I could to encourage him to step inside the shower. I even reworded the Mary Poppins song "Step in Time" to "Step Inside" and would sing it for encouragement. Finally, when I asked why he would not step in, he said, "I am not courageous enough." I questioned him further, and he told me he would die if he stepped in. After more unsuccessful reasoning, I stepped in first. Then he was willing to step in but refused to sit down on the shower chair.

It was a nerve-racking shower, with him standing up rather than sitting to give me more security. I did learn later from a friend whose mother-in-law had suffered from Alzheimer's that often those patients do not see a bottom in the bathtub and believe they will fall through if they step in. My sweet Jerry came back just as we were getting out of that terrifying (for me) shower. He looked up at me and said, "I love you." We went to the afternoon Bible class that day, and one of the ladies in the class asked if he was behaving for me. He said no. Again, I had the frustration of his being aware he was not behaving for me as he should be.

Another day, later in the stroke, Jerry had been particularly cantankerous. We had an occupational therapist coming, and he was still in the shower. The morning had been so difficult that the shower was later than it should have been. I mentioned to the therapist Jerry had been hard to work with that morning, and the therapist asked Jerry if that was true. "Yes, I was difficult this morning," he admitted. A few days later, I mentioned to the physical therapist Jerry was being my sweet guy. He replied, "Most of the time!" He seemed to be aware of the trouble he gave me at times.

Many mornings, I would find the condom catheter pulled off. Jerry also liked to pee in the bed as soon as I would uncover him. Does that sound familiar to any of you who had boys? I can still remember changing my two little brothers' diapers and needing to cover them in the process to not encourage the cool air to cause more urination. In so many ways, taking care of Jerry was much like taking care of a toddler, except I couldn't spank Jerry—although I really wanted to many days!

Scriptures like Psalm 59:16 helped refocus my mornings.

But I will sing of your strength, in the morning I will sing of your love; for you are my fortress, my refuge in times of trouble.

A fortress is defined as "a heavily protected and impenetrable building." That is exactly what I needed my God to be for me. My days needed to be heavily protected and impenetrable by Satan's attempts to discourage and shorten my temper. It was important to start each day focusing on my help rather than my problems.

It was quite an adjustment period after Jerry was home from the skilled nursing facility. There were so many scary times when he refused to get in the tub, sit on the toilet, or even talk to me. As I tried to encourage him to comply, my voice raised with my frustration. There were also times it raised when I was afraid of his falling. One evening after such a time of struggling to get him to bed, he turned to me and said, "Why are you always griping at me?" I was given a picture of what he saw in me, and it was not very Christian. Jerry helped me to work harder to have greater patience with his declining abilities.

God's pruning of me to make me more fruitful came from many different angles (John 15). I also remembered a song from *The Music Machine* my daughters had as children. The song "Have Patience" became a song I sang a lot, and the entire album is available on YouTube. The song is sung about Herbert the Snail. The words said, "Have patience, don't be in such a hurry. When you get impatient, you only start to worry. Remember that God is patient too and think of all the times when others have to wait on you." Music was a way to Jerry's soul, and he often sang with me.

While working to get the wake-up narcotics at the right level, I also experienced some aggression from Jerry. One evening nine months into the stroke, he literally pinned me down to the bed. He still had amazing strength. This was after an unusually difficult evening of his spitting out his dinner, refusing to spit out the mouthwash in our nightly mouth routine, fighting the toothbrush out of my hands, and refusing to take off his shoes to go to bed. We were both blessed to resolve the aggression issues by lowering the medication that could cause that behavior. Oh, those wonderful side effects!

During a hospital stay, Jerry carried on a conversation with me showing his mind was thinking deeply and analyzing. Here is part of the conversation that morning:

Every time I part with you, I give part of me away.

I've sought who I was and kept exploring and don't know who I am. I haven't found out who I was, or I don't understand myself. Or didn't know who I was yet. I am not satisfied with who I am or as a person. Do you know what it is to have thoughty thoughts? Deep thoughts. I had analytical thoughts on the way here. I thought I was more of an introspective person than I was. I was so surprised at who I was. I am not aware of Jerry before the stroke.

What I see is you and I and our relationship. Don't know what that is now. What does it mean that I love you? I painted a picture of it. Some part of myself, a memory bank of myself. Part of it is a zeroscopic picture of myself. The distinguishing mark of yourself is a place on the picture. Love is a picture of yourself as you see yourself. You see the strongest image of yourself. It is a picture of yourself in profile. Picture of myself as a busy person satisfying myself. Busy being yourself.

That type of conversation was rare and was a gift when it came. It was enough to give me hope from time to time as I struggled with who this man was living in the body I knew so well. A verse with special meaning after that day was Psalm 30:5b, "Weeping may stay for the night, but rejoicing comes in the morning. God was so good to me to give me glimmers of hope to see a better side of Jerry.

The end of November refreshed some memory he had not had in some time. A picture came from a friend from church in

Wisconsin. When I asked Jerry if he remembered Eileen, the sender, he told me yes and that we went to church with them. He even remembered her husband was Bill. When a neighbor was visiting one time, he used the word *quota*. Jerry immediately said, "That was what they said at my job with the Department of the Interior." This was encouraging but not long lasting. I grabbed on to each glimmer of hope of Jerry returning.

My relationship with Jerry was getting closer during this time, and his dependence on me was greater. After three and a half weeks of hospital and skilled nursing facility stays and finally being back at home, Jerry didn't want me out of his sight, especially at night. Even when I tried to go lock the doors to come to bed, he said, "I don't want you going anywhere." Of course, I never wanted to leave him at night either, but sleep was essential for my self-care, which at times resulted in my leaving him at the hospital and going home.

Another day not long after this incident, I went to the store quickly after he went to sleep, and a neighbor was there with him. I was surprised to find him awake on my return and asked why he was awake. His response was, "I can feel your presence." Whether or not that was true, I don't know, but it seemed to be. There was more than once he was absolutely aware when I was close and when I was not.

Jerry had never been a conversationalist. Now, however, the nonverbal days were the most difficult by far. There were so many parts of his care depending on my knowing what he was feeling physically and emotionally. It was like trying to make a new recipe for a delectable dessert, but all one had was the picture to go by. There was no explanation of ingredients, how much of each, or the baking time. One simply knew what the end result looked like. I read a poem addressing the way I felt during the dark times of his care.

What though the way may be lonely,
    And dark the shadows fall;
    I know where'er it leadeth,
    My Father planned it all.

The sun may shine tomorrow,
    The shadows break and flee;
    'Twill be the way He chooses,
    The Father's plan for me.

He guides my halting footsteps
    Along the weary way,
    For well He knows the pathway
    Will lead to endless day.

A day of light and gladness,
    On which no shade will fall,
    'Tis this at last awaits me—
    My Father planned it all.

I sing through shade and sunshine,
    And trust what'er befall;
    His way is best—it leads to rest;
    My Father planned it all.

God is working out His purpose.
(Cowman 1999, 312)

As I have said previously, I never believed God sent the stroke to be able to teach me so many lessons. However, God knew it would happen and had a purpose to fulfill in my life as He worked with me to care for my husband. God's ultimate plan leads to a home with Him in heaven. God knows the growth we need to make in our lives. Sometimes that growth is made through dark, difficult days. God always provides sunshine, His love, His care, His protection, and His Spirit to strengthen us on all days. His support held me up every day. My friend Jesus helped me to never have a totally bad day because "Jesus Christ is the same yesterday and today and forever" (Hebrews 13:8).

One morning after a stressful shower taking a total of one hour, I asked Jerry why he was so difficult in the shower that morning. His response was, "I am afraid you are going to drop me." It didn't really make sense because he would not let me hold him up with the gait belt or even help much. However, it did help me understand some of the fears he often did not verbalize.

The filter of tact was also gone from Jerry's interactions with people. After a visit to his rheumatologist, Jerry said, "I don't like your choice of words." Then there was the time in January when Kelly Ann was here in the afternoon. Jerry wanted to get sexually frisky, but we had company. I passed that on to her. She said to Jerry, "If you need time alone with your wife, I can leave."

His response was, "Goodbye, see you later." He just said it like it was.

One night he told me he had to be quiet because I would think he was on loco weed. (He had never used weed in his life.) We called our granddaughter a couple of days later and mentioned it to her. She suggested maybe he should buy some more weed. His answer was he should find a Mexican software developer because they always have it. Jerry was never racist, so we had no idea where that came from, but it was pretty funny.

On a Sunday morning, Jerry woke up unusually early for him, and consequently we made plans to go to church. As I was encouraging him to take a nap before we left, I told him he needed to sleep because I didn't want him so sleepy he would fall asleep in church. His response was, "Everyone else does."

That same afternoon, I fed him a potato and ham casserole for dinner. My oven apparently wasn't heating to the full temperature, causing the potatoes not to be super soft. As I was feeding him, he suddenly got up, saying he was going to the "other room." He walked to the sink and spit out everything in his mouth! Then he got ice cream for dinner. Hmm, I wonder whether he knew that would happen?

His filters of tact and appropriateness were gone. During our long stay at the skilled nursing facility, there was a nurse who had been burned over her whole body in an accident years previously, resulting in scars everywhere, including her face. She was not Jerry's nurse but came into the dining hall one day to give Jerry his medications. He took one look at her and asked, "What's wrong with your face?" I was the only one embarrassed. Her response indicated she had gotten that response from other patients.

The home health nurse aide who gave him showers from time to time at home told me in March of a funny comment. Jerry looked at her and said, "You are different. You have bumps on your chest." Even worse than that was attending Lynn's choir banquet that May. A senior Jerry had worked with came up and asked if he remembered her. Jerry made us all turn red when he said, "No but you've got nice boobs!"

One day when Kelly Ann was here helping with his care, we talked about doing something special that afternoon when he woke up from his nap. As he hugged me before getting into his recliner, he grabbed both of my buttock cheeks (as he often did). I commented, "Maybe our special activity will be in bed after your nap."

His answer was, "Dismiss her," talking about Kelly Ann. He said whatever he thought without considering tact.

Tim brought his coffee business team over one day to meet Jerry. After they visited for a little bit, one of them said on departure, "Thanks for letting us come see you today."

Jerry responded with, "I didn't have a choice."

He worded things differently with his loss of a filter. One afternoon in summer, he ran his hand up my shorts and said, "Let's play hanky-panky!" I was always happy to oblige that request for special intimate time when Jerry could seem normal to us both. It was sweet time for us.

After four hospital stays and two one-week stays in skilled nursing in thirty-four days, things began to work into a better schedule for everyone. Jerry's strength increased, especially after taking him off the antiseizure medicine that caused extreme drowsiness. God had seen me through a very dark time in Jerry's care. My dependence on Him gave me the strength I needed.

A truly different aspect of Jerry now was the toilet routine. He rarely told me when he needed to go to the bathroom. Most of his last year, he used the toilet and even wore normal underwear, which made him feel more himself. I handled bathroom time like one would with a child. After breakfast, we went to the toilet, where he would almost always have a bowel movement. After naps and before bed, he would use the urinal. It was simply a matter of sticking to the schedule. A factor that made this possible was the seemingly enormous size of his bladder to be able to need to urinate only three times a day (excluding nighttime). When something interrupted, he had accidents but was normally very sweet to work with me to clean him up.

At times, some of his distant past would surface. Right after the new year, Jerry said, "I have a wedding to do this afternoon." He had spent seven years in full-time youth ministry, and four of those were in a church where the pulpit minister didn't like to perform weddings for the public who called in. He always referred them to Jerry, who enjoyed doing them. Somewhere in his memory, that one came up, and he was sure he needed to perform a ceremony for Marcie that afternoon; he couldn't remember the groom's name.

All of us have fears, but Jerry voiced his one day in January. He told me, "I have fears." I questioned through a lot of things because he didn't want to talk, and he finally said he was fearful of his physical abilities since the stroke. He wasn't fearful of anything in the room (no delusions), mental abilities, or spiritual beliefs. I assured him I would always be here when he needed to get up and go somewhere, and I praised him on how far he had come with therapy.

The therapists once told me we were doing too much for Jerry and should let him do more on his own. I admitted I had spoiled and pampered him. Soon after that when I was taking him in for his hair cut, we put him in front of the chair, and I reminded Kelly Ann we were supposed to let him figure out how to get in the chair. "But I like to be pampered," was his response. We both thought he deserved to be pampered and kept it up.

Jerry had a degree in biology and loved all things science. One of the few times we watched a movie, I found a science documentary called *Living on Us* about the bacteria and other organisms living on and in our bodies to help them be healthy. We were eating dinner while we watched. Before he finished eating, he said, "I can't eat any more. This is gross." I was amazed his brain had forgotten his natural inclination to all things science.

Some days Jerry would say things to me I knew he didn't intend to say. One morning as I was getting ready to take him to an endocrinologist appointment, he was being particularly belligerent. When I asked him anything, no matter what, his answer was a defiant no. Then he said, "I have got to get out of here." When I asked where he wanted to go, he said, "As far away from you as I can." I knew this was the stroke talking and not Jerry, however it was still challenging and hurtful at the time.

It was always difficult for me when Jerry didn't know who I was. During a hospital stay in June of year two, Jerry had not known me most of the day and night. In the morning, I was having a discussion with him about his not knowing me. I said, "I wish you knew who I was."

Jerry responded, "I do too. It bothers me that I don't. But you are a safe character." At least he was comfortable with me and did not fear my presence. Then he said, "I can't make sense of my thoughts." It had to have been frustrating to a man with such a tremendous mind to be unable to put things together.

The first night home from this particular visit, he had gone to sleep for the night—I thought. I went in about 6:00 p.m. to give him night meds. He woke up as he sometimes did, but I could tell the look in his eyes was terror. He grabbed the PEG tube, and if I hadn't held on tightly below, he would have pulled it out of his stomach. He pulled the end off where I connect the syringe. He was afraid of me too. Finally, when I finished and backed away, he looked at me and said, "I know who you are now. I am sorry." How awful this must have been for him—something I tried to keep in mind during the tough experiences.

God continued to provide help through His Word and the many devotional books I was reading.

And He said, "Come!" And Peter got out of the boat and walked on the water and came toward Jesus. But seeing the wind, he became frightened, and beginning to sink, he cried out, "Lord, save me." (Matthew 14:29–30 ESV)

The author of the devotional had this to say:

When the Lord calls you to come across the water, step out with confidence and joy. And never glance away from Him for even a moment. You will not prevail by measuring the waves or grow strong by gauging the wind. Attempting to survey the danger may actually cause you to fall before it. Pausing at the difficulties will result in the waves breaking over your head. (Cowman 1999, 436)

This was an excellent perspective about Peter, as well as the one I now found myself in. I had to keep my eyes on the Lord rather than the confused state Jerry was in. Rather than dreading the day and what it might bring, I needed to keep my focus on God's refuge, His peace, and His strength. How true that it would be damaging to survey the danger ahead. I have heard so many stories of dementia patients and know what could have been ahead for me. I had to focus on God. The other focus I needed was the torment this must have been to Jerry's mind. Can you imagine being so terrified of things that didn't exist? How scary to hear voices in the room when there were none. How frustrating not to be able to gather your thoughts to make sense. Yes, it was difficult for me but so much more so for my sweet husband.

A conversation not long after that gave me even more insight into the convoluted thinking his brain injury was causing. This is what he said.

I am envisioning but don't know what. I am playing out scenes in my head. My mind is going backward. The scenes are going backward. This bothers me. I don't quite understand it. It started after I talked with Carla the nurse— I think it was. You act out my voice. You play out my words. It's not you—it's the other woman. She is in this room. I adopted her name of Rosarita. She is not a character as much as she is a live, acting person in the room. You don't see her because you're not here most of the time. She bothers me in that she plays out this other character.

The delusional world gave him confusion and sometimes fear, making it difficult for him to interact with me comfortably. There was nothing I could do to stop the delusions. I continued to be as supportive as I could be, sought God's wisdom, and felt the strength of the Spirit living within me for my actions.

Jerry's recovery seemed to be in one of three phases. Phase one was my favorite, when he was the clearest thinking, cooperative, and loving, and he seemed to understand what was going on. In phase two, he was not terribly delusional, but the delusions were in and out, affecting his ability to think completely clearly. He was mostly easy to manage but had brief episodes where he could be pretty difficult. He would hug in that phase but wanted nothing more than that. This was the phase where he chose not to talk to me some days. Phase three was the one we didn't have often. Praise God for that. These were the highly delusional days when he was very difficult to manage. He usually stayed in one phase for several days up to weeks or months.

Enjoy what you have rather than desiring what you don't have. Just dreaming about nice things is meaningless—like chasing the wind. (Ecclesiastes 6:9 NLT)

I realize this passage is most likely talking about material things in this life, however it truly applied to my caregiving days. I no longer had my husband the way he was before the stroke. He couldn't get up and go where he wanted by himself. We could no longer go out to the theater at night or a movie. I couldn't expect him to tell me he loved me every day as he had for all the years before the stroke. However, I was truly enjoying the husband I did have with me. The days when he was sweet were special days to be enjoyed to the fullest.

One morning a year into the stroke, I had two loads of laundry I was folding on my bed while I was trying to convince Jerry to wake up. I told him I would save all the wash rags for him to fold later in the day for his therapy. Fast-forward to that afternoon when we had a few minutes before I took him back to bed. He was sitting in the rocking chair, and I asked if he was ready to fold those wash rags. He had this huge smile come over his face and said, "I thought you would forget." My reply was he was hoping I would forget. He said, "I am living in the light of hope."

The more I thought about Jerry's comment, the deeper it became to me. His comment was "Living in the light of hope." Let's put that into a scripture that we quote often.

Now faith is confidence in what we hope for and assurance about what we do not see. (Hebrews 11:1)

We should live in the light of our hope every day of our lives. For the days of the stroke, hope is what our lives were built upon. Jerry had the hope of a healed body in the next life. He had the hope we will be together there someday. I had the hope God would continue to bless us with his recovery and me with the strength I needed for the caregiving. If we didn't live in the light of hope, we wouldn't be able to pull ourselves out of bed in the morning to face another day of affliction and chaos in this world.

Things I Learned While Caregiving with God!
1. I have learned there is plenty of cuddle time after a stroke—why not before?
2. I have learned how wonderful Jerry's hugs and kisses were; they made my day.
3. I have learned even though this Jerry was not my Jerry all the time, he delighted me with snippets of him from time to time.

Jerry joked our entire marriage, saying we had a fifty-year marriage contract, but it was renewable. When the stroke happened after forty-eight and a half years of marriage, I never dreamed we would make it to our fiftieth, and neither nor did anyone else in the medical field. However, when we got to May the year following the stroke, my thinking was optimistic we would in fact make it to our anniversary, August 6. Because according to Jerry our contract was up, it was time for a vow renewal, and plans started.

A therapist God put in our lives that June was a Christian and encouraged me. He had been an occupational therapist for thirty-seven years, and Jerry was only the third bilateral thalamic stroke he had treated. He was amazed at Jerry's recovery because the other two patients had not lived past six months of their stroke.

God was keeping Jerry alive for many reasons—from my learning to lean on God and his inspiration to so many who were blessed to know him.

The days were moving along mostly in a good routine. Jerry continued wanting me with him all the time. One evening in June when he awakened after going to bed, I asked if he wanted me to stay by him until he went back to sleep. His response was, "There is always room for you next to me." There was such sweet love between us at this time, even realizing part of his dependence on me was from the stroke effects and knowing I was his lifeline.

That same night, we discussed what the stroke had done to him. He said, "The positives outweigh the negatives!" What a marvelous attitude he had in the middle of a locked mind and body. I next commented how I wished his eyesight would come back more, to which he responded, "That is not such a big deal." His perspective on his new life was truly from God to have such acceptance and comfort with what was going on. I learned to take that acceptance as my own and enjoyed the time together.

God continued giving me strength through His word on a daily basis.

The Lord replied, "My Presence will go with you, and I will give you rest." (Exodus 33:14)

God was speaking to Moses leading the grumbling, complaining, whining, and fickle people out of Egypt. If he could be leading millions of people through the wilderness and have rest from God, I never questioned He could give me rest working with one sweet husband!

The summer even brought a day when Jerry and I had a picnic at a local park. He loved watching the children play on the equipment and being out in the fresh air. His mobility was such a huge blessing in being able to take him places in the afternoons. We walked into the ice cream shop, the coffee shop, and Panera for dinner. I used the wheelchair if we were going grocery shopping or to the doctor.

As plans were in progress for our fiftieth, I mentioned one day to Jerry that it was coming up in two months. Because we only had a fifty-year contract, I asked if he wanted to renew the vows or kick me out. He thought a minute and then said, "Let's renew." Phew! What a tease!

On the one-year anniversary of Jerry leaving the skilled nursing facility, I decided to take him back for a visit. I printed the invitations for our fiftieth event and so took them with us. When we walked into the facility, one of his nurses saw him and said, "Well, there is a miracle." The therapists could not believe how great he walked, looked, and talked. The facility doctor was also there that day and showed the same surprise. Not one of them expected him to be alive one year later. Lynn had already been practicing "Because" with him, the song he sang in our original ceremony. I asked him to sing it for them. After just singing a little, he teared up and couldn't sing any more. I guess we were both emotional about getting to the big day for us. The doctor said on our way out, "Glad I got to see you." Jerry responded with a normal comment from his past: "Glad I could be seen."

Nevertheless, each person should live as a believer in whatever situation the Lord has assigned to them, just as God has called them. (1 Corinthians 7:17a)

My assignment as caregiver was not one I would have applied for, yet God chose this assignment for me. Actually, I chose it when I promised "in sickness and in health" on our original wedding day. God equipped me for the task before me.

During June, Jerry and I enjoyed several visitors. April, a friend from Wisconsin, came for a visit. She was here for a birthday lunch for Jerry's seventy-seventh birthday with two families from church. Then there was a family birthday lunch and a Father's Day celebration. Jerry still remembered how to open presents, calling his new summer shorts "bloomers."

When we were out on different occasions, people in the public would be super nice to us. On one trip to Panera, a grandmother and her granddaughter moved to a different table to offer us a good one for Jerry to sit easily, where I could see him while ordering. Then a gentleman came up to me in line and asked if I was with that gentleman. When I said yes, he said he was paying for our meals! How wonderful to have people who wanted to help. I am sure there was a story behind them both.

At times Jerry showed more recovery, such as the day when he looked sleepy in late afternoon. I asked if he was ready for bed. His response was, "I am tired of always sleeping." He wanted to stay up more, but the stroke would never let him.

One thing God proved over and over to us by this time in the stroke was He could be counted on for whatever we needed. Getting up for specific appointment times was a huge challenge with Jerry's sleep schedule. My CaringBridge prayer warriors would be praying for every appointment where we had to have Jerry up and ready to go. When he would have a doctor's appointment, I would tell Jerry the night before that he would wake up on God's schedule the next morning, and he always did. During the entire twenty-two months of the stroke, Jerry never missed a doctor's appointment, and he was always on time! It was truly amazing to see God at work.

Even being in mostly a good phase of Jerry's care, there were still discouraging times. The home health nurses continually told me Jerry would go through phases. The thalamus controlled so much of the body's systems. When it was damaged, getting things out of balance was easy to do. One of those times was leading up to an endocrinologist appointment. He was strange for several days, causing me to wonder whether another urinary tract infection was the cause.

When the doctor evaluated his condition in her office in June, Jerry was strange enough that she advised us to take him to the ER to be checked out. They would do a urinalysis there. Upon arriving at the ER, Jerry's confusion was more concerning than it had been in quite some time. Even though he did not know who I was, he did not want me to get too far from him. They did every imaginable test, always considering another stroke. They finally decided his thyroid was not stable; he had hyperthyroidism.

After treating me poorly before leaving for the doctor that morning and then not knowing who I was in the ER, when Jerry looked concerned, I asked what was bothering him. He said, "I am afraid now that I have finally figured out what is important, they will take it away from me." Next, I asked what was most important. He answered, "You." Of course, I couldn't tell whether this was a deep, wise conclusion or whether he was remembering the many tests they had taken him away from me to do when in the ER. They kept him overnight for observation in the ER, and I stayed with him through the night to be sure he had what was most important to him there with him. My presence was calming to him when he woke up delusional in the night. His subconscious knew who I was even when the conscious did not.

It was always encouraging for me to hear the perspective of others watching my family care for Jerry. On a trip to a local coffee shop with Lynn and David in June, the two women next to us handed us a note when they got up to leave.

To the family next to me:
I just wanted to take a moment and tell you watching your family totally made my day. The love you have for who I can only assume is your father brought me to tears. We need more people like you here on our earth. Thank you from the bottom of my heart for touching my life today just by doing what you obviously do all the time, which is showing

compassion for others. I wish you love and happiness. I wish I could hug you right now.

Lynn followed them to the car and did hug them. She saw them later at the same coffee shop and updated them on Jerry's progress at that point. People needed to see us lovingly caring for those we loved. Jerry recognized the day was an overall good one ending with cuddling time in bed. When I told him before he went to sleep it had turned out to be a good day, he said, "It was a very, very, very good day."

Once again, 1 Corinthians 7:17a applies.

> Nevertheless, each person should live as a believer in whatever situation the Lord has assigned to them, just as God has called them.

We should act as Christians not only when things are easy for us but always. Marriage is not for the weak at heart; it takes work throughout life to make it work. The caregiving was the most challenging for me (us), but it was also the most fulfilling and produced the most spiritual growth of my life.

At times Jerry was able to think about his new life. One day I told him he was a miracle because he was supposed to die from this stroke a long time ago. He responded, "Was my not dying living through it or surviving it? I want my not dying to be living. Is it living? Is it half living? It is physical? I want the other half to be spiritual. I dearly love the idea that there is life after the stroke." It was so sweet to know he recognized he had survived the stroke and was living. Another day soon after that, he told me, "I decided to be happy. I knew I could be happy or unhappy but decided to be happy because I have all the chances to make the best of it."

In early July, we discussed his memory of life before the stroke. He said, "I remember the life that came before, but I don't remember what it was. I don't remember what I don't remember. But that's not to say I didn't have it." Then I asked if he remembered people who visited. "I remember people but not where or when. I remember bits and pieces." I thought what a blessing for him not to have regrets for what used to be! This thought was a big part of why he seemed happy most of the time. He had no regrets for what he could not do because he couldn't remember that part of his life. However, one discouraging piece of not remembering was one day when he told me, "I love you but don't remember why or when." At least even without the memories, he still loved me. I was grateful for his love.

In late July, we made another trip to the skilled nursing facility to see the weekend staff we had not seen in our previous visit. After our visit, I asked if he remembered being there because he had spent one hundred days in that facility. His question was, "Did you see me there?"

"Yes," I told him, "I was there every day."

He replied, "I'm sorry, I don't remember it at all." The brain injury erased negative memories along with positive ones.

When I tried to question him another night, he told me I was making him think too much, and that wasn't enjoyable. The speech therapist told me the thought process would really tire him out. Another day he told me, "If you love me enough, you won't ask me to talk." I needed to hear him talk now more than ever, but most days it was not to be.

Jerry's neurology visit in mid-July received great remarks. Jerry walked back to the exam room, leaving the wheelchair in the waiting room. The doctor was surprised at how well he was doing and the number of hours he was able to stay awake. It seemed the four to six hours was so little to me, however given full recovery without wake-up narcotics was only one to two hours, the doctor was impressed. The doctor said Jerry was lucky to have me—another affirmation of my caregiving!

One of the special visitors who came to see Jerry in July was a gentleman from the Dominican Republic, Rafael. Jerry took several mission trips with our church in Wisconsin, and the team met this young man when he was high school age. Education there was only free through grade school, and consequently Rafael was not attending school for financial reasons. Jerry and others saw great potential in him. Several of the team, including Jerry, committed to help Rafael through school. They paid for high school and his bachelor's and master's degrees in the Dominican. He then completed his doctorate in education and was working on a second master's at the time of his visit. He mastered six languages. Jerry had mentored Rafael, encouraging him to set goals and then reach them. Two of the men in the congregation in Wisconsin drove him the fourteen hours down here to see Jerry after arriving from the Dominican for his first visit to the states, at Rafael's insistence. It was an awesome visit. My husband was such a special man and touched many lives.

Psalm 139:23–24 reminded me of a needed lesson.

Search me, God, and know my heart; test me and know my anxious thoughts.

This described me several mornings. I found myself telling God what the schedule should be. It was difficult not to be anxious about it. When I finally backed off and didn't try to wake up Jerry but let God take over, of course it worked out! It seemed strange the psalmist asked God to search me to know my heart when He already did. But the testing did show whether I had enough faith. In order to let God take the reins, I had to relax and quit fretting about the schedule and what I thought was best.

The months of June and July were busy with preparations for our big fiftieth vow renewal on August 5. Our anniversary was August 6, but because it was a Sunday that year, I moved it to Saturday. It would be a difficult day without the extra stress of church that morning. I worked on preparing a slide show of our fifty years of marriage. The exercise of putting it together helped me remember all the good times of our life together. How I would have loved to share those pictures with Jerry, allowing us to laugh and cry together about the stories behind each picture. I asked Jerry in late July if he wanted to keep going in our marriage. He said, "Unless you can find a reason to kick me out, I'd like to stay around."

Jerry gave me another confirmation of our love close to our fiftieth. We had made it to church one Sunday, which was a rare happening due to his sleep schedule. When we got back home, as I was putting him down for his nap, I said out loud, "Thank you, God for letting this happen."

Jerry's response was so sweet. "Thank you, Lord, for letting Lois happen." I was touched.

My friend and planner Kelly Ann helped me think through the invitations and the arrangement of the room, the food, flowers, and other decorations. Lynn worked with Jerry for two months relearning the two songs he would sing for the service. "Because" was the song he sang in the original ceremony but decided to end the time with him singing "Once I Had a Secret Love," an old Doris Day song. He sang that one to me on our first date. I asked my two daughters to stand with Jerry as our bridesmaids. My younger brother, James, was asked to come from Tulsa and walk me down the aisle. I wore my original wedding dress, and Jerry was dressed in a nice suit. Kelly Ann made silk flower corsages, boutonnieres, and my bouquet. Granddaughters and grandsons worked at the guest book and served.

My daughter Kara, grandson Alex, and granddaughter Cassidy arrived from Georgia on August 2 for our big day. It was Kara's second visit since the stroke and the grandkids' first visit. (They had been here for my big seventieth birthday celebration five weeks before the stroke happened.) Jerry had been delusional the night before, not knowing me or his daughters from the pictures. However, on their arrival, we were waiting in the driveway. He knew them and was so happy to see them.

Jerry had a delusion that evening of wanting to go to the red barn in the yard. I helped Jerry work through it while they were there for support. They all complimented me on how I handled the situation. After this long, it had become second nature to me to talk him down calmly if possible.

The two daughters shopped to purchase matching dresses for their bridesmaid role. They also talked through the questions I had for them about cremation. I talked to the salesman about plans but needed their input on whether they needed an actual service with the body before cremation. There were so many decisions to make without being able to talk them through with Jerry. The family was here to decorate the building for the celebration on Friday night and help with all the last-minute preparations.

Here are some funny things Jerry said during the few days before our big fiftieth. I was kissing him and asked if it was too much. He said, "Yes, but I can handle it." The next morning, Kara was helping him get dressed. He looked at me and said, "She loves me more than you do."

Later, when he was going down for his nap, I said, "Just for the record, I love you more than Kara."

His reply was, "Just for the record, I know that."

If we had a nickname for Kara, it was always Carrot Top for her red hair. That day for some reason, he called her Kara Dumpling. Later she said, "So what do I call you?"

He said, "I don't know, but it better not be Jerry Dumpling."

When he got back in the car after his hair appointment, I said, "You look sharp."

He replied, "I just saw the sharpener." After that, Kelly Ann was the sharpener rather than a beautician.

The day of our fiftieth was truly a gift from God. Several of my relatives came from Texas, including my sister from Boerne. My brother and other relatives came from Oklahoma. Our adopted family from Wisconsin surprised us by showing up at the party. My two high school friends came from Oklahoma and Texas. Jerry's schedule worked well. He enjoyed talking to all the people who attended. Our son-in-law, Tim, officiated the ceremony. Jerry stood for the whole fifteen minutes, with daughters holding him up. He sang beautifully, and most people cried. It was truly a beautiful day and the true climax of our twenty-two months together.

The schedule for the afternoon was from 1:00 to 3:00 p.m., with the ceremony being first. The rest of the time was a come-and-go reception. Jerry was totally done by 2:30. Alex and Kelly Ann helped me get him home, undressed, and in bed. He stayed awake for about another hour with dreamy stars in his eyes. The day was beautiful for him as well. For me, the memories are still precious. For Jerry, sadly they were gone by the next day. (To see a video of the service, go to YouTube and search for "Lois Cox 50th vow renewal video.")

Therefore I tell you, whatever you ask in prayer, believe that you have received it, and it will be yours. (Mark 11:24)

What a joy it was to have prayers answered. I prayed for Jerry to be clear thinking, and he was. I prayed he would truly enjoy the day, and he did. I prayed he would be awake, and he was for the important parts. I prayed to be sitting and resting here after it was over, saying how good the day was, and I did just that. It truly was a very good day. I prayed for peace for me, and someone actually said to me, "You have such peace." God is good and truly amazing, isn't He?

The fiftieth vow renewal was a gift from God to hold me up through the rest of Jerry's life and beyond. It was such a sweet memory for me to remember the commitment we made and stuck with through sickness and health. I am forever grateful to God for this amazing gift.

Things I Learned While Caregiving with God!

1. I have learned that God provides.
2. I have learned caregiving is emotionally, physically, and spiritually exhausting but also the most fulfilling work you will ever do.
3. I have learned you can put your life on hold by reading the right books, keeping projects to do, journaling, and connecting through your faith for strength.

The hospice nurse who came later in Jerry's stroke explained what we had been through in his stroke life was like a roller coaster ride since February 24, 2016. Jerry finally topped the last hill and was racing to the bottom at record speed. The fiftieth was on the incline to the top of that hill, as were the next few months. The ride was exactly like that, with some hills higher than others and some rides down falling faster than others. He was getting ready to reach the highest hill now.

Soon after the family left the next week, Jerry had an appointment with the new primary care physician taking over our records. One of the things he asked Jerry was about his jaw surgery back in 1973. He responded with, "Yes, it was a mandibular osteotomy." I was amazed he remembered that because I certainly did not. After we left, he said he liked the new doctor. He said, "He made me feel important." The practice was for him to face Jerry, and I sat behind them against another wall if they needed me.

Jerry made it clear to me he wanted to be with me all the time possible. One afternoon, he heard me texting Lynn that I needed bananas and would try to go get them once Jerry was down. My neighbor was so eager to help me in that way. However, when he was still awake and not looking, I asked if he wanted to go with me to Walmart to get the bananas. His reply was, "Hooray, I get to go with you." God blessed us in many ways during the caregiving. This closeness was one of them.

About a week after that, I thought Jerry was in bed asleep as I started laundry and the dishwasher. When I sat down in my rocker about ten feet from him, his eyes were open. When I went to ask what he needed, his response was, "I just need you." Then shortly after that, we had a storm at night with very loud thunder. When I went in to check on him to see if he was okay, he said, "I see you as my storm shelter."

I have mentioned Jerry waking up on God's schedule many times during the twenty-two months. The biggest challenge and most amazing intervention by God came in mid-August when, after checking some lab work, the endocrinologist wanted a new set of labs done that needed to be done at 8:00 a.m. Home health didn't have a nurse who could come that early. He had been awake only three and a half hours the day before the required test. There was a plea to God once again to perform His schedule miracles. With morning traffic, we needed to leave the house at 7:30. When Lynn arrived to help me at 7:15, Jerry was sitting on the bed dressed. We were in the car at 7:20. The traffic was light. God took care of everything!

We enjoyed such a wonderful time of Jerry being sweet and loving. He was discharged completely from home health and was doing so well. Almost two weeks after our fiftieth, I had eyelid surgery. When I returned from the procedure, Jerry had not slept because he was worried about me. Lynn asked if he wanted to pray when I left, and he did. She said he prayed a lovely prayer, thanking God for the doctor who worked on me and praying for my quick recovery.

We ended up with another hospital visit due to low sodium levels. When the sodium level gets low, it can cause confusion among other things. It affects the brain's ability to work properly. He was talking strangely for several days, which alerted me to something being wrong. The only way to treat low sodium is through IV therapy, resulting in an ER visit. As we were driving over to the hospital, I asked Jerry questions, which he was not answering. I finally asked why he wouldn't talk to me. "I don't find it worthwhile to talk to you," was his reply. Well, okay! Guess he told me. He finally got into a room and on a bed about 2:00 p.m., and I told him he could go to sleep now. "I can't go to sleep because no one is waiting for me on the other side," he said. I asked who was waiting for him, to which he replied, "Ghostly people wait for me when I go to sleep." That was disturbing, but he said they weren't scary. Low sodium levels do have strange results on people.

The hospital stay resulted in much more than low sodium levels, with more vomiting, blood pressure and heart rate too elevated, and low oxygen levels. I spent two nights at the hospital due to all the problems he was having. With his inability to communicate properly to staff, he needed me by his side. He was also much calmer with my presence beside him.

I returned home after a five-day stay, and this verse was in my morning reading.

> Therefore do not worry about tomorrow, for tomorrow will worry about itself. Each day has enough trouble of its own. (Matthew 6:34)

Now, here was a verse for the caregiver. Taking Jerry home could create all sorts of worry and concern over how he would do at home. Typically, he did so much better at home than at the hospital. God was so good to us to provide strength for Jerry as well as for me.

A huge benefit from another hospitalization was renewal of home health services again. That meant getting more physical therapy sessions to get Jerry's strength back. They tried to assign a different therapist to Jerry—a male this time. When I asked Jerry if that would be okay, he said in a very down and depressed voice, "I guess that will be okay." We ended up with Jenny again—she was much prettier. When this new therapist finished our visit, he said he understood why everyone at the agency thought so much of Jerry. He was known as a sweet patient there as well.

> For we are to God the pleasing aroma of Christ among those who are being saved and those who are perishing. To the one we are an aroma that brings death; to the other, an aroma that brings life. And who is equal to such a task? (2 Corinthians 2:15–16)

Jerry gave off the sweet aroma of Christ wherever he went. Our love for each other also was a sweet aroma, making an impression on people wherever we went—the ER, the doctor's office, the coffee or ice cream shop, and here at home to the home health personnel. Even in caregiving, I could spread the aroma of Christ to those we touched. God helped me to be equal to the task. There is a wall plaque in my bathroom that says, "If God brings you to it, He will bring you through it." This is so very true!

We still had days when Jerry didn't know me. One of the funny ones was following the last hospital stay. When David arrived after school, he did not know him. When we told Jerry he was named for him and asked his name, Jerry didn't know his middle name either. We finally told him he was David's grandfather, and I was his grandmother. "So we are married?" he responded. "That's the best thing I have heard all day." At least he wanted to be connected to me.

When life is good, enjoy it. But when life is hard, remember: God gives good times and hard times, and no one knows what tomorrow will bring. (Ecclesiastes 7:14 NCV)

That is so true! When things are good, we need to fully enjoy the moments. The hard times provide such opportunities for growth. Hard times help us appreciate the good times. As the verse says, none of us knows what tomorrow will bring. When Jerry had a good day, I needed to enjoy every minute. When days were hard, I needed to rely on God for what I could learn through the experience.

When Jerry woke up the morning after the day described above, I asked if he knew me this morning. "No," was his response. I showed him his wedding ring and mine and confirmed with him we were married. The next thing he did was a riot. He grabbed my breasts, one in each hand. I could hear his mind saying, "Well, in that case, I might as well make the best of it." A day in September when he did know me, he told me *love* couldn't begin to describe how he felt for me. There were many sweet days to offset the more difficult ones. Our cuddling times of intimacy were very special to us both during these days.

As you have read, Jerry was pampered and was told how sweet and wonderful he was daily. One night when Jerry was going to sleep, we had a conversation letting me know we had gone too far.

Lois: "You are a sweet guy."

Jerry: "There are a lot of sweet guys but only one really sweet guy."

Lois: "Who?"

Jerry: "Me."

Lois: "You are stuck on yourself."

Jerry: "If you are going to be stuck on someone, might as well be me."

Maybe we over did it building him up!

The deeper into the stroke we got, the more I found out what the thalamus controlled. Jerry could easily get overheated on a walk when in physical therapy. His body was not able to regulate body temperature and at times required ice packs to cool him. His sodium levels were affected by the thalamus, along with blood pressure, sleep, and his immune system. Balancing these organs without the brain stem functioning as it should was a huge challenge. The injured brain continued to give him periods of delusional thinking, especially if he slept too long for his afternoon nap. Dreams were vivid and often continued after he woke up.

> But it is the spirit in a person, the breath of the Almighty, that gives them understanding. (Job 32:8)

The Holy Spirit needed to work overtime in my life to give me the understanding I needed to give Jerry the proper care. How amazing it is to have the breath of the Almighty within us to help, guide, and empower us with understanding for every situation arising.

Even though there were difficult days, God kept reminding me of His care and love for us.

> Are not two sparrows sold for a penny? Yet not one of them will fall to the ground outside your Father's care. And even the very hairs of your head are all numbered. So don't be afraid; you are worth more than many sparrows. (Matthew 10:29–31)

Sparrows are so plentiful partly because they were brought to New York City in 1851 from the Middle East and Northern Africa and became an aggressive species. God had the balance of nature in place, and man messed it up. They aren't even a pretty bird in my estimation. But God notices every one of them who is killed by anything. Most of the human population is a flock of sparrows— nothing out of the ordinary. However, God still loves and cares for each one of us in a very special way. He knew every time Jerry had a delusion, had high blood pressure, had vomited, had a UTI, and was being obstinate, and every time I was discouraged, lonely, fatigued, and even had a headache. He takes notice of everything going on with us no matter who we are. I am more valuable than a sparrow!

God needed to be caring for me. This was also a time during the stroke for me to finalize financial details. I took over all the finances the day of the stroke, such as paying bills, doing taxes, and making purchase decisions. However, I needed to set up a trust, be sure I could be in charge of his Social Security account and have the cremation services paid for ahead of time. All this is discussed in more detail in chapter 16—the practical side of the stroke. Our main bank account was still in Wisconsin, resulting in my needing to move all direct deposits to our local bank. There were so many details outside of Jerry's care causing additional stress. God's calming presence was needed on a minute-by-minute basis.

But now, this is what the Lord says—he who created you, Jacob, he who formed you, Israel: "Do not fear, for I have redeemed you; I have summoned you by name: you are mine. When you pass through the waters, I will be with you; and when you pass through the rivers, they will not sweep over you. When you walk through the fire, you will not be burned; the flames will not set you ablaze." (Isaiah 43:1–2)

Here is my paraphrase:

This is what the Lord says, he who created you, Lois, he who formed you, Jerry: Do not fear, for I have redeemed you; I have summoned you by name: you are mine. When you pass through the stroke, I will be with you; and when you pass through the requirements of the federal government, the paperwork will not sweep over you. When you walk through the ups and downs of caring for a stroke patient, you will not be overcome; depression and loneliness will not overtake you.

God always saw me through the toughest days. I was and am a detail person who wanted to take care of everything. That was why all these loose ends gave me such grief: I wanted everything in place and in order for whatever happened. And as Jerry often quoted from scripture, it says, "It came to pass," but it never said, "It came to stay." I could hold to that promise.

It was also a promise I held onto during the delusional days we had through that fall. There were such challenging days, but God gave me another verse to help me get through.

Praise the Lord. Praise the Lord, you his servants; praise the name of the Lord, Let the name of the Lord be praised, both now and forevermore. From the rising of the sun to the place where it sets, the name of the Lord is to be praised. (Psalm 113:1–3)

I needed to spend my days in praise of God's awesome care of us, His loving kindness, His answers to all my prayers, His knowing the limits I could take and giving me good days following the tough ones, and His creations in nature in my backyard. My days were all about where I put my focus.

Jerry was a listener, and that did not change after the stroke. If anyone was in the house talking, he wanted to be where he could hear. During times I thought he was asleep, he would surprise me, such as one night in early October. Each night after I put him to bed, I would read a devotional to him and then pray with him. As soon as his head hit the pillow, his eyes closed, and he appeared to be asleep. This particular night, I read the devotional, prayed, and then went to finish cleaning up the bathroom from cleaning him up. As I walked by, he said, "There is a lesson in there for you."

"What, from the devotional?" I asked.

"Yes," he replied. He was not only listening but thinking about what he was hearing.

I reread the devotional, and yes, there was a lesson in there for me. Here is a quote from the reading.

The education of our faith is incomplete if we have yet to learn that God's providence works through loss, that there is a ministry to us through failure and the fading of things, and that He gives the gift of emptiness. It is, in fact, the material insecurities of life that cause our lives to be spiritually established. The dwindling brook at the Kerith Ravine, where Elijah sat deep in thought, is a true picture of each of our lives. (Cowman 2016, 683)

The scripture used was 1 Kings 17:7, "Some time later the brook dried up."

It was an excellent thought for me to think about the loss of Jerry. I was losing him a little each day, watched his life fading, and the felt the emptiness of time alone while he slept. I was like Elijah sitting by a brook and watching it dry up before my eyes. However, as it dried up, my faith was increasing, and Jerry's life was decreasing. Jerry knew I needed to read that one again.

As clear as Jerry's thinking was that night, a couple of days later, it was just the opposite. Here was the conversation that morning.

Me: "What are you thinking about?"

Jerry: "I'm planning the New York Marathon."

Me: "Are you running?"

Jerry: "Well, I have so much time on my hands, might as well."

Me: "So we need to walk around the block more?"

Jerry: "Ohh—if that's what it takes."

You have to realize Jerry was never a runner. He actually hated exercise. When he was getting ready to climb a fourteen-thousand-foot mountain in Colorado, he would plan the last possible date he could start his training to be able to make the climb. At least he was trying to think of something productive to do with all his time, and he was not thinking about his physical limitations.

As much as that one did not make sense, a few days later, here was the conversation.

Me: "Are you ready to get up?"

Jerry: "We're done."

Me: "With getting up?"

Jerry: "With getting up in the mornings. We'll get up in the afternoons."

Later in the day when I asked him about it, he said, "That was just a rash statement." This conversation was after his morning wake-up time had gotten later and later, and often it was noon before he opened his eyes. The exceptions were when we had a doctor's appointment, and God woke him up on time for those.

Scriptures like the following helped keep my focus.

I press on toward the goal toward the prize for which God has called me heavenward in Christ Jesus. (Philippians 3:14)

Aren't you glad we are not pressing on for just the end of this life? There would certainly be no hope there! We get older and feebler, we have more aches and pains, and the mind isn't working so well. Just the thought of getting out of this life of struggles is something to make me happy. And with Jerry, wow, what a hope for him to look forward to: a life without a stroke where his body and mind will work perfectly, whatever the body will be. It seems that old age is just a waiting game for the next life. The goal has always been heaven, but it seems more real now than in my thirties. What an exciting goal to have.

God came through with help so many times. The endocrinologist wanted to do a test where I needed to collect all

Jerry's urine for twenty-four hours and bring it in so they could do lab work that day. There were just a few hiccups in the collection test. First, I had to have a new Foley catheter collection bag for night. A bag used once already has existing bacteria. Second, he would have to have a night when he didn't pull off the catheter. Third, it couldn't be a day when he decided to urinate in the shower. Fourth, it couldn't be a day when he urinated when he sat on the toilet after breakfast! Just a few things to consider. The day I finally did the test, Jerry felt pressure to need to go on demand. However, with God's help, we managed to collect all we needed, take it to the lab, and have the blood drawn for the test. His help got us through a lot of stressful doctor requirements.

Philippians 4:6 came up that morning as I was collecting this test.

Do not be anxious about anything, but in every situation, by prayer and petition, with thanksgiving, present your requests to God.

The timing in my daily devotionals was totally in God's hands. Yes, I was praying more, but I was not successful at not being anxious. There was still growth in my faith to come!

His physical therapist in October told me Jerry was doing the best mentally and physically—the best ever in her time working with him. He had changed to a new wake-up narcotic when we had to move to a different pharmacy due to insurance refusing to pay for the drug he had been on or any type of those drugs. We were all feeling good about his progress and his future. This newer drug of the same kind was giving him a better clarity of mind than the old drug. I would always wonder about all the things we did not know. Perhaps had he been on this drug sooner, he would have had a better functioning mind earlier. But wondering what could have been was not worth wasting my time.

It seemed we had reached a pinnacle in his recovery. He was thinking more clearly, remembering some things from one day to the next, putting words together to make more sense, and even offering prayers at times. All of us were enjoying this season of a better place. It was obvious he was processing conversation and questions better.

I am the Lord, the God of all mankind. Is anything too hard for me? (Jeremiah 32:27)

Of course, I believed God could completely cure the stroke for Jerry, but He didn't. Why? Sickness and dying are a part of living because of the sin of Adam and Eve in the garden. I knew for me, the lessons I had learned over the past twenty months at that time were enormous and would not have happened without the stroke. I am certainly not saying Jerry's stroke was for my learning, but I did learn a tremendous amount. There were times when we needed to look forward to our heavenly home. If life was all rosy here with no physical ailments, would we long for heaven?

Yes, we were in a better place in Jerry's recovery, however Jerry was still living in a compromised body, with much of his thinking ability locked. God has a better life for us after this one. So why didn't God heal Jerry when he could? I don't have an answer for that. It had certainly been the prayer of many, including myself. Jerry was a very sweet, contented patient who was not in arthritic pain as previously. By most standards, Jerry's life was less than comfortable. Yet he had no complaints, woke up happy, was well taken care of, and was loved very much. He had a comfortable life.

During this time, Jerry even attended his men's Bible study at church on Tuesday mornings at 10:00 a.m. three times. I felt like I was leaving my child at day care with all the worries about whether he would need me, spill his coffee, need to go to the bathroom, miss me, and more. He enjoyed being with his guys, listening to the conversation, and hopefully having a little independence from me.

Jerry always needed to be reminded of my love, as we do with God's love. One day he woke up from his nap wet and messy, and I proceeded to clean him up. Somewhere in the process, I reminded him that I loved him. "Even when I am dirty?" was his question. Even after all my care, he was still amazed to know my love was there for him.

The next day, he had been praying for his older brother, Marvin, who had had a fall. He was struggling with the words to say—a common occurrence for him after the stroke. I reminded him of Romans 8:26.

> In the same way, the Spirit helps us in our weakness. We do not know what we ought to pray for, but the Spirit himself intercedes for us through wordless groans.

This is a great promise for us all but particularly with someone after a stroke who is struggling to find the right words. Jerry's prayer always got to God in perfect condition thanks to the intervening of the Spirit.

Things I Learned While Caregiving with God!

1. I have learned how valuable handicapped parking spaces are.
2. I have learned what a blessing online shopping is for homebound caregivers.
3. I have learned the meaning of crying out to God—literally.

The family gathered around our Santa for Christmas as Jerry was preparing to go home.

Jerry wasn't always up for conversations of a deep nature throughout the stroke, but there were times sprinkled throughout those twenty-two months when discussions happened. One of those was in November after the stroke, after the very difficult time of several hospital and skilled nursing facility stays. He told me he was tired of being this way (meaning what the stroke had done to him). When I asked him if he was ready to go home to heaven, his response was, "I'm not sure." The next morning, not prompted, he said, "Yes, I want to go home." I knew he meant his heavenly home and not his physical home.

The next time I brought heaven up was in February starting our second year. We were discussing the journey we were on in his care and that the journey would only end when one of us went to heaven. I hoped for his sake I would be the last to go to be able to continue his care. Then he said he didn't want to go to heaven without me, but I explained going together would most likely mean a traumatic accident for us. His real thought about going was he didn't want to leave me here alone. He was always my protector and wanted to continue to be that for me. Since his death, I have felt the care of God so dramatically in my life. Jerry didn't leave me here alone!

A discussion in the second April one evening followed a great time visiting with friends from Texas and Wisconsin. I told him I was glad God was letting me have some good time with him before he went home to heaven. Jerry's response back to me was,

> I don't know if it is even reasonable to wish for heaven. We wish for too much. I want to wish for heaven, but I want to wish for time away from heaven too. I want to stay here with you. It bothers me to be sick, but I know at the same time what it means: it means to not be sick. I remember not being sick. It is hard to be sick now. I remember not being sick. I want the end of being sick but fighting with the end of it.

His mind was struggling with leaving me here because he had taken the role of protector for me in our marriage very seriously. He was, however, aware of the stroke's effect on him.

Jerry started his last days with me on October 26. I knew that day God was preparing him to go home. It was after breakfast when he asked if I heard him vocalizing. Here was our conversation.

Me: "Of course I did, and I enjoyed it much. I would love it if you sang all day. Why don't you sing some more?"

Jerry: "I am listening to the angels singing."

Me: "You hear angels singing?"

Jerry: "Yes, don't you?"

Me: "No, I don't."

Jerry: "There must be something wrong with you. They sing to me a lot."

231

Me: "When?"
Jerry: "A lot at night."

Later, when I put him down in his recliner for his nap.
Me: "Are they still singing?"
Jerry: "Yes. Don't you hear them?"
Me: "No."
Jerry: "I'm sorry."
Me: "Do they sing all the time?"
Jerry: "Just when I ask them."
Me: "Whom do you ask?"
Jerry: "Peter."
Me: "You see Peter?"
Jerry: "Yes, don't you? You are standing right beside him."

After his nap, I asked about the singing angels again and how long he had heard them. He said since the stroke. I'm not sure why he never mentioned it to me before. Perhaps this was one of the reasons he stared at the ceiling so much during the stroke. Because he died a little more than two months after this revelation of the angels singing with him, for me it was a sign God was getting him ready for the greatest singing role yet—the heavenly choir!

The conversation continued another day.
Lois: "Are the angels singing?"
Jerry: "No, Peter just came out."
Lois: "What is he doing?"
Jerry: "Getting ready for practice."
Lois: "Angels need to practice?"
Jerry: "No, I have to practice. Can you leave now?"
Lois: "You want me to go away?"
Jerry: "Yes, I have to practice."

One morning when I asked if the angels were practicing with him, he told me not yet because the angels were late. Knowing my husband as I do, it was more likely he was late getting there! I was able to record and upload to YouTube two of the songs the angels taught him. (These can be found by going to YouTube and searching "Lois Cox Jerry practicing an angel song.") They were short snippets but very different from his normal singing and from what I expected. How precious to have that connection with the angels in preparation.

In one other conversation about singing with the angels, I asked if he sang tenor or bass with the angels. Jerry was a phenomenal bass, however there are more tenor solos than bass solos, resulting in Jerry being a little jealous of tenors. To answer me, he put one of his hands on his hips and proudly stated, "I sing both."

Jerry's humor at times amused me. I asked what he was thinking about after a period of cuddling, and he said he wanted a little Kimono girl. I couldn't figure out at all what he was talking about, but as I asked more questions, he wanted me to have another baby—a Japanese one. I went into all the reasons that was not possible, starting with the fact I am not Japanese, nor do I have the body parts left and working to have a baby. I also reminded him I had my hands full taking care of him and couldn't take care of a baby. As I was getting up, I asked what he was thinking about now. He said, "Well, the last one was such a bombshell, I won't tell you what I am thinking of now." At least the mind was processing!

> Are not all angels ministering spirits sent to serve those who will inherit salvation? (Hebrews 1:14)

God certainly sent the angels to minister to Jerry throughout the whole stroke. How precious for our heavenly Father to be sure to minister to Jerry with his brain injury. If angels had been singing to him since the stroke (although he couldn't remember back that far usually), they were comforting him in the journey in ways I could not.

Before he went to sleep a couple of nights later, I could tell he was hearing the angels sing, so I asked if he would sing one of the songs for Kelly Ann and me. He did hum a tune from the angels. It was so cool that God was teaching him some of the songs ahead of time. I just wish there wasn't something wrong with me so I could have heard them too!

The second time Jerry made it to the Tuesday morning men's Bible study, he was in deep thought when I went back to get him. We both had some time away from each other, which I asked about when we got back in the car. However, when I asked if he enjoyed spending time with his guy friends away from me, he said no because he didn't like to be away from me. The attachment was getting stronger as we went through our journey together and as Jerry drew closer to the end of his life.

Let us run with perseverance the race marked out for us. (Hebrews 12:1b)

My race for now was caregiving. It required tremendous perseverance to keep going day after day. So many days I just wanted to be finished with this race, however I knew that meant Jerry would be gone from my life. The sweet, touching days helped me get through the more challenging ones. When you are running a race as this passage indicates, the resting only comes after the race is completed. There would be no long-term rest in my caregiving role until it was over at Jerry's death.

Some days, Jerry was so empathetic with my tasks to complete. We went to the bank to make the necessary changes to our account there and add it to my newly created trust. After having just moved all the direct deposits from our Wisconsin account to the local one, I was thrilled not to have to start over with a new account. Jerry was sitting there with me and said, "If I had known I was going to cause so much trouble, I would have done something different." During our married life, Jerry had taken care of all the financial details. His desire now was to take that burden back from me. I was touched. I reminded him he had no control over having the stroke.

A primary care visit in early November near the end confirmed Jerry was doing great. His coloring was good, but he had gained weight. I tended to spoil him with trips to the ice cream shop and zucchini and pumpkin bread for breakfast. He thrived on my pampering. I told Kelly Ann in front of Jerry later that he wouldn't be having any more pumpkin or zucchini bread for breakfast. You should have seen the look on his face: it was a combination of shock, disappointment, and disbelief. Of course, I continued to spoil him, knowing the stroke would result in his death.

This was evident when a couple of days after that visit, I asked him if he had a good life. He said yes, there wasn't anything he needed. He also said he was content. How many people in any condition would have answered in that way? And yet twenty months into his serious stroke, he stated he had a good life and needed nothing. This was an excellent lesson for me. My time with him gave me an abundant life as promised in John 10:10.

By mid-November, Jerry was starting to sleep more. He had been up to six or more hours of awake time before that time, however that moved quickly down to only four hours or less a day. The longer he slept each day, the less mobile he was when awake.

About the same time, when trying to do physical therapy exercises with him, he was not following instructions well. When the therapist had discharged him a month earlier, she said he was processing commands the best he ever had. Now, a few weeks later, that part of his thinking was slowing down considerably. This phase of his care was new to me. We seemed to be on a slow decline with nothing I could do to slow it down. One of his delusions during this time was seeing Peter and Paul. God seemed to be preparing him for the last journey.

God helped us have a wonderful Thanksgiving. The timing was all in God's scheduling to allow Jerry longer naps but still be up to go to our daughter's home for the Thanksgiving meal, visit with friends (and eavesdrop on their conversations), and usually be sweet. Delusions seemed to become minor in the last phase of his life.

During the stroke days, Jerry had entire days when he refused to talk to me, which created bigger problems for me. There were times I needed to know whether he hurt, whether he was hungry, whether he was cold or hot, and so on. To do proper caregiving, I needed to know these things. God reminded me of the days I don't talk to Him enough. The difference, of course, is God knows everything about me whether or not I tell him. However, as hurt as I would be when Jerry refused to talk to me, it helped me realize how hurtful it was when I refused to talk to my God on a regular basis.

Jerry continued to bring humor into my caregiving. One morning in late November, I went in to find Jerry holding the condom catheter in his hands, still connected to the tubing. As soon as our eyes met, he said, "It was an accident." What a precious guy, and often it was hard to be angry with him over these things.

Early in our last December, I had a very disappointing week, with Jerry being more fatigued and less cooperative. The sleepiness in the mornings was making it difficult to finish breakfast. The afternoons often were a little strange with Jerry's mental state, causing problems with getting out when we needed to. He was much weaker in getting up and balancing. Things were definitely slowing down for Jerry, however he had done this before and bounced back. We all thought this was just another one of those times.

> But as for me, I am poor and needy; come quickly to me, O God. You are my help and my deliverer; Lord, do not delay. (Psalm 70:5)

I was certainly praying this prayer as we entered into the last few weeks. I was questioning decisions I was making about his care and imploring God to be right beside me every day. For Jerry, perhaps he was praying for the Lord to come quickly because his body was already in shutting down mode. God was our deliverer— for Jerry to get to go home finally to a new body, and for me to have rest from the job of caregiver.

God was giving me a blessing of more quiet time while Jerry slept more. A well-timed devotional in early December was based on Matthew 14:23b, "He went up on a mountainside by himself." Jesus needed time alone with His Father, as strong as He was. Why would we think we could make it with less quiet time? Here is a quote from that devotional:

> Crows travel in flocks, and wolves in packs, but the lion and the eagle are usually found alone. Strength is not found in busyness and noise, but in quietness. (Cowman 1999, 825)

Of course, I spent time alone during the twenty-two months of caregiving, but Jerry was sleeping more now. I had even more time to ponder our life together, his life to this point, what the outcome would be to this declining phase, and whether I was truly ready for him to die. I took more questions and concerns to God. December wasn't a typical time to be able to sit in my garden for meditation there, but my sunroom with its rocking chair became my "meet God" place.

Living in total quiet as I did most days was such a blessing in many ways. My house had never been this quiet, with Jerry singing so much of the time when he was home. He did best now with a quiet house, especially when he slept. I played Christmas music when he was awake to let him enjoy the season. Just as Jesus went on a mountaintop to pray in solitude, I sat in the quiet of my house, prayed in solitude, and prepared myself for whatever was coming.

Promises and comfort continued to come from God's well-timed scriptures on these days.

> For I am the Lord your God who takes hold of your right hand and says to you, "Do not fear; I will help you." (Isaiah 41:13)

I needed to hear from God that I needed not fear because He would help me. By the end of the first week of December, Jerry was noticeably weaker, causing more difficulty in getting him up to the shower or even just up. Next, he started not wanting to chew as much. He would opt for a protein shake rather than trying to eat even scrambled eggs. Upon reading back through my journal, I discovered the chewing problems started back in August, with mention again in September and October. The decline was certainly longer than I had thought but was very slow before we got to late November. However, God promised to help me, and He did when I needed it the most. I was watching my husband decline day by day, and there was nothing I could do to slow it down.

On Sunday, December 10, we hosted a Christmas party for Tim's afternoon class of senior citizens in order for Jerry to be able to attend. It was difficult to get him awake for it, but he did enjoy the time of singing and fellowshipping with these people. As soon as they left, I needed lots of help to get him back to bed with his added fatigue.

Jerry had three doctor appointments in December. Hindsight is always so clear, and I should have moved him to palliative care and cancelled them. Home health was still coming for their weekly visits but did not suggest any changes. As a new caregiver, I was struggling to do the best I could. The appointment on December 11 was a difficult one in getting him out of the car, onto the exam table, and then back home. Mobility was becoming an issue after being blessed with mobility throughout the stroke.

By early December, meals were a bigger challenge. He was so sleepy that he would often eat with his eyes closed. The egg and cheese omelet was now too difficult for him to chew. I opted often for a protein shake, soft breads like pumpkin bread with no nuts, or hot cereals such as Cream of Wheat. Dinner was often soup. The fact he was still eating told me he wasn't ready to be completely done with living here. My stroke-nurse friend was a valuable source of information during these stressful days. The days showed a more lethargic Jerry in all ways.

Going places was getting much harder because of the process of getting in and out of the car. He was more unsteady when walking and continued to keep his eyes closed much of the day even when awake. The decline was clearly escalating. Giving him a shower moved to the point of needing help to get him in and out. His mental alertness was also noticeably less.

This was the Christmas season, and devotional scriptures centered around that theme. On December 16, Luke 2:10 provided.

But the angel said to them, "Do not be afraid. I bring you good news that will cause great joy for all the people."

Of course, I knew this was talking to the shepherds who were afraid of such an unusual sight—angels in the sky singing to them. However, it helped me not to be afraid as I was approaching Jerry's death. I put my hope in the great joy for all people of the world—the promise of salvation through this Savior born in a manger.

On December 17, some teens from Tim and Lynn's church came with communion for Jerry. We didn't realize it at that point, but this turned out to be his last communion service before communing directly with Jesus in heaven. We were remembering the gift Jesus had made of His life to give us life. Jerry would soon be celebrating that gift in heaven.

Cleaning out Jerry's mouth both morning and evening became difficult as well. He would refuse to spit out the rinse water and generally not understand what was going on. His final doctor's appointment was one I called on my neighbor Bert to help with, knowing it would be too hard for me to get him there myself. Jerry had a bed bath that morning because he would not get up for me. The walk to the car that morning was with difficulty in each step.

The next day when the home health nurse came, I asked her to contact hospice for me. They had skipped a week with a home visit, and those two weeks were certainly a downward spiral for Jerry. She advised me to let Jerry sleep and not get him up if that was what he wanted. He never got out of bed again after the Monday doctor's appointment. I found it strange that I had to ask for hospice to come. I would think the home health nurses would have been able to see signs earlier than I was detecting them. They may be required to wait for the request of the caregiver; it can vary by the state in which one lives. They called hospice to come the next day.

I went to bed Tuesday, December 19, not feeling well, and on Wednesday, December 20, I woke up even sicker. It was a day for Kelly Ann to be there, which allowed me to head to a local urgent care and return with steroids, antibiotic, and a deadening mouthwash. The medications along with the overwhelming need to care for Jerry allowed me to keep going until after his death—then I crashed and was really sick.

Hospice arrived early that afternoon. The nurse asked many questions, with my retelling the last five weeks of decline. Next, she went back to meet Jerry, who was in a semicomatose state. She explained there were two stages of dying: transition and active stage. Jerry was now in the active stage. Upon looking back, I could see the five weeks of the transition stage. She recommended I stop his tube feedings—a decision I was not ready to do that day. How difficult it was to stop feeding my husband and make that decision for him. The nurse explained that when his body was ready to be finished with digesting any food, he would throw it all up, or it would come out around where his PEG tube entered his stomach.

After she gave me this news, I did a tremendous amount of crying. Knowing this day was coming did not prepare me for the actual day's arrival. We all know our deaths are inevitable. Those who are wives know statistically they will probably be widowed. I had now watched Jerry go through a very difficult recovery for twenty-two months, and the best option was for him to finish this life and go on to a perfect body. I knew that, but it didn't stop the tears. I was crying as I wrote this chapter (as I did through many of them). Death is so permanent, so final, a true end of this life as we know it.

The purpose of hospice is to keep the patient as comfortable as possible through the remainder of his or her life. Those who have been able to describe the pain of dying say it is like the ache all over of the flu, only worse. For that reason, they provide painkillers—for Jerry, it was liquid morphine.

Jerry actually did help in the decision to stop the tube feedings. The next day after the hospice nurse came, I heard the sounds of vomiting at 1:00 a.m., 3:00 a.m., and 6:00 a.m. that morning. Cleaning him up in his semicomatose state was more difficult than before because he was not able to move for me at all. My friend the stroke nurse had told me it would be clear when I needed to stop feeding him, and it was!

As I was sitting there holding his hand and crying out to God, it dawned on me this was an answer to prayer. I had prayed for some time now that when the end came, God would make it easy for Jerry, not painful, and not long and drawn out. God was answering that prayer; I had to accept what I knew was really best for my sweet guy.

Jerry continued to throw up all day even with nausea medicine. The nurses estimated death could come any day, but most predicted he would live no longer than a week. Hospice takes over all the medical care from that point on. All his previous medications were stopped and only the new ones administered. All prescriptions were delivered to the house along with a new hospital bed—one with a motor to raise and lower the bed. They also brought in a suction machine to help with the aspiration complication of vomiting. All diapers, bed pads, and anything else we needed would be delivered to the house. An aide would be there three days a week to give bed baths along with a social worker and chaplain. The nurse visits would be two or three days a week, however they were on call twenty-four hours a day.

Not only was hospice readily available, but God was even closer now.

Yet I am not alone, for my Father is with me. (John 16:32b)
God was with me as I sat up all night and read Psalm 23 over and over again. He was with me when I cried and cared for Jerry. I was never alone during the hospice days.

As difficult as the timing was, being in the middle of the Christmas season, it was good for Lynn. Her last day of school before Christmas break was the day we put Jerry into hospice. She was available to spend time with her dad during his last days. Ecclesiastes 3:11 tells us there is "a time to die." Jerry's time was coming even if it was the Christmas season.

On Friday, I tried giving him his high blood pressure medicine with only one-fourth cup of water. However, it came right back up. When I questioned the nurse, she said I was interrupting the body's natural dying process. Not only was I not feeding him, but now I was not hydrating him. That afternoon the nurse aide came to give him a bed bath. This was the same aide we had earlier in the stroke who told us Jerry was her favorite because of his singing. When she asked him to sing, he sang "Amazing Grace," and of course we all cried. I am quite sure his singing prolonged his life. Singing was such a part of this man, and the fact he sang through and to the end of the stroke was a tribute to the power of music.

On the eve of December 22 and into December 23, God gave me a wonderful Christmas gift. I have talked about how much Jerry slept the entire twenty-two months of the stroke. He was now sleeping more than ever. And yet at 11:45 p.m., Jerry was awake. Of course, I sat beside the bed to see what he needed. He wanted to talk! When I said I couldn't understand and asked if he would like his dentures, he said yes, he would. After dentures in (and mouthwash for me at Jerry's request to take care of my night bed breath), we were ready for a discussion. I asked if he was hungry or thirsty, and he was thirsty. I got a glass with water, and he sipped a tiny bit but never wanted more. (This little bit of water resulted in more vomiting and later caused us not to even offer it when he asked.)

We started talking about his going home, and I asked if he was scared to go to heaven. "Yes and no," was his reply. As we talked, he was not scared of being there but of the process of getting there, which is understandable. He reassured me of his love for me. He didn't want me to cry, but I told him how hard it was not to do so. We kissed, held hands, talked about our life together, our children, our grandchildren, and much more.

We talked about people he would see in heaven. He said he would tell Moses hello for me because Moses is my favorite Bible character. Jerry thought his was Peter. Our daughter Kara had two miscarriages, so I told him how great it was going to be to see two grandchildren we never met. He wondered if they would love him, but I told him not to worry about that. Everyone who knew Jerry loved Jerry! He promised to give them a hug from Grandma as well.

I asked if he had any pain, and he assured me he did not. He did say he wanted to complain, which surprised me. His complaint was that I complained about his not complaining! How very sweet. I tried to explain how hard it was to know what he needed if he didn't complain when he hurt. We talked about his life since the stroke, and he assured me he was well taken care of during the twenty-two months. Of course, he didn't remember all the details. As a climax, he sang, "Once I Had a Secret Love" to me again.

After we talked for an hour, he was sleepy again. I crawled in bed beside him, and we continued to hug and hold hands for another thirty minutes until my coughing forced me up. I was singing God's praises for not only this time of his being awake but also to be alone. We had wonderful helpers coming in and out with hospice, family, and friends. When Jerry was awake, however, I enjoyed being together with him to share our love. I didn't want to be selfish with his time when others were here, so God made special arrangements just for us. Praise God for knowing all my needs and taking care of them.

I remembered when my mom was dying with pancreatic cancer, she and Dad would talk about so many memories of their years together. She and Dad talked, laughed, and shared some things with us we had never heard. The first cake Mother made, she was careful to find the pans that fit the batter she had made perfectly coming up to the brim. Of course, it cooked over in the oven! Dad said it was a very hard, tough cake, but he ate it. She turned out to be a great cook with more experience. Mother slept a lot as well during her last days, but I still remember this. Her eyes would open, and she would say, "I'm going to see Flo." As she was sleeping and thinking about heaven, her excitement grew every time she remembered someone else who was waiting for her there.

She named many people and Bible characters during that time of growing anticipation. Mother had her mind intact, not like Jerry's injured brain.

After more vomiting on Christmas Eve, Jerry had a peaceful Christmas day. The nurse who came that day gave him twenty-four to forty-eight hours to live. I crawled in bed with him for the afternoon and slept close to my sweetheart. His grandson came by to see him. This was his first experience with death, and at age twelve, he was touched deeply. He texted me the day we put Jerry into hospice, concerned about how I was doing. His sweet, sensitive heart was touched by my pain, and he wanted to help lessen it. That night, Jerry sang several hymns with the family and also sang "Because" to me again, helping to make the day truly special in the love we shared for over fifty years.

Early the next morning, I woke at 4:00 a.m. to see Jerry's arm stretched out to me. I climbed in bed with him and slept in the crook of his arm for an hour. Hospital beds are definitely made for one person; I was held in by the bed rails. These were special times for us as a couple. Jerry wanted me close, and I rarely left his side.

Our Christmas celebration was not until December 27, as we waited for our granddaughter Kinsey to arrive from Dallas. There were eight of us in the bedroom surrounding Jerry's bed. He had his Santa hat and scarf on in the middle of present opening. Even though Jerry was asleep, I know he was aware of what was going on around him.

I spent as much time at night as I could in bed with him just to be close. He could always sense my presence, but I wanted to be sure he knew I was right there for him. Let me emphasize again that hospital beds are made for one person only. It takes only a short time before the bed rails in your back become very uncomfortable. But this was about Jerry—not me.

By December 28, he slowed down even more. I found myself waking up at night to see if he was still breathing. I had the grandkids help me take down the Christmas decorations. The sight of them was not one I wanted when my husband was soon to leave us. The sitting and waiting were very difficult.

December 29 saw Jerry's blood pressure dropping to 90/80 and his breathing slowing down. The hospice nurse indicated these were more signs of his body closing down. I was reminded again of Psalm 56:8 (NLT).

You keep track of all my sorrows. You have collected all my tears in your bottle. You have recorded each one in your book.

God was working overtime during the hospice days to track all my sorrows and collect my tears. His book had several pages added, recording these ten days.

The family was there in the evening, and Jerry tried to sing with us again but couldn't get it out. His breathing was becoming more labored. We all knew this was the night God would take him home. Before the family left, they moved Jerry's bed right next to mine for me to hold his hand all night. I had heard the term "death rattle" before but now was hearing it from my precious husband. I could hear all the phlegm in the back of his throat, but the suction could not reach it. I wanted to do anything I could to help ease the struggle to breathe. I held tight to his hand all night and found it very difficult to sleep. Finally, around 4:00 a.m., I dozed off as his breathing became less labored. When I woke up at 5:30 a.m., my sweetheart was gone. I looked over at him and said, "Till death do us part." His hand stayed in mine all morning until they took his body away around 11:00 a.m.

The family was called, as well as hospice. The nurse was very understanding, allowing us as much time as we needed with Jerry. When he first passed, I looked at the body and had second thoughts about cremation. However, as the color drained from his face and the body got colder, it was so evident Jerry was no longer in this body that had failed him so miserably. He was in his new body in heaven. Kelly Ann cut a little of his hair as a keepsake. They allowed me time to lie in bed next to him for one last time.

I hung onto the verse in Psalm 116:15.

Precious in the sight of the Lord is the death of his faithful servants.

God was so excited to take Jerry home and heal him of every ache, pain, failing body part, and locked brain. His audition to the heavenly choir was accepted, and his choir robe was fitted and waiting for him. He has probably sung every minute he has been in heaven because he sure did here on Earth.

Jerry was home at last. His life here was over, but eternity was just beginning. Yes, my heart has a huge hole in it, never to be filled again in the same way as he did. My twenty-two months with Jerry had ended, but the new life of sharing God's story had just begun. God rewrote my story!

Things I Learned While Caregiving with God!
1. I have learned that Jerry was ready for heaven when it came.
2. I have learned that hospice is a great organization to guide you through the end of life.
3. I have learned now I can look back on this experience with great joy, knowing I did all I could for the man I loved.

16 - Planning for the End and Living Day to Day – the Practical Side

The following tips are useful to prepare for caregiving.

Seeking legal advice from an elder care attorney

1. If you do not have long-term care insurance, or if yours does not cover what you thought it did, discuss financial concerns. What can a nursing home legally take of your assets to pay for care if the patient is a spouse? This will vary if it is a parent or child.

2. Check your life insurance to see whether it can be assessed for critical illness or a nursing facility if they have critical illness and long-term care riders. Others allow you to receive a cash benefit upon diagnosis.

3. What are the criteria for a living will in your state? Will advanced directives suffice through your medical facility? A living will states your desire to donate body parts when they are viable after your death. Advanced directives list your desires of being kept alive medically or allowed to pass naturally without intervention.

4. Do you have accounts that should be liquidated prior to death?

5. Do you qualify for Medicaid benefits? What are the parameters?

6. Can a trust and an estate plan be beneficial for future? Their usefulness can vary according to the state where you live. The attorney can advise you what would be beneficial.

7. How can Social Security and Medicare benefits be accessed to pay the cost of a nursing facility?

8. What is guardianship, and when might it be needed?

9. If you do not have a financial power of attorney, a medical power of attorney, and advanced directives, set one up.

Helpful information to know before meeting with admissions for a skilled nursing/long-term care facility

Here are some base line questions they could potentially ask.

1. Do either of you have life insurance?
2. Prepaid burial plans?
3. Health plan names and details.
4. What are your VA options and benefits?
5. Disability plans?
6. House debt (if own a home)
    a. Value of home:
    b. Monthly mortgage payment:
    c. Principal and Interest payment:
    d. Escrow:
    e. Total:
7. Other homes or businesses?
8. Any other debts?
9. Monthly income itemized
    a. Salary:
    b. Social security:
    c. Pension/retirement income:
10. Annuities?
11. Return on investments (ROI)?
12. Other income sources?
13. Monthly expenses itemized
    a. Household related
    b. Personal spending
    c. Budget necessary to meet basic expenses if standard of living is scaled back.
14. Investment portfolio itemized:
    a. Stocks, bonds, cash?

b. Savings? Interest rate?

c. Any other assets (land, inheritances, collectibles, LLC ownership, etc.)?

15. Financial goals for the next five to ten years.

16. Attorney of record?

17. Financial planner of record?

18. Estate plan?

19. Under what scenarios would you have your loved one at home with home health or long-term care?

Yes, they really do and can ask these questions to be sure they will be paid before you are admitted. If you qualify for Medicaid, the questions will go in a different direction. Benefits vary dramatically from state to state. Here are the Oklahoma guidelines for 2019.

Oklahoma Medicaid Eligibility Information 2019

Medicaid Eligibility Requirement	Single	Married
2019 Oklahoma Medicaid Income Limits	$2,313	$2,313
2019 Oklahoma Medicaid Asset Limits	$2,000	$4,000

What to look for in selecting a skilled nursing/long-term care facility

1. The greatest detail about how the facility is meeting nursing standards is to check its reports binder. It should be located close to the front door, but ask the nursing staff if you don't find it.

a. The binder includes the state surveyor's audits checking for compliance with state and federal regulations and the Center for Medicare and Medicaid Services guidelines. These may not be easy to read, but the director of nursing or minimum data set

(MDS) nurse can explain it to you. That nurse is responsible for collecting the data for the reports for the facility.

 b. The reports can contain specific observation taken during an onsite audit, in addition to concerns and complaints filed to the state and how they were addressed.

 c. Look for the observations that were noncompliant or a deviation from the standard of practice, which includes either the frequency of the occurrence or the degree or severity of the error. There will be errors in any facility, but there should be a plan of correction noted.

 d. Look for reports of fall, safety, medication errors and types, and infection control. It is more important to check for how the facility is working to improve these errors than that they have them.

2. If applicable to your situation, ask about dementia special units and hospice care.

3. Also ask about the ratio of nurses and certified nursing assistants to patients.

 a. Ask about what the Medicare minimum requirement is and then how the facility meets that or goes beyond.

 b. You may also ask about the acuity level in a specific hall, meaning how many patients require additional assistance for getting in and out of bed or toileting.

 c. Night shifts will typically see a reduction in staff.

4. Ask what the standard time is for checking a patient both during the day and at night. If you become aware these are not being met, ask to see the director of nursing or the facility administrator.

5. On each visit, the staff should greet you in a pleasant manner.
   a. When you walk into a facility, the overall physical appearance and smell may also tell you something about the care and concern for patients. The staff should greet you in a pleasant manner.
   b. If possible, go during a mealtime to check the food being served to the patients. Many facilities use government-supplied products, possibly making healthy meals more difficult to serve.
   c. Don't be afraid to ask lots of questions.
6. Look into the therapy rooms to see how the therapists work with the patients.
7. Look for outside courtyards to be sure patients can be taken outside for fresh air on a regular basis.
8. Ask to see the activities director to check what is planned for the patients on a weekly basis.
   a. It was important to me to have a church services held in the facility every Sunday. Local churches may come in to provide this or the facility may have its own chaplain.
9. Therapy dogs come in to see the patients in some facilities, but in my experience, only a few facilities offer music therapy in Oklahoma City.
10. Be careful to talk only to the staff and not to patients or caregivers because of Health Insurance Portability and Accountability Act (HIPPA) restrictions.
11. Remember that the best facilities will have staffing issues on some days. They do the best they can to staff to requirements, however there are some shifts with nurses working a double shift to cover, creating fatigue situations for the staff.

12. Proximity to your home is important for ease of visiting regularly, even daily.

13. Get references from friends, relatives, healthcare providers, and social workers on facilities they have heard about in their circles.

14. Once you have moved to hospice, remember the hospice provider is there to meet your patient's needs as well as yours. If you are not satisfied with the hospice you choose, do not feel obligated to continue with them. There are others you could contact and interview.

Tips for once you have settled in at home

Physical Aids

1. When purchasing grab bars for the home, be sure they are ADA approved. Look for their seal. Assist bars are not as strong.

2. Clear plastic corner guards are great for all the corners to protect from wheelchairs and walkers. Both grab bars and corner guards can be purchased at hardware or home improvement stores. You will see corner guards in medical facilities—the plastic shield for corners. The clear ones don't show and can also protect from everyday wear and tear in a home.

3. A baby monitor will give you security when you need to be in a different room or outside. These can be purchased on Amazon or many stores carrying baby products. Note: I started with an app on our iPhones—one the receiver and one the sender. However, it drains the battery on the phone in about thirty minutes.

4. Walkers need to be purchased by the size of the person. The physical therapists can guide you as to size needed.

5. Walkers can be made narrower by mounting the wheels on the inside of the walker rather than on the outside. You can

reduce its width by several inches this way, which is helpful getting through older doorways.

6. A transfer chair (I purchased mine from Walmart) is much lighter in weight (twenty-six pounds) and, for me, so much easier to handle. A wheelchair weighs in the fifty-pound range and caused great challenges for me.

7. A hospital bed is provided by Medicare when either ordered by a physician or the social worker at the hospital. What they provide includes one with motorized lifts for the head and feet. However, if you want the whole bed to be motorized to go up and down, you have to pay an additional one hundred dollars per month over what Medicare covers. If you have the bed for thirteen months, they will contact you to see if you want to purchase it; however, what Medicare has paid covers the cost to you. The mattress is not particularly comfortable and may need an additional either egg crate topper or gel topper; both can be purchased from Amazon. It can take up to four weeks to make the necessary arrangements. When you return the bed (they will pick it up), you are left with the mattress because they cannot take it back. If a bed is ordered through hospice, it is fully motorized and delivered the same day as ordered.

8. An EZ Slide Sheet is a marvelous product for helping to pull your patient up in bed. It has handles on each side and a slick material on the bottom. You can read about it online at ezlifts.com. It was also helpful to have the foot of the bed against the wall and the head of the bed to the open room. This allows the caregiver to stand behind the head to grab the handles of the slide sheet (or just the bed pad) and pull the patient up with the EZ Slide Sheet.

9. Plastic or vinyl tablecloths were useful to put beside the bed at night to catch any drips from the catheter bags or vomiting.

10. If possible, without extra expense, move a cabinet close to the bed to hold necessary supplies for the patient. Having things easily accessible will help you in the long run.

11. When moving a hospital bed into your home, think carefully about room placement. It was best for me to stay in the room with Jerry to hear all sounds at night. I moved my bed close to the wall to accommodate the bed for Jerry.

Cleaning Tips

1. Hydrogen peroxide takes out blood stains as well as fecal matter stains. Squirt on before putting in the laundry.

2. Foley catheter bags that are going to be reused should be rinsed out with plain water; keep some water held in them until the next use.

3. A laundry drying rack in a bathtub is a great place to hang Foley bags as well as fabric bed pads.

4. A soiled bed pad (with either urine or fecal matter) should be washed within twenty-four hours. Otherwise, it will need to be rewashed to reduce odor issues.

5. Drying the bed pads on a rack rather than in the dryer will prolong the life of the plastic backing.

6. A good supply of wash rags can be wet with warm water for cleaning up. They are easier on the skin than wipes with chemicals and can be rewashed and reused.

7. Be sure to bring home hospital wash basins. They are great for holding wash rags, cleaning out the patient's mouth in bed to catch liquids, vomiting into, cleaning out finger and toenails, and any number of other uses. When I changed Jerry in bed, I used two: one for clean and warm washrags,

and another for the used ones. Using washable wash cloths saves money and is easier on the patient's skin.

8. Bring home any supplies brought to the hospital room if you can use them. Once in a patient room, they must be thrown away even if unopened. Supplies can include briefs, powders, creams, disposable bed pads, unused catheter bags brought in but not used, wipes, first aid supplies, and the wash basins used for bed baths (as well as pillows in some facilities). Not all hospitals give actual bed baths anymore but have bed bath wipes. Ask for a true bed bath. The wipes leave a film on the patient's body.

9. An office chair mat beside the bed gives something wheelchairs and walkers can roll on while protecting carpet from bed spills.

10. Once the caregiving days are over, a good carpet cleaning is in order. You will also probably need to have your carpets restretched. Wheelchairs and walkers rolling over carpet do a good job of stretching it the way it should not be stretched, causing lumps.

Nursing Tips

1. A barrier cream is excellent to use on the skin to guard against rashes developing from skin being too wet or irritated by feces. It is also useful if you are using a condom catheter with adhesive on it. Daily use of these can cause breakdown of the skin, but barrier cream helps. I found switching from the latex to the adhesive ones every other day was the ultimate solution.

2. If using condom catheters, it helps to trim the pubic hair regularly to keep the hairs from getting caught in the adhesive. Shaving the hair will cause irritation to the skin.

3. When hiring a nurse aide from an agency, they typically have a four-hour minimum whether the aide stays one hour

or four. The cost when I was checking was eight dollars for four hours. They do try to send the same aide every visit, allowing the aide to get to know the patient.

4. Palliative care is nursing care to maintain comfort but not take aggressive action with the patient. It is not "giving up" on the patient but rather deciding not to treat issues aggressively (such as Jerry's thyroid problems) when they would not change his quality of life in the long term.

5. There are pharmacies that don't take insurance. This is a benefit if your insurance denies coverage on a medication the doctor believes necessary. The cost is considerably less because you are not paying the billing cost to insurance companies of most pharmacies.

You should address these tips as soon as possible, even if you are not currently a caregiver.

Financial Tips

1. See a lawyer to obtain a financial power of attorney. Without this, your hands may be tied regarding financial papers and monies you are entitled to have. Your spouse and children may be beneficiaries, but that does not go into effect until death.

2. Check to see if a trust would make sense in your state (it doesn't in every state). By having a trust in place, everything goes to whomever you want it to without having to go through probate which can be costly and take a long time.

3. If you don't have your will in place (this can be in the trust), be sure to complete one and make sure it is up-to-date.

4. Make arrangements (if you haven't) for your burial or cremation desires. Prepayment and decisions for these services should be made before the death happens. You will make more logical rather than emotional decisions.

5. Be sure to talk to your loved one about death and the person's desires. It gives you great comfort to discuss with each other what is coming together. You shared life together—why not be open about sharing death?

6. If your loved one spends any time in a skilled nursing facility or long-term care, be aware of what the facility can legally take to pay the bill. If you have long-term care insurance, you will be covered for part of it.

7. Be aware of how much income you will lose when your loved one dies. Knowing mine would be cut in half helped me decide what I needed to spend while I still had the two incomes to prepare for that day.

8. If you have a joint banking account, be sure you will be able to access the funds when needed. It is also a good idea to have another adult to be a signer on the account in case you are not able to sign either.

9. To be able to make any changes or arrangements with Social Security for another person, you need to complete the paperwork to become a representative payee. They do not recognize a power of attorney—that is only for state business but not federal. The application process will take three months. Once completed, you are required to turn in a yearly summary of how you spend the other person's money.

10. The other option is to legally become another person's guardian. This must be done in court and can cost several hundred dollars. It must also be renewed yearly according to my attorney. This could vary from state to state.

Address these items as soon as you can—some now and some when you know you will become a caregiver.

Prepared for ER and Hospital Stays

1. You should have a healthcare power of attorney on file with your doctor's office. You should also file one with the hospital you expect to use so the doctors there have access to it. If you don't have one, get one right away. This includes your Do Not Resuscitate (DNR) and Do Not Intubate (DNI) wishes and whether you want a feeding tube to sustain life.

2. When the ambulance comes, they like to have a copy of the DNR and the medication list in the ambulance. I kept the medication list on the computer and printed one as soon as I called the ambulance. It changed often enough that I didn't keep copies on hand. I had copies of the DNR on hand.

3. Keep a bag ready with toiletries for your loved one and for you to have what you need at the hospital. I also had a bag ready with a change of clothes for the patient to use when coming home. Once Jerry was in the ambulance, I had forty-five minutes to an hour before he was settled in a room for me to see, giving me time to grab what I needed.

4. Have one point person to call who will contact others you want to be informed.

5. After I discontinued Jerry's phone because he couldn't use it, I had a landline available at home. My thought was to be sure to have a phone to call 911 or family on if my only cell phone was not working. After his death, I purchased a security system and can call for an emergency services using the security system if my cell phone is not working.

Family Checklist after Your Loved One Has Passed (Adapted from Signature Cremation and Funeral Care, 447 SW 89th Street, Oklahoma City, OK 73139)

1. Send acknowledgment cards for flowers, memorial donations, food, and spiritual remembrances. This may be out of style in some circles but very much appreciated.

2. Transfer of real estate

    a. Apply for homestead and disabilities

3. Notify insurance companies and file claims
    a. Life insurance
    b. Medical, health, disability, travel, and accident insurance
    c. Retirement benefits and annuities
    d. Homeowners insurance
    e. Car insurance
    f. Change of survivor's beneficiary

4. Apply for appropriate benefits
    a. Social Security survivor's benefits. Note: If applying for spousal benefits, take your marriage license with you to the Social Security office.
    b. Veterans burial and survivor's benefits
    c. Pension benefits (contact spouse's place of employment)
    d. Workmen's compensation benefits
    e. Civil service benefits
    f. Retirement benefits

5. Notify financial planner or stockbroker
    a. Change ownership of joint or solely owned stock
    b. IRA and retirement accounts
    c. Transfer bonds
    d. Mutual or other funds

6. Notify bank
    a. Change all jointly held accounts
    b. Cancel direct deposit benefits payment
    c. Reestablish safe deposit box
    d. Reestablish all outstanding mortgages, personal notes, etc.
    e. Apply for credit life insurance, which may exist on loans, credit cards, and mortgages

    f. Certificate of Deposit (CD)

    g. Individual Retirement Account (IRA)

7. Notify credit bureaus (Note: notifying one may notify all)

    a. Transunion: PO Box 1000, Chester, PA 19022, www. Tranunion.com

    b. Equifax: PO Box 105069, Atlanta, GA 30348; www. Equifax.com

    c. Experian: PO Box 9530, Allen, TX 75013; www. Experian.com

8. Notify Department of Motor Vehicles/title agency

    a. Transfer titles of all registered vehicles

    b. Cancel driver's license

    c. Cancel voter registration

9. Notify all credit card companies

    a. Apply for credit life insurance if a policy is held in the deceased's name

    b. Cancel all individually held credit cards of the deceased

    c. Change all jointly held accounts

    d. Apply for a credit card in your own name, if needed

10. Notify attorney, accountant, and tax consultant

    a. If a will must be probated

    b. If your will needs to be revised

    c. For income tax purposes

11. Advance planning—You may want to consider prearranging your funeral. It's a sensible, caring way to relieve your loved ones from the burden of having to make decisions during an emotionally difficult time.

Jerry always wore a Santa hat during the Christmas season. This was December 2018.

The night Jerry slipped into his heavenly choir robe, Saturday, December 30, 2017, I slept eleven hours. My body could finally sleep without keeping one eye and ear open to the needs of my sweet guy. This brought tremendous relief but also tremendous guilt. I was able to fall asleep without a worry *because* Jerry died. My patient was no longer in my care, and how I missed him!

Hospice picked up the hospital bed the day he died, as well as other medical equipment. Kelly Ann cleaned up his bedroom, making it no longer look like a hospital room. It was both a welcome change and a heartache. Caregiving duties were over. I should feel total relief, which I did, however the pangs of guilt would not go away. I learned from others this was a normal response. For months after Jerry's death, I would feel this guilt because I was able to get up and go any time I wanted to, stay as long as I wanted, eat what I wanted, not eat if I wanted, travel when I wanted, and nap and sleep when I wanted. My freedom came as the result of the end of Jerry's life.

Kara, my Georgia daughter, arrived on Monday after Jerry's death to stay with me for a week. The sickness of the hospice days was now able to flourish in my body with no caregiving responsibilities. I slept a lot while she worked to help clean out things. There were closets and cabinets in need of attention, which she is excellent at tackling with her organization skills.

Jerry's cremation allowed me to be sick and not have to do a funeral service immediately. Out of the seven brothers in the Cox family, now only two remained. The older one, Marvin, was himself too sick to travel. Bob, the younger one, wanted to be there, and I coordinated with him for the best time to hold the celebration of life service for Jerry. With the schedule my daughter had at school with contests and other choir activities, we finally decided on February 24, 2018, exactly two years from the day of the stroke. This gave me time to plan, time to grieve alone, time to adjust to life without caregiving activities, and time to heal.

Cremation has become more acceptable in recent years. Years ago, only those who were too poor to afford a funeral decided on cremation. Today, it is more socially acceptable and, to be quite honest, a more financially responsible choice. Jerry's wisdom fifty years previously in choosing to be cremated was now the best option. The family sat down and carefully planned his celebration of life service. Jerry was such a special human being, and therefore, his service had to be special and include lots of song.

Rather than a eulogy by a minister, we chose to have family and friends share Jerry's role in their lives. The following roles were included.

- Jerry as a brother
- Jerry as a youth minister
- Jerry as a friend

- Jerry as a father and classroom volunteer
- Jerry as a grandfather
- Jerry as a father-in-law
- Jerry as a husband (I presented this one)

Linda, the dear friend from Texas, came to sing "I Will Rise," and granddaughter Kinsey signed it beautifully with great emotion. Linda then joined Kelly Ann and Lynn in a trio rendition of "Amazing Grace, My Chains Are Gone." Windsong Chamber Choir sang a song, as did Lynn's students from Moore High School. My son-in-law, Tim, led congregational and upbeat singing. This service was videoed and can be searched on YouTube by typing in "Lois Cox Jerry D Cox Celebration of Life Service." It was a two-hour service but was well done by all who participated.

The seventeen years before our move back to Oklahoma were in Wisconsin. For that reason, I returned to Wisconsin and held a second celebration of life service there on March 24, one month later. There were a few changes there as follows.

- Jerry as a father figure
- Jerry as a backpacker
- Jerry as a grandfather
- Jerry as a neighbor
- Jerry as a coworker
- Jerry as an elder
- Jerry as a mission team member
- Jerry as a missionary
- Jerry as a husband

Music there was performed by the church choir and the Good News Singers, a group in which Jerry took part. Both services honored Jerry as I believed he should have been.

Jerry's cremation ashes have been surprising to me for the comfort of their presence. The box of his ashes sits on the nightstand on his side of the bed. I say good morning and good

264

night to him on many days. There are also days when I fuss at him for leaving me. The first five weeks after his death, my hot water tank went out, the stove needed a repair, the microwave quit and had to be replaced, the printer finally quit, a leak developed under the dishwasher, and even the pump in my pond failed me. I really fussed at Jerry's ashes during those days as I moved quickly into the role of widow taking care of everything!

When I went to Wisconsin for Jerry's second service, of course I took the box with me. However, that started a practice of taking him with me on trips. His ashes sit on the floorboard in the front, held in by a small ice chest to keep him from falling over. I talk to him and feel comfort in his presence.

So far, I have his ashes under a magnolia tree in my front yard given to me by friends in Wisconsin in Jerry's memory. The sweet fragrance of the blossoms reminds me of sweet memories of Jerry. In the back garden, I planted a yellow rose bush with his ashes. He always called me his Yellow Rose of Texas, which is the reason I chose yellow. It is very meaningful in my garden because of the special place it was for both of us, and it continues to be one for me. The only legal place to spread ashes is on your own property, however this is rarely followed or enforced. I do enjoy his ashes sitting in the bedroom and traveling on car trips with me. The picture at the beginning of this chapter shows my first Christmas without him. Jerry wore a Santa hat from Thanksgiving through Christmas, causing many fun exchanges with children in public.

Upon returning from the Wisconsin service after spending two weeks visiting with friends there, my new life was in front of me. What was I to do now? I was now a widow but was not sure I liked my new role. The house was empty of Jerry's presence, especially his song. How I missed and still miss his song in my house and my heart. I was now at the congregation where my daughter was a member and started to get involved there.

Jerry's severe erosive osteoarthritis previous to the stroke made travel too difficult to do more than visit our children and grandchildren. I had always been an independent woman (a major advantage now), so I decided to visit people from our past together. When I contacted people to come visit, I asked them to let me speak on the lessons God taught me during the twenty-two months at their churches while there.

During the first year after Jerry's death, I drove twenty-three thousand miles in my car alone, traveled to fifteen states by car, and flew to California for Jerry's brother Marvin's funeral. I was also blessed to visit the Pacific Ocean, the Atlantic Ocean, and the Gulf of Mexico. Each body of water and beach provided much-needed time to grieve, talk to God, write, and be in my favorite place. My trip back to Colorado also gave me time in God's marvelous Rocky Mountains. During those travels, I spoke eight times on caregiving, including two in the Oklahoma City area. Preparing and presenting how God took care of us during our twenty-two months together was healing for me. Renewing old friendships was marvelous.

As everyone says, the firsts are difficult times to endure. My birthday came in January, followed by Valentine's Day in February. My daughters helped get me through these times. Father's Day and Jerry's birthday are both in June and often in the same week. My daughter here took me to a beautiful park and out to lunch for our anniversary in August. Thanksgiving was filled with lots of people at my house, helping tremendously to keep me occupied. For Christmas, we drove to Kansas and Missouri, staying at an Airbnb and enjoyed snow tubing. It was great fun and nothing like a traditional Christmas at our house.

Also during the first year, I attended a GriefShare session, helping me process even more through the grieving journey. My grieving blog has contributed to my healing as well. It is located on my website, https://22monthministry.com, under the blog tab if you would like to follow me. A sweet part of my grieving has been napping in Jerry's recliner. This was a recliner I bought for him after the stroke; it was just his. I have found it very comforting to nap in his special chair with the prayer quilt draped over the back.

In March of my second year without Jerry, I made a trip to Israel and Egypt with a tour group. As I was telling Jerry I couldn't take him with me this time, I stopped and said, "Why not?" I took ten small bags of his ashes and spread them around places in Israel and Egypt. Each bag was then labeled as to where I left him. I have continued this practice with my other travels. When I told one of the men in our tour group I had left Jerry's ashes on the top of Mt. Sinai, he said, "When Jesus returns, He will have a hard time finding Jerry." My response was, "Not for my God. He is awesome, and nothing is too hard for Him."

In February 2020, I went to Ecuador for a medical mission with my church. Jerry would have enjoyed it so much, and I feel his presence with me each time I leave town. It is carrying on Jerry's practice of going on mission trips during his lifetime.

Chonda Pierce, a Christian comedian, said in one of her YouTube videos, "Being alone is not bad. Being lonely is terrible." This is so true. Her husband died after thirty-three years of marriage due to a sudden stroke. I was well prepared for being alone due to Jerry sleeping so much of our last twenty-two months together. But being lonely comes on the most unlikely days and with the most unusual triggers. I can be playing some Christian music and hear a deep bass note, and tears stream down my face upon remembering my bass. Worship services almost always bring tears during some part. When attending musical functions for my daughter's program, I need Jerry there, with him smiling in pride and enjoying the students, his students, and the music. I am often lonely with people around me. There are difficult days for sure.

Year one was all the firsts with a certain newness. Entering year two was more difficult than expected and brought the recognition of the permanence of my widowhood. It is just not a phase—Jerry is truly gone. My life must continue without his song, wisdom, hugs, and presence. In my grieving, however, I am always thankful I had a husband and relationship worthy of this grief.

God has given me a purpose: to share His testimony of care and providing for every one of our needs during my caregiving days. I plan to spend the rest of my time here sharing via this book and speaking engagements. Nothing I learned should be wasted but needs to be shared to inspire and encourage others in similar situations.

The life of a widow—maybe that will be my next book!

E

Appendixes

1 - Things I Learned While Caregiving with God!

On February 24, 2016, my life changed forever when my husband, Jerry, suffered a bilateral thalamic stroke. Upon reflecting on the twenty-two months, here are some things I learned.

1. I have learned life is unpredictable. Be sure you end each day with those you love knowing it!
2. I have learned the tear ducts never run dry.
3. I have learned God is in control—not our healthcare system.
4. I have learned a loving home environment is therapeutic.
5. I have learned to extend forgiveness to any who have wronged you before it is too late to do so.
6. I have learned if you don't make that call today to reach out to someone, you may not get another chance.
7. I have learned the true meaning of "in sickness and in health."
8. I have learned patience.
9. I have learned how valuable handicapped parking spaces are.
10. I have learned how to put on a condom catheter after Jerry was asleep in the dark, using a flashlight, and how to keep draining catheter bags from stinking.
11. I have learned a brain injury really can require twenty hours of sleep a day.
12. I have learned how much I truly miss Jerry's gorgeous bass voice singing every day.
13. I have learned caregiving is emotionally, physically, and spiritually exhausting but also the most fulfilling work you will ever do.

14. I have learned that grieving doesn't wait until the end but is a process day to day.
15. I have learned that what you do today will ensure you have no regrets tomorrow.
16. I have learned that the Bible has the answer to every problem and concern, and it is the source of joy and peace that cannot be understood.
17. I have learned how journaling through CaringBridge is the best way to create a community of support while creating a place to transparently share the struggles of a dependent patient.
18. I have learned that the promises in the Bible are true—every one of them!
19. I have learned God will weave the threads of your life, positive and negative, into a beautiful tapestry if you allow Him to do so.
20. I have learned how valuable good neighbors are.
21. I have learned there is no better way to start the day than with God.
22. I have learned that home health is one of the best ways Medicare spends our tax money.
23. I have learned that God provides.
24. I have learned that Jerry was ready for heaven when it came.
25. I have learned how important it is to have family support, and how much it hurts when I don't have it.
26. I have learned no matter how attentive my caregiving was, I still missed things, and he still had ER visits and hospital stays.
27. I have learned what a blessing online shopping is for homebound caregivers.
28. I have learned people are what is important in life. Possessions require money, repair, cleaning, and storage;

often have to be move; and eventually have to be sold or given away.

29. I have learned there is plenty of cuddle time after a stroke—why not before?
30. I have learned a garden is a place of God's beauty and a solace for a gardener.
31. I have learned the meaning of crying out to God—literally.
32. I have learned that every day has more to be thankful for than it has problems.
33. I have learned how valuable a phone call or visit from a friend is.
34. I have learned how much you miss corporate worship when I can't attend but also how meaningful worship in my living room could be with just Jerry and God.
35. I have learned you can put your life on hold by reading the right books, keeping projects to do, journaling, and connecting through your faith for strength.
36. I have learned sacrificial caregiving is not the norm, unfortunately.
37. I have learned how wonderful Jerry's hugs and kisses were; they made my day.
38. I have learned how your priority list changes overnight when your spouse has a stroke.
39. I have learned to experience delusions and hallucinations through Jerry.
40. I have learned Satan will take any opportunity to try to move in on a dedicated Christian because he has a brain injury.
41. I have learned even though this Jerry was not my Jerry all the time, he delighted me with snippets of him from time to time.
42. I have learned that when you give up your life for someone, God gives you a new life.

43. I have learned you have to fight for your loved ones as an advocate to get the care they need and deserve.
44. I have learned that hospice is a great organization to guide you through the end of life.
45. I have learned now I can look back on this experience with great joy, knowing I did all I could for the man I loved.

2 – My Favorite Devotionals from the Twenty-Two Months

A note about these devotionals: Each day, I included a devotional for my readers (and for me). They are here listed by the day they appeared in my CaringBridge journal. Because they were written on those days, they are written in present tense.

Day 130

It is transparent day. As I said earlier in the week, this hospital visit was a chance to get some information. I got information I needed and information I didn't want to hear.

Let me start with the passage for the day.

But now, this is what the Lord says—he who created you, Jacob, he who formed you, Israel: "Do not fear, for I have redeemed you; I have summoned you by name; you are mine. When you pass through the waters, I will be with you; and when you pass through the rivers, they will not sweep over you. When you walk through the fire, you will not be burned; the flames will not set you ablaze." (Isaiah 43:1–2)

God made me who I am and Jerry who he is. He also made our bodies, originally perfect, but because of the introduction of sin in the Garden of Eden, our bodies start dying the day we are born. Strokes and other illnesses are a part of this broken world. It is very comforting to know God has redeemed us, knows us by name, and calls us HIS! What an amazing thought! He is on our side and holds us up through all the difficulties of life.

I feel like I passed through the waters on February 24 when Jerry had his stroke. What a day of shock and total upheaval that was. Hearing your husband has had a severe stroke was devastating and the future looked bleak, especially when you talked to the doctors. I started this CaringBridge the next day and began to share my thoughts, feelings, fears, and prayer requests then and receiving support from every one of you. He helped me get through the waters of those first hospital days and weeks.

We moved to the skilled nursing facility and entered the river. All around us were doubtful caregivers not believing Jerry would ever leave the facility. Progress was slow but steady. We went from a limp rag doll to a man who insisted on walking out of the nursing home on June 17 and did! The rivers did not sweep over me, but we floated along on top in His life raft.

We entered the fire when we went home. Yes, I was able to transfer him from bed to chair to walker, give him a shower by myself, feed him, and care for him but with great stress. As his independent streak became stronger, he became more challenging not even taking his medicines without a fight. The week brought doubt, fear, stress, and finally a fall. The fall brought us to the ER and now seven days back in the hospital. The week has given me back a PEG tube for feedings, hydration, and water without a fight. However, the week has also given Jerry two sedations and recovery from a fall. He has gone from walking around the house with the walker easily to not being able to balance on the edge of the bed. Realizing we can't go home without help has been depressing, causing fear, doubt for his recovery, and stress.

Do I believe I will be protected from the flames? Absolutely. But flames are flames and there will be pain to get through. The doctor said we must be prepared that this level of mobility may be the new baseline. Learning even more about a thalamic stroke and the way it limits his body's ability to recover from any trauma including a common cold is excruciating. Yes, I have always known that with a stroke, he would eventually go down, but his miraculous recovery has put that far in the future in my mind.

275

What is best for Jerry? I keep asking myself that question as I see him lying in bed mostly asleep. He is comfortable but is in bed! I want him to come back to his state of mobility around the house and to sing every day. I never knew how much I would miss the singing but wow, do I ever! God has brought me through a lot. I have seen miracles through prayer and am very thankful for that. I have sacrificed my own life to give to his care and am blessed to do so. I also want to be aware of what is coming to a point. I need to know how fragile he now is because of his brain injury. I need to be open to whatever God wants for him—for us. I don't want to selfishly say, "God keep him here at all costs!" However, I want him back!

Like I said, this is transparent day. God has been phenomenal through these 130 days, and I have never doubted his presence, care, and concern. Maybe He has been preparing me gently for what the future could hold for us. I know He has let me see his power at work and that has brought glory to Him throughout the recovery process. I have fears, doubts, questions, and hope for our future. Pray God will keep me open to His will for us both!

Day 136

These things I have spoken to you, that my joy may be in you, and that your joy may be full. (John 15:11 ASV)

It is possible to have joy even in these circumstances. God is still in charge and is planning a great home for us some day without any pain or strokes. I strive for more joy in each day because of those promises. More joy in my day would put more joy in Jerry's day. More focusing on the blessings and less on the difficulties!

Day 140

Love, love, love this verse in 2 Chronicles 20:15 (and the song):

He said: "Listen, King Jehoshaphat and all who live in Judah and Jerusalem! This is what the Lord says to you: Do not be afraid or discouraged because of this vast army. For the battle is not yours, but God's."

We seem to fight our battles as they are all ours, but God wants to fight them for us. Why wouldn't we want Him to? He knows the enemy better than we do and has all the resources to fight them. Turn it over to God and sit back and wait for the victory.

Day 144

Better is one day in your courts than a thousand elsewhere; I would rather be a doorkeeper in the house of my God than dwell in the tents of the wicked. For the Lord God is a sun and shield; the Lord bestows favor and honor; no good thing does he withhold from those whose walk is blameless. (Psalm 84:10–11)

I believe I live in God's courts each day as He encourages and strengthens me. This is truly the best place to be. Yes, I would love for Jerry to be totally healed, but it is wonderful to watch God at work right in my little house! He lights my days with His scriptural sunshine, the physical sunshine, and the beauty of my garden. He shields me from so many difficulties such as depression, pity, and other things I could be feeling because of my position with Jerry. I trust He will continue to give me favor and honor and good things will keep coming!

Day 155

When all our enemies heard about this, all the surrounding nations were afraid and lost their self-confidence, because they realized that this work had been done with the help of our God. (Nehemiah 6:16)

Nehemiah and his construction crew rebuilt the walls of Jerusalem in fifty-two days! We would still be getting the building permits here. However, it was so fast, the enemies realized this could not have happened without God's help. This scripture reminded me of Jerry's recovery being called miraculous. The health care professionals realized this recovery could not have happened without some intervention from above. How awesome when our lives show the power of God!

Day 161

Be joyful in hope, patient in affliction, faithful in prayer. (Romans 12:12)

I like this verse better than James 1:2 that tells us to consider our trials pure joy. This verse puts the joy in the hope which is so much easier to do. We have so much joy in better times and a better life after this one. Being patient in affliction is also easier than being joyful. I am not saying patience is easy in any circumstance, but for me it is easier to achieve than the joy. I have already talked about the patience I need to take care of Jerry. I was telling Kinsey last week I didn't remember asking God for more patience, but I sure have the opportunity to develop it! I was seen as a patient person at the nursing home, but I want to call and say, "You should see me now!" I must have sung through an entire album of songs from YouTube this morning trying to get Jerry awake enough to get up. For me to wait two and a half hours from eyes open to actually making a move to get out of bed is just not my personality!

The last part of the verse is "faithful in prayer." That is where I want to thank each of you who daily read my journal. Your faithful prayers are so meaningful to me and so powerful in Jerry's recovery. The word faithful is not understood well in today's society of living together and not making a commitment to be faithful to one person for life. Faithful means hanging in there when we don't think our prayers are heard but continuing to offer them up. So, thank you for all your prayers daily!

Day 165

Though the fig tree does not bud and there are no grapes on the vines, though the olive crop fails and the fields produce no food, though there are no sheep in the pen and no cattle in the stalls, yet I will rejoice in the Lord, I will be joyful in God my Savior. The Sovereign Lord is my strength; he makes my feet like the feet of a deer, he enables me to tread on the heights. (Habbakuk 3:17–19)

What is described here is pretty bleak—nothing to eat because the crops have failed, no sheep or cattle. And yet, he still rejoiced in the Lord. We don't have to have things going right to be able to praise God and look to him for our strength. The example of having feet like a deer indicates we can be on very treacherous ground and still have stability if we depend on God. Remembering the Colorado mountains I climbed, my feet were not like a deer but unstable. But in our walk through life, even over rocky ground, climbing steep mountains and entering deep valleys, God can give us an unnatural stability through it all.

Day 192

Here is a verse I still struggle with in my journey.

But he said to me, "My grace is sufficient for you, for my power is made perfect in weakness." Therefore I will boast all the more gladly about my weaknesses, so that Christ's power may rest on me. That is why, for Christ's sake, I delight in weaknesses, in insults, in hardships, in persecutions, in difficulties. For when I am weak, then I am strong. (2 Corinthians 12:9–10)

Paul said he delighted in weaknesses, insults, hardships, and persecutions. I am accepting more all the time the growth that can happen with hardships; however, I am far from delighting when they come. I believe I have accepted the struggles at this point, but delight—no, I am not there yet. I do enjoy the new closeness to God and how my faith has grown. But what it took to get this point has

279

not been pleasant—certainly not delightful. I still have a long way to go to get to this point.

Day 194

So the people grumbled against Moses, saying, "What are we to drink?" (Exodus 15:24)

We are all familiar with how much the Israelites grumbled throughout their forty years of wandering. This was a verse from one of my devotionals this morning. What the author pointed out in this one was that this happened three days after they had walked through the Red Sea on dry ground and watched it fill up again and drown their enemies! What short memories they had and continued to forget not only through the forty years but beyond. But then I thought about the times with Jerry's care that I go to God in prayer saying I just can't do this—it is too hard! How quickly I have forgotten the last time He pulled me through a tough spot! How quickly I have forgotten the people He has provided along the way to hold me up. How quickly I have forgotten the wonderful comments here of encouragement from each of you. I am sure God gets just as frustrated with my forgetfulness as He did with those Israelites so many years ago.

Day 206

Then they cried to the Lord in their trouble, and he saved them from their distress. He sent out his word and healed them; he rescued them from the grave. Let them give thanks to the Lord for his unfailing love and his wonderful deeds for mankind. (Psalm 107:19–21)

Never had I cried out to the Lord before the stroke. Yes, I had prayed fervent prayers during my life, but now I cry out to Him on a regular basis. The promise He will save me from my distress is something to hold on to throughout the day. I pray for the healing but also know it is a very slow process. God created the brain so very complex and the healing process is not totally understood. Do I

280

believe God could heal Jerry instantly? Yes, I believe He could. I also know He doesn't choose to do that at times. Death entered the world because of the sin in the garden. The process of a dying body is the result of that complete with strokes, cancer, heart attacks, etc., etc. We should not be attached to this world and the aging process helps us long for our eternal home in heaven. However long this process takes—either complete recovery or God takes Jerry home—it is a process and will increase not only my faith but of many around me. Praise God for that.

Day 224

Surely the arm of the LORD is not too short to save, nor his ear too dull to hear. (Isaiah 59:1)

I love this verse. God's arms are long enough to rescue us from any predicament, plus He will always hear us. He is not hard of hearing even when we whisper or say a prayer in our hearts and minds. It reminds me again of our physical limitations here on this planet. I thought of the little two-year-old who was grabbed by an alligator at Disney World in the summer of 2015. The dad tried to grab him, but his arms were too short. Not so with our God. Not only is it amazing He can hear my prayers and calling out for help but those of everyone else in the world—at the same time! Is comforting to know I am never out of His reach!

Day 236

Blessed is the person who trusts in the Lord, making the Lord his trust. He will be like a tree planted by the water that sends out its roots by a stream. He won't fear when the heat comes, and his leaves will be green. In a year of drought he won't be concerned, nor will he stop producing fruit. (Jeremiah 17:7–8)

I believe God has spent my lifetime helping me put down deep roots of faith for this time with Jerry. I was raised by godly parents, in church regularly, learning scriptures in many Sunday school classes. My mother suffering with pancreatic cancer as well as my aunt with breast cancer gave me an example of godly women facing their own death with anticipation. Does this mean I don't get discouraged? Of course not, but my faith in God helps me endure through the hardship. Does this mean I was excited to spend the afternoon and evening in the ER? Of course not, but God strengthened me physically and emotionally to see lots of doctors, nurses, and needle sticks for Jerry.

The deeper the roots are, the more secure the tree is to whatever nature sends its way. Native plants are like that. I have a chart of several showing some of the roots for these "wildflowers" are six feet deep. No wonder they can survive years of drought! Our faith in God sees us through whatever difficulties come our way. Here is a mathematical equation from the *I Am STRONG* book: "God's Strength + My Weakness > My Strength + No Weakness." (Dickerson 2016, 42) Now don't you want to order the book to read?

Day 239

Today's verse comes right from the garden.

Therefore, since we are surrounded by such a great cloud of witnesses, let us throw off everything that hinders and the sin that so easily entangles. And let us run with perseverance the race marked out for us. (Hebrews 12:1)

I transplanted two rose bushes in the garden last year. One of them was surrounded by all sorts of volunteer flowers and weeds so thick this year that I couldn't see the rose bush anymore. In August, I finally went to that part of the garden and pulled out all the plants around it. The bush looked so pitiful and actually looked dead. I trimmed it back and planned to pull it out at the end of the season. Well, getting out all the "hindrances and sin" that surrounded it, the bush was able to come back and thrive. We can't thrive as a Christian when sins crowd our lives, whether they are easily seen or taking over our thoughts.

Day 264

Nehemiah said, "Go and enjoy choice food and sweet drinks, and send some to those who have nothing prepared. This day is holy to our Lord. Do not grieve, for the joy of the Lord is your strength." (Nehemiah 8:10)

This is one of those thoughts I have read a hundred times and even sung a song with these words. However, this morning, it really hit me where my strength comes from. It is essential to have joy in the Lord to have His strength. This doesn't mean every day I must go around being a Pollyanna but need to have joy in the salvation He offers to us daily. More of my prayer needs to be joyful and thankful than give me, give me, give me as is so easy to do. Some days my needs seem overwhelming. In one of my posts last week, I used the verse in Matthew that God knows our needs before we ask Him. If that is the case, I really don't have to spend my prayer time listing my needs from A to Z. Yes, He wants us to ask Him for help but more of our time should be in thanksgiving and being joyful. Our joy can be seen in the way we handle everyday stress and just our overall personalities. Our joy in Him is our strength!

Day 276

Here is a favorite of mine in I Kings 19:11–13.

The Lord said, "Go out and stand on the mountain in the presence of the Lord, for the Lord is about to pass by." Then a great and powerful wind tore the mountains apart and shattered the rocks before the Lord, but the Lord was not in the wind. After the wind there was an earthquake, but the Lord was not in the earthquake. After the earthquake came a fire, but the Lord was not in the fire. And after the fire came a gentle whisper. When Elijah heard it, he pulled his cloak over his face and went out and stood at the mouth of the cave. Then a voice said to him, "What are you doing here, Elijah?"

God, of course, has the power and might to come to us any way He chooses. He could cause an earthquake bigger than any we have yet experienced here in Oklahoma to get our attention. The Oklahoma winds help us understand the powerful wind example as well as the tornadoes in our state. God speaks to me the most effectively in the quiet of my garden. The thought of a powerful God whispering in my ear goes along with the picture I used a few days ago saying God is sitting beside us on a bench holding our hands through the difficult times. When you are sitting with a friend on a bench, it is a quiet time of sharing thoughts and feelings. Whispering brings Him closer to me in our relationship than His booming voice echoing from across the valleys. And how often can I hear his voice saying, "Lois, what are you doing here?"

Day 338

About Benjamin he said: "Let the beloved of the Lord rest secure in him, for He shields him all day long, and the one the Lord loves rests between his shoulders." (Deuteronomy 33:12)

When I first read this, my thought was, how fortunate for Benjamin to be loved by the Lord. Then rethinking, I said to myself, "But I am beloved by the Lord!" I am secure in my Lord. There is no other security in this life. I cherish the thought that God shields me all day long from so many of Satan's darts—discouragement, fatigue, loneliness, depression—and keeps me positive throughout the day. But the best part of this scripture is the picture of Benjamin resting on the Lord between His shoulders. I love to watch a small child sleeping on his father's chest, feeling the breathing pattern of his dad, and listening to whatever dad is saying or singing. One of Lynn's favorite memories of growing up about her dad was sitting in church with her head on Jerry's chest to listen and feel his bass voice singing the hymns. It is a beautiful picture of God's love for us!

Day 351

Before they call I will answer; while they are still speaking I will hear. (Isaiah 65:24)

We know God wants us to pray with our requests and needs. However, this says God hears us even before we pray to Him. God knows our hearts better than we do. He has our answer ready before we submit our prayers. It reminds me of our care of our children as infants. As parents, we knew their needs when they obviously couldn't ask. They were totally dependent on us as parents to care for them. Just as we knew what they needed to grow normally, God knows even more what we need as His children to grow spiritually. This verse is a huge promise to hang onto.

Year 2, Day 28

The LORD your God, who is going before you, will fight for you, as he did for you in Egypt, before your very eyes. (Deuteronomy 1:30)

I love this verse. The Israelites were getting ready to go into the Promised Land where there were actual giants. And yet God told me, I am going ahead of you and will take care of it. I hear God telling me that He is going ahead of Jerry's fall and will take care of us. He will take care of my physical body. I hurt so much when I got up this morning after two bed changes in the night. I asked for God's strength for the day, and He went before me into the day and helped me feel so much better! God is in my future preparing the way for Jerry and I!

Year 2, Day 32

But the pot he was making of clay did not come out like he wanted it. So the pot-maker used the clay to make another pot that pleased him. (Jeremiah 18:4)

When we lived in Wisconsin, a favorite place for us to visit was Red Wing, Minnesota, a little over an hour away. I had seen Red Wing pottery (and Red Wing shoes) all my life, but now I was visiting where it was made. One of the shops had a potter throwing pots on a wheel. It is truly amazing what the potter can do with pressure here and there to shape a beautiful pot. I also watched the potter literally squash the pot he was making, roll it in a ball, and start again.

The potter keeps putting pressure on the pot until he gets the perfect pot shape. Then, of course, it needs firing, painting, and sometimes firing again. If you were the clay, it would not be pleasant with the pushing, squashing, firing, painting, and final firing. But the end result is a thing of beauty. The potter is pleased.

I wonder how many times God has had to squash me into a ball and start over? He certainly did on February 24, 2016. Each day, He is pressing into a new place to shape me like He wants me. I feel like I have been fired in an oven at least once. God will keep working with me until He has created a beautiful servant ready to do His will. Ouch and wow!

Year 2, Day 37

You are the salt of the earth. But if the salt loses its saltiness, how can it be made salty again? It is no longer good for anything, except to be thrown out and trampled underfoot. (Matthew 5:13)

I have heard lessons on being the salt of the earth all my life. It has always been explained as we are to preserve the earth as salt preserves foods. One of my devotionals this week had a different take on it which I like a lot. Suzanne Davenport Teitjen described sheep needing to drink three times as much water as the food they eat. Because they won't do this on their own, the shepherd has to put out blocks of salt to encourage their thirst. Once again sheep are shown as pretty needy creatures with little chance of survival without their shepherd. The author said that just as the block of salt makes the sheep thirsty and want to drink, we are as salt to the earth to make people around us want more of what we have. Our lives should give them a thirst for more! I like that interpretation more (Aughtmon 2016).

Year 2, Day 47

You turned my wailing into dancing; you removed my sackcloth and clothed me with joy. (Psalm 30:11)

This scripture was in the last chapter of our book, *The Twenty-Third Psalm for Caregivers* (Leal 2004). We finished it last night, since Jerry was awake so much, and I often read to him. Joy is not an emotion only available when everything is going your way, no one you know is sick or suffering in any way, you have all the money you need to pay your bills, you feel great and look great, and your husband has not had a stroke. Joy is provided by God and the many blessings He brings to us each day in whatever situation we happen to find ourselves. There is great joy in caregiving. There is joy in the quiet mornings I get to spend with God without the time crunch of leaving for a job, taking care of children, or having to be anywhere on a schedule. There is joy in the people I have met who have come to see us, the therapists, the nurses, and other stroke patient's wives. There is joy in so many answered prayers and miraculous recovery. There is joy in my garden and the wonders God is growing there. There is joy in never being alone. There is great, great joy in being a child of God.

Year 2, Day 52

By faith Abraham, when called to go to a place he would later receive as his inheritance, obeyed and went, even though he did not know where he was going. (Hebrews 11:8)

Of course, I realize none of us really knows where we are heading in this life, do we? However, we can often make plans based on different variables. When we decided we needed to move to warmer weather three years ago and get closer to family, we planned for Jerry to volunteer in the classroom and for me to get a job using my newly acquired PhD teaching at the university level. We sold our house, bought one here, and made the move. Everything was going according to our plans (except for finding a job for me) until February 24, 2016. That is when God said to me, "I am calling you to a place even though you have no idea where it is, how to get there, and what to do when living in this new place." He gave me a full-time job with very long hours and multiple benefits. It probably wasn't by faith at first that I started this journey but started out because of a wedding vow I took many years ago. However, as I have moved along this journey of now fourteen months, it is only by faith in God I can continue to move forward each day.

Year 2, Day 72

First a quote from Zig Ziglar, an author and motivational speaker: "The more you complain about your problems, the more problems you will have to complain about."

And now what God says about it.

Do all things without grumbling or questioning, that you may be blameless and innocent, children of God without blemish in the midst of a crooked and twisted generation, among whom you shine as lights in the world, holding fast to the word of life, so that in the day of Christ I may be proud that I did not run in vain or labor in vain. (Philippians 2:14–16 ESV)

It is so easy to fall into complaining or grumbling about things in life, isn't it? The Amplified version expands it to say, "questioning the providence of God." Guess I had never thought about my grumbling or questioning being against God's providence for our lives. If we don't have enough money in our lives, perhaps God is teaching us a lesson we need to learn. If we are grumbling about our spouse, maybe we need to focus on their good traits like we hope they do with us. If we are complaining about an illness, maybe we need to learn more empathy for others dealing with chronic illness and pain. As Ziglar says, complaining multiplies your problems rather than taking them away. Putting this with the benefits of being thankful in all circumstances and you have the way God would prefer us to lives our lives—in gratitude to Him. And if we live this way, we are without blemish and a light to the world. Wow—that is a lot for just not complaining.

Year 2, Day 120

The Lord will fulfill his purpose for me; your steadfast love, O Lord, endures forever. Do not forsake the work of your hands. (Psalm 138:8 ESV)

Apparently, the Lord is working on fulfilling His purpose for me right now. I am to be an encourager through this journal. I am to be a caregiver for my husband. I am to find things to keep me busy and content staying at home most of the time. I am not totally sure what my purpose will be after this is over, but can imagine a few scenarios. We are so blessed God's love is steadfast and will never end. There is never a day when I get up and have to wonder if I am loved by God today. I don't have to worry I did something bad enough to lose His love. With that kind of love, I cannot doubt whatever purpose He has for me.

Year 2, Day 161

But seek first his kingdom and his righteousness, and all these things will be given to you as well. (Matthew 6:33)

The big part of this verse to me is "all these things." What do "all these things" mean? For my last seventeen months, it means the strength to get up each day. It means creating a more intimate relationship with God. It means receiving encouragement from people around the country. It means having some very meaningful worship services in my living room. It means developing a special relationship with my husband. It means valuing every day as a gift from God. It means more meaningful time with God in prayer. It means receiving answers immediately when I am desperate for help with Jerry. It means learning so much medical information. It means being a patient advocate extraordinaire. It means having a meaningful, purposeful life!

Year 2, Day 190

Let us not become weary in doing good, for at the proper time we will reap a harvest if we do not give up. (Galatians 6:9)

This scripture caught my attention quickly even though I have read it all my life. Weary is a word I can relate to in my current role. There are days when it is physical fatigue and days when it is emotional fatigue and most days a combination of both. There is a harvest to look forward to in the future. However, I believe there is a harvest in this life as well. There are days when my back is weary of changing the bed at 2:00 a.m., but there is the harvest of knowing Jerry is dry and able to sleep well. There are days when I am so weary of Jerry not knowing me, but there are days of harvest when he wakes up and tells me he loves me. I grow weary of days of the same routine with Jerry day after day, but then there is the harvest of such a sweet patient. I grow so weary of the constant caregiving of medications, feeding, bathing, exercising, and toileting, but there is the harvest of so many medical professionals telling me Jerry is where he is because of me. Weary—YES. Harvest—YES, right now!

Year 2, Day 223

Finally, my brethren, be strong in the Lord, and in the might of his power. (Ephesians 6:10)

The great thing about this scripture is the strength is in the Lord. It isn't in us. What a relief to know we don't have to rely on our own strength. There are so many days I feel totally drained of any strength. The only way to get out of bed is knowing God will provide the strength when mine falters. When I wake up in the morning and have my quiet time with God, I never know what Jerry will throw at me during the day. I don't know if he will be sweet or cantankerous. I never know when the next ER visit will be. I never know when the next delusional day will be. What I do know is my God is faithful and will provide what I need each and every day. If I need to change a light bulb, I can try to reach it myself, but know I am not tall enough. But if I grab the step ladder, it is an easy reach. Those are our days. We can only stretch so far, but God is there to make up the difference.

Year 2, Day 233

How often in your life have you wished things would just slow down so you could rest awhile? I thought of that this afternoon sitting for three hours in the garden with my husband. The world came to a stop February 24, 2016 for us.

Then I thought of the verse again.

Be still, and know that I am God; I will be exalted among the nations, I will be exalted in the earth. (Psalm 46:10)

Not only did God still us both but made it easier to know Him through this time. He has given Jerry and me a totally different life together but many days a precious life of special moments and plenty of time to be together. Yes, there are those days when I feel totally alone because Jerry doesn't always talk, but then God gives me days like today. In many ways, I feel like a fenced-up dog who just wants to get out and run free. But God reminds me there is a season for everything and now is the caregiving season. Paul after his conversion went to Arabia for three years to get himself ready to preach (Galatians 1:17–18). God knows how long I need to get me ready for whatever He has in mind for me next.

Year 2, Day 293

I brought you up out of Egypt and led you forty years in the wilderness to give you the land of the Amorites. (Amos 2:10)

From time to time, we need to reflect on how God has been with us through our lives. God has been good to us in our marriage. Yes, we have had difficult times before, including lots of financial struggles, the deaths of family and friends, family relationship struggles, and health issues before the stroke. However, God has seen us through everything, and we were never totally without food and always had a roof over our heads. But remembering the times when God always took care of us helps me to know this is no different. I know that death is a part of life and remember my mother not wanting to go through the process. Our death will take us home to heaven, but the process of the illness or whatever takes us is the difficult part. Spending some time remembering the good times with God will help you get through the tough times.

3 - Personal Psalms

These are the psalms I wrote during my first year of my grieving journey.

Alone!

Alone! I find myself alone!
God Himself said, "It is not good for man to be alone."
And yet I find myself alone—a woman no longer with my man.

He is not alone but walking the golden streets in God's presence.
He has ended his life on Earth, his life after a stroke.
He wanted to stay with me but wanted to go home too.

I rejoice in his new life, his new body, his new home.
I rejoice this life of struggles, pain, heartache is not all there is.
I rejoice his death was "precious in God's sight."

And yet, I am alone!
My life is starting over alone.
I am traveling to see old friends—alone!

But You, O God, are here to keep me from being alone.
You are beside me every day as I carry on in my new life.
You make me secure as I lie down at night and rest.

I praise You, O God, for caring that I am alone.
I praise You, O God, for knowing every tear I shed.

I praise You, O God, for meeting my every need.

I praise You, O Jesus, for shedding your blood for me.
I praise You, O Jesus, for being my friend when alone.
I praise You, O Jesus, for walking beside me every day.

I praise You, O Spirit, for indwelling me day to day.
I praise You, O Spirit, for the strength to keep going.
I praise You, O Spirit, for guiding my words as I speak.

Yes, I am not alone!
My God, my Jesus, and my Spirit walk with me daily!
My husband is gone, but I am never alone.

Precious Memories Psalm

Is "Precious Memories" just the name of an old hymn used at
funerals?
Are there precious memories surrounding other events in our
lives?
Or people in our circle of family and friends?
Are precious memories valuable to create and then remember?

Precious memories are the substance of what we have left.
They are the ingredients scrapbooks are made of mingled with
photos.
They are what makes holidays and vacations special and worth
repeating.
Hallmark built their business on the precious memories of
society.

While precious memories are carried from birthday to birthday,
Anniversary to anniversary, holiday to holiday, and song to song.
Precious memories are especially valuable when you lose a
precious person.
They help keep that person alive in your thoughts, writing, and
speaking.

I have precious memories of fifty years of marriage to my sweet
guy.
Memories of our courtship, including falling in love with his
bass voice.
Memories of early marriage and involvement with our faith in
God,

And memories of becoming parents together.

There are precious memories of moving from home to home
And job to job as we took our family on the road, creating
memories along the way.
There are career memories, ministry memories, raising children
memories,
And daughters getting married memories adding to our family.

Precious memories were heightened with the birth of
grandchildren.
Each new life brought unique memories with that child.
Memories we created to cherish throughout their lives and ours.
Memories to carry us through our golden years.

Then the precious memories came to a difficult time of my sweet
guy's stroke.
Could this time give me memories I would want to keep or
painful memories?
Would God's Word be true in walking beside me and carrying me
through this time?
Yes, these would be memories, but would they be precious
memories?

And yet here I sit on the other side of caregiving for twenty-two
months during the stroke,
And the precious memories flood my soul as the old hymn says.
Memories of holding hands to help Jerry walk to the car to go to
the coffee shop.
Memories of lying in bed beside Jerry just loving him and him
loving me back.

There are precious memories of recovery far beyond medical predictions.
Memories of my sweet guy, of amazing doctors, nurses, and therapists with progress.
Memories of hugs, kisses, and closeness beyond my dreams after a stroke.
Yes, precious memories of my caregiving days held up by God.

The most precious memory of all is the celebration of our fiftieth anniversary.
It was one year ago today as I write this on August 5 when we renewed our vows,
When my sweet guy sang "Because" to me as he had done fifty years previously,
And memories of once again vowing our love till death do us part.

When death did part us five months later, the precious memories were created,
Even as we held hands that one last time this side of eternity,
Even as my sweet guy took his last breath here and his first one in heaven,
Even as our time as husband and wife ended but the memories lived on.

Yes, precious memories stay with me today and will forever hold me up.
Memories of a life well lived together sharing, loving, giving, and being.
Memories of a marriage committed to God and each other,
Precious memories to carry me through my journey of grieving.

Praise God for precious memories of life and love, of joy and
sorrow,
Of success and failure, of anger and reconciliation, of pain and
healing.
Memories are what we have when events end, when holidays are
over,
When vacations are finished, when friendships end, when life
ends.

Precious memories—thank You, God, for each one!

These next five psalms were written during my visit to the
Emerald Coast of Florida, Georgia, and South Carolina in August
2018.

Walking in the Sand

This morning I walked along the beach,
Barefoot in the edge of the ocean waves.
The water rolled over my feet,
Momentarily making the sand insecure.

The bigger the wave, the more unsteady I was.
My feet searched for solid footing.
But the wave rolled back into the sea.
And once again my feet were sure.

It's tiring walking along water's edge,
Always looking for the steady ground.
The waves never cease to roll,
With differing force all night and day.

As I walk through life, it is like sand.
The waves of trouble constantly come.
They batter my days from young to old.
Just like ocean waves, they never end.

But as each wave of difficulty
Comes and goes with differing force,
Once subsided, my footing once again

Is settled, and I feel solid ground.

My God keeps the feet from slipping.
My Jesus holds my hand as I walk.
My Spirit gives me inner strength.
I can keep walking on the beach of life.

Waves of difficulty will never stop,
As constant as the ocean waves,
But God's love will also never stop.
Keeping me sure footed till the end!

The Ocean

The ocean is a place of comfort,
Of peace, joy, solitude, and confidence.
It is the promise of God to me.

Ocean waves never stop rolling in.
The tides come and go every day.
It is always there awaiting your visit.

Some waves are small, rolling to shore.
Others are mighty, holding surfers aloft.
Tidal waves show unstoppable power.

God's love never stops covering us.
From day to day; it is secure.
We can leave it, but He awaits our return.

God's love comes to meet our needs.
Some days a small whisper,
And when needed, it totally smothers us.

The ocean is amazing power!
God's love is surrounding power!
And both are never ceasing! Praise!

People

God makes people in all sizes and shapes.
Being at the beach brings it all to light.
Short, tall, bumpy, and smooth;
Little, big, from young to old.

God loves them all no matter what size,
No matter what age, color, or shape.
Each a creation from God above
Is here for a purpose—to love and serve.

If God loves each and every one,
Who are we to question their worth?
Our love for each one must be there too.
For God to love all them and me!

Ocean Sounds

White sounds—those comforting noises.
They help you calm down.
They help you go to sleep.

The sound of waves crashing,
As the foam rolls up on the shore,
Ending that one wave forever.

Wave after wave come crashing,
Morning, noon, and night they come.
The roaring sound calming the soul.

Why would something so powerful,
So potentially destructive,
And never ending produce peace?

The powerful sound of the ocean
Is the powerful sound of God.
It demonstrates His constant being.

The comfort is in knowing He is there.
He is in control of everything.
His power gives us peace and security.

Rest well, oh weary one!

The Tides

Each evening the tides begin to rise.
Ever so slowly the water inches up.
The shoreline disappears as it rises.

Each morning the tide begins to lower.
And again, ever so slowly the water inches down.
The shoreline comes back into view.

The moon's pull is the mighty force
To create this daily ocean action
That happens daily, monthly, yearly.

In and out as regular as a ticking clock,
As dependable as the rising of the sun,
As consistent at winter melting into spring.

God is the force behind it all.
His power is dependable, is consistent.
More important, His love is the ultimate force!

The Lighthouse

The fascination of lighthouses.
What is it? Why so enticing?
Why am I so drawn to them?

They guide the sailor's way
Safely to the harbor from the sea,
Warning of perils along the way.

Their beacon at night shines afar,
Giving hope to the captain of ships,
Alerted to dangers and their port is in sight.

God is my lighthouse, always there,
His light shining night or day,
Showing us the way safely home.

I will keep my eyes firmly on the light
To guide, direct, warn, and show the way.
My path to make clear through my life.

The rest of the poems continue from here.

The Waterfalls of Life

Inspired by Linville Falls, North Carolina

Water rushing, constantly rushing,
Falling over rocks ever downward,
Ever flowing with no end in sight.
Where? Why? What? Comes to mind.

Water running ever on its path,
Slowing only for a pool to rest.
Then back to the swirling rapids
And the rush builds again.

Life is like a waterfall moving,
Starting so small so far from here.
Then building and growing as it moves
Slowly emptying at the end.

As you rush through life,
Enjoy the calming pools.
Rest to gather strength
For the rapids still to come.

God is with you in the rush,
And He provides the pools of stillness.
God guides your moving path
By creating the channels of life.

The pools of stillness are God's reprieve,
His way of providing a time of peace.
Draw close to Him in the quiet,
And He will meet your needs.

The stillness gives needed rest
And helps to build your strength.
He draws us close to Him
To prepare us for what is next.

Welcome these pools of respite.
Grow in the times of quiet.
Because soon you will move again
To the rapids of busy life.

Some day the waters of your life
Will reach its end here
And empty into the ocean of God's eternity,
Where the pools of His love and peace await.

The Path

Inspired by the hiking path at Linville Falls, North Carolina

The path led me from the parking lot.
It was tree-lined, covered with shade.
The shelter all around covered my head,
Giving me a feeling of security as I hiked.

The goal as I hiked was the rushing falls.
I followed along the guided path,
And the reward of the views to come
Kept me going over the ups and downs.

As I walked along the defined path,
I noticed many side paths off the main.
Their destination was a mystery to entice
The hiker with the lure of the unknown.

The path also had rocks scattered as I walked,
Causing me to take caution with each step.
Many stairs took me to the goal of the view
With handrails to use to steady my steps.

Some of the path was downhill and easier to travel,
While other parts were uphill traveled with effort.
The downhills were easier, creating a respite,
But the uphill took greater strength and focus.

As I walked along the path using ever-increasing strength,
I came upon a bench—a place of rest and renewal,

A place to sit, breathe deeply, and refresh
To once again move farther down the path.

The view at the end of the long and lovely path
Was worth the rocks, steps, upward, and downward
Bringing me to see beautiful Linville Falls,
Giving me rest, peace, joy, and beauty.

My path through life is similar in many ways.
God defines the path through the beauty of abundant living.
He lays out the goal at the end of our path
And provides eternal rest, peace, joy, and beauty.

But along the way, it is often challenging travel.
There are rocks of discouragement, depression, and death.
Some rocks are easy to step over in my way,
But others take faith and strength from above.

God often provides handrails for me to hold
As the path goes sharply up or down.
Some paths in my life move easily down,
But others take greater strength to upward climb.

Many paths along the way cause my attention to stray.
The mystery of the side path draws me away.
Should I see where that path leads into the woods
Even though it is away from my goal ahead?

God gives me my path and holds my hand each day
To strengthen me every day to move toward the goal.
The path is clearly marked if I seek Him,
His Word becoming my GPS—God Positioning System.

But Satan also wants to be my guide along the path,
Providing many side paths to lure me away,
Putting rocks in my life to slow me down,
And wanting to lead me astray with his deceit.

Follow the defined path God provides.
Take the benches of rest in His sheltering arms.
Turn to Him for strength along the way
And arrive safely at the goal—the view of your heavenly home.

A New Era

Inspired by opening the renovated auditorium at Alameda Church of Christ, 9/30/18

Today at Alameda, our congregation opened a new era.
We worshiped the first time in our newly renovated auditorium.
Our excitement is growing due to the newness of the building,
But more for the newness of the vision of the shepherds.

It is a new era in the life of this body of Christ.
A new era of committing to carrying out the great commission,
Of reaching out to the community where our building abides
To create a dynamic church, making a difference in our city.

My own life is in a new era now as a widow.
It is not with the same excitement I start this era.
There are many unknowns in the era of a widow's life
As I must travel without the companionship of a husband.

Now I travel alone through the tasks of life.
My house and heart are empty of my husband.
He is no longer blessing me with hugs, kisses, and song.
My heart is heavy with the grief I feel.

But the new era also has a renewed purpose.
God not only held me up though my caregiving,
He continues to hold me up each and every day.
I do not feel alone because He holds me close.

When the waters of baptism wash over you, erasing sin,

A new era begins for the fully forgiven Christian.
The new life takes away the guilt of all past sin
And gives grace to cover the future life to come.

The new Christian is not walking that life alone.
The gift of the Holy Spirit is given to indwell.
Providing strength, wisdom, guidance, and fortitude.
Never alone but filled with the presence of God.

Embrace the new era of being a Christian today,
Whether you are brand-new or saved many years past.
God's mercies are new every day, giving a new beginning.
Each day is a new era of your life living in God's mercy.

Communion

The simple wafer is taken from the tray.
As I put it in my mouth, my mind is focused.
The symbol of Christ's broken body in my body,
Reminding me of the excruciating pain he endured.

The juice in its little cup comes next.
Blood was shed as Christ's body was pierced.
The liquid flows down my throat to remind me
Of the precious blood that flowed just for me.

Remembering is what communion initiates.
Reminding me of the salvation that's mine.
Rejoicing for the sacrificial Lamb's death.
Rededicating my life back in service to God.

The Changing Colors

Autumn is here, showcasing the hues of color.
The trees are ready to shine in their glory.
Bringing a beauty to delight all those who see
The orange, yellow, and golden fading into brown.

Our forests build through the year in preparation
For their time of grandeur to again return.
The leaves glisten, sparkle in color for all to see,
The winds giving a rustling sound of fall.

Then they die and fall to the ground in mounds.
Children play in the dry, crackling heaps.
Gardeners rake, stack, mulch, and compost.
And all prepare for a season of seeming death.

Trees are bare, bushes naked—all their leaves gone.
Flowers have frozen—all the green has disappeared.
There is no life in nature—all is brown.
Winter is soon to come—a period of no growth.

But is this truly a time of death and no growth?
Is life over when the skeleton of limbs appears?
Why did God give us a season of death?
Everything looks so bleak, still, and silent.

God is giving a time of rest and rejuvenation.
A time of silence when deep beneath the soil,
Roots are soaking in nutrients in preparation

For a new season of growth in spring.

Our lives have seasons mimicking nature,
Seasons when we pull back from activity.
Times when we too need to rest and rejuvenate,
Turning to God to refuel our souls.

The autumns of our lives leading us to winter
Are times of turning to God for nourishment.
Draw close to Him to soak up His love,
To be ready for the coming season of new growth.

The 23rd Psalm for Caregivers

The Lord is my caregiver; I shall want for nothing.
He makes me lie down and take an afternoon nap.
He leads me beside a running stream.
He refreshes my inner strength.
He guides my decisions as I go through this life.
Even though there will be difficult, impossible situations,
I have no fear of the future because God is beside me.
The world cannot attack me because God's Spirit is within me.

There are times when I must face those who make me
uncomfortable.
However, your presence is always there to hold me up.
I am assured God's goodness and love are constant companions.
They will be with me throughout this life and into the next,
Where I will live and praise God forever.

Holiday of Grief

Cheer is everywhere as we enter December.
Stores play joyful Christmas music.
Neighborhood lights brighten the winter nights.
Santas await children in all the malls
To hear the wishes of their little hearts.

Gift suggestions bombard the shopper
Through internet, newspaper, phones, and social media
To bring happiness to all their recipients.
Parties and concerts clutter our calendars,
Filling our days with holiday activities.

But it is my first—another first.
I've had my first birthdays and Valentines,
My first Mother's and Father's Days,
The first vacation in an empty car,
My first Thanksgiving—but now it comes.

Christmas alone—no need to hang his stocking.
Christmas caroling without my amazing bass.
No Santa hat waiting for my husband's head.
No children in stores sidling up to my Santa
To be noticed by my loving husband.

The tears flow with so many reminders.
The tears won't stop with the memories.
The tears are this year's Christmas decor,
The tears of missing my sweet Santa.
The tears of my first Christmas holiday a widow.

The joy of the season is still found
In the same memories that make me cry,
But most of all in the birth of our Lord.
That joy surpasses all the grieving
And promises a reunion some day.

Christmas is all about family, yes.
But when part of that family leaves,
Whether by death, divorce, or other choices,
It leaves an empty hole in the Christmas heart.
A hole never to be filled again.

Yes, joy to the world, the Lord has come!
Find the joy where the joy belongs.
Reach out to those hurting this season.
Cry with them, pray for them, hug them.
The joy is not in the present but in the eternal.

Remember the hurting and those alone.
Take your joy and soothe their hurting.
Send a card, take a gift, sing a carol, say a prayer.
Christmas may not be the most wonderful time of year.
To those it isn't, share your Christmas spirit.

4 -Cover Symbol Explanation
SYMBOL GLOSSARY

The butterfly on the front cover represents Lois's Journey with Jerry, the transformation that occured through that process, and ultimately letting jerry fly away. Contained within the butterfly's wings are many symbols. Below are their meanings.

 Flower: Growth and Life

 Sun: Light, Holiness, Clarity, & Victory

 Cross: Faith

 Drop: Purity, Struggle, and the Blood of Jesus

 Heart: Love

 Mountain: Journey, Struggle, Alone But Not Alone

 Infinity Sign: Eternity

 Three Stars: Trinity, Promises, Prayers

 White Wind Pattern Around Butterfly: The Spirit, Flight

American Psychiatric Association. 2018. "What's the Difference between a Delusion and a Hallucination?" *PsychCentral.* https://psychcentral.com/lib/whats-the-difference-between-a-delusion-and-a-hallucination.

Armstrong, J. R., and Mosher, B. D. 2011. "Aspiration Pneumonia After Stroke, Intervention and Prevention." *Neurohospitalist* 1 (April): 85–93. https://www.ncbi.nlm.nih.gov/pmc/articles/PMC3726080.

Aughtmon, S. F.; Faulkenberry, G. F.; Fox, G.; Goyer, T.; Gay, T. L. S.; Hinck, S.; Jordan, R. B.; Marshall, E, K.; Matthews, D. N.; Meacham, G.; Ruchit, C.; and Tietjen, S. D. 2016. *Mornings with Jesus 2017.* New York: Guideposts & Inspirational Media.

Aughtmon, S. F.; Faulkenberry, G. F.; Fox, G.; Goyer, T.; Hinck, S.; Jordan, R. B.; Marshall, E, K.; Matthews, D. N.; Meacham, G.; Ruchit, C.; Tietjen, S. D.; and Yoshuio, I. 2017. *Mornings with Jesus 2018.* New York: Guideposts & Inspirational Media.

Beattie, Melody. 2001. "BrainyQuote." https://www.brainyquote.com/quotes/ melody_beattie_134462

CaringBridge: Free Personal, Protected Websites for Every Health Journey. 2018. https://www.caringbridge.org.

Caswell, J. 2015. "When Stroke Affects the Thalamus." http://strokeconnection.strokeassociation.org/Spring-2015/When-Stroke-Affects-the-Thalamus.

Cookson Hills Wildlife Management Area. 2010. "Great Plains Narrow-Mouth Toad (Gastrophryne olivacea)." https://www.wildlifedepartment.com/ wildlifemgmt/swg/t35p1/WMA/G_olivacea_CH.shtml.

Cowman, L. B. 2016. *Streams in the Desert.* Grand Rapids, MI: Zondervan.

Davis, Katie. 2011. *Kisses from Katie.* New York: Howard.

Dickerson, John S. 2016. *I Am Strong.* Grand Rapids, MI: Zondervan.

Drennan, Miriam. 2016. *Devotions from the Garden.* Nashville: Thomas Nelson.

Fields, L. 2016. "The Healing Power of Gratitude." *Reader's Digest* (October). https://www.readersdigest.co.uk/health/health-conditions/the-healing-power-of-gratitude.

Get Palliative Care. 2018. "What Is Palliative Care?" https://getpalliativecare.org/whatis.

Google Dictionary. 2018. "Anxious." https://www.google.com/search?q=anxious+definition&rlz=1C1CHBF_enUS806US806&oq=anxious&aqs=chrome.1.69i57j35i39j0l4.4909j1j7&sourceid=chrome&ie=UTF-8.

Leal, Carmen. 2004. *The Twenty-Third Psalm for Caregivers*. Chattanooga, TN: AMG.

Lucado, Max. 2012. *Great Day Every Day*. Nashville: Thomas Nelson.

Lucado, Max. 2007. *3:16, The Numbers of Hope*. Nashville: Thomas Nelson.

Mercola, Joseph. 2018. "Most Americans Suffer From Nature Deficiency Syndrome." https://articles.mercola.com/sites/articles/archive/2017/07/13/ecotherapy.aspx.

Mercola, Joseph. 2018. "The Health Benefits of Going Outside." https://articles.mercola.com/sites/articles/archive/2017/07/13/ecotherapy.aspx.

Meyer, Joyce. 2012. *Trusting God Day by Day, 365 Daily Devotions*. New York: FaithWords.

Rice, Helen Steiner. 2012. *A Collection of Faith, Hope, & Love*. Uhrichsville, OH: Barbour.

Seladi-Schulman, Jill. 2018. "Everything You Need to Know about Thalamic Strokes." Healthline Newsletter (April 13). https://www.healthline.com/health/ thalamic-stroke.

Stanley, Charles F. 2011. *Life Principles Daily Bible*. Nashville: Thomas Nelson.

Voskamp, Ann. 2016. *The Broken Way*. Grand Rapids, MI: Zondervan.

Williams, F. 2012. "Take Two Hours of Pine Forest and Call Me in the Morning." *Outside Magazine* (November 28).

Woolsey, Steffany. 2014. *I'll Be Praying for You*. Nashville: Thomas Nelson.

Unless otherwise noted, scriptures are taken from the Holy Bible, New International Version, YouVersion. Life Church/YouVersion, Edmond, OK.

Lois A. Cox, PhD, has roots in Dallas, Texas, but met her husband, Jerry, at Oklahoma Christian College, Oklahoma City, Oklahoma, in 1966. They married in 1967 and started a life together of serving God in several locations. Seven of their years were in full-time ministry in churches in Midwest City, Oklahoma; Tulsa, Oklahoma; and Ft. Collins, Colorado. Most of Lois's career has been spent in education at the high school, technical college, and university levels. Lois holds four degrees in education, including a PhD completed in her late sixties in instructional technology and online learning.

On February 24, 2016, Lois was plummeted into the role of caregiver for her husband, who suffered a rare and serious bilateral thalamic stroke. The next twenty-two months were spent in full-time care of Jerry in skilled nursing facilities, hospitals, and at home. Jerry passed away on December 30, 2017. Since that time, Lois has been focusing on sharing her experiences with others to encourage and teach them to depend on the Lord during similar stressful times. Her book, *Caregiving with God: Twenty-Two Months with Jerry*, was written during her first year of grieving. She also regularly writes a grieving blog and is available for speaking engagements to share her experiences firsthand. Contact her at 22monthministry@gmail.com or through her website, https://www.22monthministry.com, where you will find her blog and information about speaking.

CPSIA information can be obtained
at www.ICGtesting.com
Printed in the USA
BVHW080034051221
623259BV00017B/372

9 781661 039202